after college... what?

a career exploration handbook

by
Newell Brown

Director, Career Services, Princeton University
and formerly United States Assistant Secretary
of Labor, Employment and Manpower

M. W. LADS PUBLISHING COMPANY
New York / Philadelphia

Foreword: To Undergraduates

Many of you, if what I hear from day to day is any measure, are finding the necessity of making up your minds about the future an anxious business. Some of you have been waiting for lightning to strike and it hasn't yet, or have been hit several times and face a choice, or are not comfortable with a decision tentatively made. Others of you are wondering whether the answer could be found if you could get around to applying the research-consultation approach you habitually use in putting together a term paper. But you've been too busy with more pressing matters. Or the resources available haven't fitted your needs of the moment, in one way or another. Or possibly you've been reluctant to inquire, either because you feel a little guilty about having let the matter slide or because this seems to you a little like sex and marriage: it's a highly personal thing which books are not likely to have answers to and which you just don't feel like discussing in depth with members of the older generation. So who wants another lecture!

No book is going to solve your problem, if you have one. But a book which attempts, as this one does, to set down, with an eye to your particular circumstances and within the limitations of the printed word, what would happen if you approached a good career counselor and asked for the "works," might be helpful.

Such a counselor would not provide you with "ten easy steps to an occupational happy-ever-after." He would be aware that career exploration is indeed a very personal and emotion-charged process and that career planning, if one's aim is to fix on a sharply delineated course with the expectation of being able to follow it over the years, is today pure nonsense. He would make available to you brief but comprehensive information on the job options you probably have. And he would believe that you will probably best serve society by best serving yourself and so would not attempt to make your decisions for you.

Thus, the first half of the book has to do with self-understanding, so far as it relates to career exploration, and the second half with the six fields of work and the 62 kinds of work most likely to occupy collegians. Neither contains any advice on the conclusions you should reach. Between them, however, is an informal, self-administered exercise which may help you in matching up yourself with those among the alternatives before you most likely to provide a "fit" in terms of values.

I hope you will find it useful. If it isn't, you can always drop it — unlike a counselor who proves to be useless — in the wastebasket.

Newell Brown
Princeton 1968

Contents

Part II — What the Choices Are

Appendices:

Preface

The choice of how to make one's living is crucial, for the work a man does makes him what he will become. The blacksmith pounds the anvil, but the anvil also pounds the blacksmith. The clam's shell turns golden in the brown depths of the ocean, and in far more subtle ways is a man's mind colored by the course of his life. So when a man chooses his labor, he chooses his future self.

From To Catch An Angel by Robert Russell.*

In exploring careers, you would be best served by a program composed of three elements. The first would be face-to-face discussion with a counselor. In such a meeting, if the counselor were a good one, he would be primarily a listener and a source of information. His aim would be to help you acquire a thorough understanding of yourself, to think through your own problems and to come to your own conclusions. He would avoid recommending decisions. The second element would be reading up-to-date, objectively written publications on careers and way stations such as graduate schools. The third would be testing, to the extent that you and the counselor were agreed that the results might add something new, or clarify doubtful points, or stimulate thought.

Without access to such a program, you will perhaps find this book helpful. First, it is addressed to you and your colleagues, not to scholars and professional practitioners in the career-counseling field. Second, it goes into the process of choice in some depth, with particular emphasis on the non-logical ingredients which inevitably will and should influence your ultimate

---

* New York: The Vanguard Press, 1962. p. 150.

decisions and which, once identified, can help you in making them. In effect, it attempts to tell you what emotional aspects of decision-making a good career counselor listens for and suggests and explores and explains. The various sides of this process are illustrated by case histories.

Finally, it contains brief descriptions of all the *fields* of work (government, education, profit-making enterprises, private non-profit organizations, self-employment and the Military Services) and of most of the *kinds* of work which occupy the college trained, and that section is introduced by a chart cross-referencing these fields and kinds of work and a self-administered "matching-up" exercise. The purpose of the chart is to clarify the relationships between kinds and fields of work and also, by ticking off most of the 360 degrees of the job horizon of interest to collegians, to help you to avoid the danger of focussing too early on those most familiar to you. Careers which Liberal Arts graduates can pursue with little or no more supplementary "pre-vocational training" than is required for those in other under-graduate disciplines are indicated by an asterisk. The exercise provides a means by which you can roughly relate your particular emotional wants and needs and urges to those which each of the kinds of work are likely to satisfy or frustrate.

As to tests, those which are not administered and interpreted personally by someone trained in their use — and meaning or lack of it — can do more harm than good. This is especially true of the "do-it-yourself" variety offered to the general public. Thus, this book makes no attempt to provide the testing element of good counseling.

If, first, career decisions had little influence on a man's life; or if, second, satisfactory ones could usually be made thought-lessly; or if, third, they were being made thoughtfully by most students; or if, fourth, effective assistance were everywhere available; or if, finally, choice could be put off until one got around to it, there would be no point in writing this book.

I do not believe any of these things are true. In the first in-stance, the view expressed in the introductory quotation seems to me self-evident. The issue is not simply how you will make a living, it is also how you will make a life. In the second, I know of no systematic evidence, actually, that proves that those who take their job decisions seriously live happier and more useful lives than those who do not. It seems likely to me that they do, though, and unsystematic observation supports the belief. I do know, in the third instance, that many student decisions made at graduation are half-baked, as the students themselves will often admit. The word they sometimes use in their Senior year to describe their state of mind is "panic," not a condition conducive to thoughtful decisions. I also know, considering the fourth point, that expert career counseling is not everywhere available (or, if available, acceptable to some students) and the same applies to good career libraries. It is in this area that I hope the book will be helpful. Finally, the immediate post-college decision, and many of those later on, obviously can't wait. Millions of men and women across country must make up their minds each year, ready or not.

Certain matters you might expect to find in a book on career exploration are not dealt with, either because information or help is probably at hand or because they are not as important as those which are discussed. These matters include how to job hunt; check-lists for comparing job offers; psychotherapy as a step preliminary to exploration, where indicated; military service requirements (as contrasted with options); such short-term careers as the Peace Corps; training programs; and post-graduate education. However, where formai schooling beyond college is required or advisable, the individual job descriptions in the latter half of the book so indicate. Publications containing reliable information on most of the rest of these matters are listed in Appendix C.

In my judgment reasonable brevity is essential to the usefulness of a book of this kind. But when one is trying to cover anything as complex as human emotions and careers and as many-faceted and kaleidoscopic as the world of work in the United States (some 25,000 distinguishable occupations known by some 40,000 job titles, and rapidly changing), a concern for brevity posed a problem. I have resolved it by being selective and suggestive in many places; by cutting corners ruthlessly on occasion; and, sometimes, by unavoidable oversimplification. I beg the reader's tolerance for these admitted limitations.

In conclusion, I should like to express my deep appreciation to Dr. Seymour L. Wolfbein, Dean of the Temple University School of Business Administration and former United States Deputy Assistant Secretary of Labor for Employment and Manpower; Mr. John S. Obecny, Jr., Director of Placement, Newark College of Rutgers University; Mr. Arthur J. Horton, Director, Development Office, Princeton University; Mr. Henry H. Callard, Director of Teacher Preparation and Placement, Princeton University, and Colonel Douglas H. Patterson, Commanding Officer, Princeton University R.O.T.C., for their expert and thoughtful editorial suggestions; to Mr. Richard Woodward for research assistance; to Mr. Laurence B. Chase for editorial assistance; to Mr. William T. McCleery for prodding me way back at the beginning; to Miss Lee Williams for long hours at the typewriter and a watchful eye on the text; to the hundreds of undergraduate friends who, largely unknowingly, have contributed in various ways to this book; and to my wife, Alice, who participated in all these activities and who managed against heavy odds to provide me with the time and encouragement I needed to put the book together. I hold none of these, however, responsible for the opinions expressed or for whatever gaffes may have been committed.

N. B.

*   *   *

It is the author's intention to update and republish this book periodically.

A WORD TO THE LADIES

I address you on the assumption that you are doubtful about the importance to you as a woman of reading further — or even of thinking seriously about a career at this time. If I'm wrong, read on. If I'm right, give me five minutes to try to change your mind.

Your doubt, if any, is probably based on one or more of three prevalent points of view. You may be entirely cheerful about the prospect of a lifetime, once beyond the diaper stage, of continued housekeeping, cooking and children tending, of teas and bridge and good works, of grandchildren and hobbies, of serving and following your man. Or you may think that the world of interesting work is essentially a man's world, or that it would be impossible to combine a career with your primary role as wife and mother. Or you may feel that it will be time enough to worry about the whole business when your children are finally off to school.

Many women, of course, live careerless but happy and constructive lives. Many others, however, who originally thought homemaking would be enough and gave no thought to a possible career, find themselves later on wanting to undertake rewarding paid work outside the home. Today these usually land in jobs not worthy of their talents or remain uncomfortably at home. The point here, it seems to me, is that the early twenties may be too soon to make a commitment to careerlessness. And this is a decision you may well be making, if you elect to ignore the possibility of a career now. And it might be added that one day, going to work may not be a matter of free choice. Among other things, the standard of living you and your family want may not be possible on your husband's salary. Too, the costs of education are rising astronomically, and, again, your man could die or be disabled. Whatever their reasons, in any case, nearly half the women of working age in America are employed at some time each year.

As to the question of whether or not a rewarding career is a possibility for you, the answer is emphatically "yes," though undertaking it in some cases may not be easy. Acute shortages exist today in many kinds of professional, technical and managerial work. Thirty-two of the "largest and most promising [for women]" careers are described in the pamphlet "Job Horizons for College Women," up-dated and republished periodically by the Women's Bureau of the United States Department of Labor. They are given in the note on page xiv and are among the 62 kinds of work described in the second half of this book.

"All very well," you may say, "but my continuing home duties and the prejudice against women in many of these occupations, or both, rule out serious consideration of them." In your mother's time you would have been right pretty much across the board. As far as getting out of the house is concerned, you wouldn't have had the many labor-saving devices which today drastically reduce the time spent on household chores. As to prejudice, serious shortages in many challenging kinds of work didn't exist then, or at least weren't recognized. The nation hadn't come to realize that its single largest untapped source of brain power was probably its non-working, college-trained women. As a result, little had been done, as is increasingly being done today, to modify training and working opportunities to meet the married woman's special needs — limited hours of availability and the necessity of remaining close to home. Employers are fast finding that they can't afford prejudice. This is not to say that time, distance, and prejudice problems no longer exist. It is simply that they are not prohibitive, as they once were.

They are considered to be, however, by many women. This may be one reason for the phenomenon of the proportion of women in professional, technical and kindred careers being smaller today (37 per cent of all so employed) than it was in 1940 (45 per cent). Whatever the reason, you won't be trampled by other women in the rush to enter such careers if you embark on them.

About combining work with home-making, I know of no authoritative study to demonstrate that the two don't generally mix well — with particular reference to the continuing welfare of husband, children and home. In fact, a recent and well-received book entitled *A Complete Guide for the Working Mother*, by Margaret Albrecht,* takes quite the opposite view. But basically it boils down to the sort of person you are. For some women work and home won't mix. For some no harm will result. And for some a satisfactory career outside the home may even be vital to happiness within it.

What about the idea of waiting until the children are in school to decide about a career? In the first place, this may come sooner than you think. The chances are even that the last child in a completed family will go off to kindergarten when the mother is 32. At whatever age this happens, as it eventually will, can you just pop into the job of your choice if you decide to go to work? The chances of doing so will depend heavily on what you do just after college and during the time that you have had to stay at home. Due principally to the technological revolution, the content of most jobs of probable interest to you is steadily changing. People working at them year in and out must study constantly, both formally and on the job, to keep up to date. Thus, if you have little or no work experience at the outset or take any old job to mark time and then lose touch with the world of work while at home, you may face, first, the choice of what career you want, and, second, and almost certainly, a long, perhaps prohibitively long period of training or retraining in order to be able to pursue it. Your alternatives, then, are to take a job, as a salesperson or clerk, for instance, below your capacity, or to stay at home. If, on the other hand, you choose your college courses and your first job, if any, judiciously and if, while at home you keep in touch with "the state of your art" by such activities as taking occasional courses, attending professional meetings, reading relevant journals, and maintaining membership in professional organizations, then a degree of "skill rustiness" may be all you will have to overcome before job hunting. As with challenging jobs themselves, the opportunities to train for them and to keep track of what is new are increasingly being adapted to meet the limitations of the married woman.

---

* Garden City, N. Y.: Doubleday and Company, Inc., 1967.

And that is my case. The possibility of a rewarding career, if you want it later on, definitely exists. The surest way to keep the option open, whatever your present persuasion, is to give serious thought to the matter right now.

*   *   *

Note: Accountant, bank officer, biological scientist, counselor, dietician, engineer, home economist, insurance agent and broker, interior designer and decorator, lawyer, librarian, mathematician, medical technologist, musician and music teacher, nurse, occupational therapist, personnel worker, pharmacist, physical scientist, physical therapist, physician, programer and systems analyst, real estate agent and broker, recreation worker, religious worker, retail store buyer, secretary, social scientist, social worker, statistician, teacher, and writer and editor. These are the thirty-two largest and most promising careers for women.

Part I
Ways to Explore

Introduction

Your parents probably fall into one of four groups in regard to how they think you should go about deciding on your career.

The "Father Knows Best" (or, as least, "Grown-ups Know Best") School is perhaps the largest.

Next come those who would have you solve the problem logically. Draw up two lists, one of abilities and interests and the other of possible careers, say they; then, using pure reason, find the best match between the two.

Then there are the "Trial-and-Errorists" whose apparent assumption is that collegiate skulls are so thick that only repeated contact with stone walls can make an impression.

Finally, there is the "Hands Off" School which holds that parents should remain simply spectators (and usually apprehensive ones) as their offspring search or fail to search for answers.

None of these schools is either wholly right or wholly wrong. Now, almost 60 years after career choice first became an object of serious study, there is still no generally accepted standard against which to judge right and wrong on how people should and do make job decisions. Certainly your parents' advice can be helpful. But it can also be useless or harmful and, for several reasons to be considered later, should always be regarded with skepticism. Again, knowing your capacities and interests and something of what the world of work offers is usually essential to making sound choices. But you can no more look to pure reason for the ultimate decision on your career than for the decision on whom you should marry. As to trial and error, it is true that most people will change jobs several times and one should therefore remain flexible. Careers today are almost always built of a succession of decisions, not just one at the start. But to leave initial and later choices entirely to chance when some guideposts are available would surely be stupid. As to neutrality, while it should be the ultimate parental posture, if it is carried to the extreme of refusing to discuss the matter or make suggestions along the way, it may deprive the searcher of useful guides and ideas.

All of this falls far short, of course, of providing you with a tidy formula for finding a satisfying job. It is doubtful if such a formula will ever be devised. Choosing a job is a highly complex and personal matter. But it may be possible to improve on current methods of helping a person to get his bearings and set off in a promising direction and to avoid needless zigs and zags and unnecessary breaks in stride. That is what this book as a whole attempts.

This first part is composed of four chapters. The opening chapter examines certain assumptions in connection with career exporation which have undergirded the thinking of most professionals and laymen over the years, which are still prevalent today and which are questionable if not manifestly false.

The second chapter deals with those human dimensions which have traditionally and properly been considered relevant to good choice-making: intelligence, aptitudes, interests, physical capacities, family background and achievements.

The third discusses the emotional influences which have or should have a bearing. Feelings, often contradicting reason and often subconscious, will play a major role, both at each point of choice and, later, in the degree of enjoyment you get from your job.

The final chapter suggests a variety of ways in which you can learn more about yourself and the world of work.

Chapter

1

Eleven Fallacies

WHEN YOU GO actively seeking help in deciding what to do with your future—or unintentionally invite it because your indecision is manifest—take a hard look at the "facts" you turn up. Some may not be that at all. Your parents and peers and other well-wishers — and some professional counselors, as well — may be unaware that recent research has disproved or raised questions about some of the plausible assumptions of yesteryear on how career choices should be made. Or they may base their suggestions on traditional but clearly illogical concepts.

As a matter of clearing the decks for ensuing discussion, let's examine the more serious and widespread of these fallacies.

Fallacy #1 — Interests Go Hand-in-Hand with Aptitudes:
You can expect to be apt in those kinds of work in which you have interest and to be interested in those kinds of work for which you have talent.

So far as is now known, there is no truth in this assumption, with one minor exception: the scholastically apt tend to have scientific and linguistic interests and to be uninterested in social welfare, business detail and business contact occupations. Otherwise it is impossible to predict that, say, an interest in surgery will ensure dexterity and scientific aptitude; or that competence with figures means a liking for accounting.

At issue here is the connection between interests and aptitudes, not the importance of considering them in making job choices. Both should be taken into account, but there may well be no relation between them.

5

Fallacy #2 — Base Career Decisions on Advice:

You should rely heavily on the advice of others in making up your mind about what to do with your working life.

Among the sources of information more or less relevant to career choice is the advice you are likely to get, solicited and unsolicited, from those around you. If you've gotten beyond the point where you automatically turn a deaf ear to all advice from any quarter, you may be wondering how seriously to take what is said on this subject by whom.

None of your advisers, I think, except the obvious fools, can safely be tuned out. But what they say should not be swallowed whole. All of these people, to the extent they talk in terms of "You should . . ." or "You ought to . . ." make this or that choice, suffer from one or more serious limitations.

Let's start with your father. In the first place, his knowledge of what kinds of work are and will be available to you is limited. He knows a lot about his own work and the changes to be expected in it, but unless he has made a day-in, day-out study of other kinds of work, his information about most of them is bound to be fragmentary and probably out of date to boot. His concept of what engineering, or social work, or government service, or selling is today — and may become 10 years hence — may be far wide of the facts. Even those who study occupations full time in these days of rapid change can't keep up with all the developments.

In the second place, your father's interests, attitudes, values and strengths and weaknesses are different in at least some degree from yours. You are probably well aware of this, but he may not be. Many fathers consider their sons (and sometimes their daughters), by definition, chips off the old block. "I know my boy like a book," one sometimes hears. On this assumption they have been known to give advice with a confidence equalled only by its irrelevance.

Finally, your father is just that. As you'll one day discover for yourself, most parents can't help being deeply concerned about their children, whether they show it or not. Their own happiness, their pride, their emotions are inevitably involved in what becomes of you. Thus, though they often are unaware of it, they simply can't think entirely objectively where your future is concerned. Your other relatives suffer from the same three disabilities in varying degrees.

Others of the older generation — professors, pastors, friends, employers — have the same disabilities, excepting those resulting from blood relationship. In addition, some may have an axe to grind. Summertime bosses and professors whom you have impressed may, quite naturally, urge on you a career in their own kinds of work, advice that must surely be suspect under the circumstances.

Close friends at college can be a somewhat different story. They may know more about what turns you off and on than any adult. But the chances are that they know less than members of the older generation about the working alternatives you have.

Professional career counselors may also be among your "advisers." They shouldn't be but some are. If in an interview you find a counselor telling you what's best for you, he should be taken no more or less seriously than any other adviser, except that he should be able to tell you more about your work alternatives. But he doesn't know *you* any better than the others do, and that is the point. If, on the other hand, he asks questions, listens, spends the time trying to help you think through to your own decisions, and confines his suggestions to such matters as how you might go about deciding, and where to get more information, about careers and yourself, then he can be very helpful — as can anyone else who follows this course.

Whether they "know best" what's good for you or, far better try to help you decide for yourself, most "advisers" are worth listening to, however. Many have information about the world of work and, perhaps, insights about how you function which may be important to your decisions. It's a matter of winnowing the useful information from the chaff of unwelcome advice without losing patience — and then going ahead and making your decisions yourself. Such decisions, difficult as they may be, are the only kind that are likely to be right for you and, thus be ones with which you can live comfortably.

7

Fallacy #3 — Seniors Should be Ready to Make Career Decisions:
*You should be ready to make firm decisions about your
career, or at least about the best next step, not later than
your Senior year at college — some would say earlier, when
you choose your major. If you claim that you are still at sea,
it's just that you don't want the academic party to end or
haven't given the matter sufficient thought.*

Most studies of "vocational maturity" do indeed indicate that
the average undergraduate late in his college career has at least
shortened his list of alternatives and is ready to try out one or
another of them. But these studies are careful to stress the word
"average." Some young people can make decisions with which
they feel comfortable even before they get to college. Others can't
do this until they have been out for years. For these a firm
decision not to make a firm decision as they complete college is
the best one. If this were accepted with understanding by interested onlookers, life would be more bearable for all concerned.

Like physical maturity, readiness comes to men and women at
different ages and cannot be substantially speeded or slowed by
outside pressure, though accumulating relevant information can
help. Vocational maturity is not a discrete facet of personality
moving at its own pace, but rather one of several — physical,
emotional and intellectual — jointly involved in the overall grow-
ing-up process.

Your parents and counselors, if they badger you for vacillat-
ing, probably stress three points, all irrelevant, as evidence that
you should be ready to decide. They say that you have reached
your majority and are better trained than any of your collegiate
predecessors. They point out that more than half of your contemporaries, those not going on to college, made job decisions at
the time they left secondary school. And they remind you that the
next steps available to you after college, excepting required
military service (for men) and the Peace Corps, VISTA, the
National Teacher Corps and a few other employments similarly
temporary in nature, all have clear long-run vocational implications. There are few ways, they tell you, in which you can further
put off at least tentative career decisions.

While I am arguing that erudition does not necessarily breed decisiveness and that necessity is not always the mother of readiness (as anyone who has observed the garb of people escaping from a flash fire in the early morning would agree), one has to concede that some decision must be made at graduation. If you are unready and if the temporary employments mentioned above are unacceptable or impossible, there is one good rule of thumb: Do something that leaves the maximum number of career doors still open. Business, government and private school teaching, among other fields, all welcome a competent, undecided Senior, providing he or she can honestly say that he might be interested in making that field a career. And graduate work to the master's level over a broad range of disciplines, particularly in education and the liberal arts, forecloses relatively few kinds of work you might later find appealing — and may open up the door to some.

If you go in for such "temporizing," you can cherish a comforting thought. Your welcome to a variety of careers and many graduate schools may actually be warmer if you have waited to firm up your thinking for a year or two or three. Many employers and admissions officers, because they have become skeptical about the stability of the choices made by Seniors at graduation, prefer men and women who have been "out" for a while.

And another word of possible comfort, this time for your parents. There is little chance that when you are ready to decide you will procrastinate for the fun of it. Indecisiveness in itself is not a comfortable state, for one thing. For another, you would be delighted to be relieved of the outside pressures indecisiveness usually generates. And finally, unless you are unusual, you envy those among your peers who know where they are going, or say they do. In these circumstances the fact is that, if unsure, you would be more apt to feign decisiveness than confess confusion.

It might be noted, in conclusion, that students often do not move from unreadiness to readiness overnight. Many, previously at sea, find themselves beginning to have preferences but wonder how seriously to take them in the light of their past vacillation. Since "vocational maturity" is inextricably tied in with growing

9

up in general, such students may find some clues by assessing their maturity generally. They should regard the finality of their conclusions with skepticism if they:

—— Are still engaged in establishing their personal independence, *vis-a-vis* their families.

—— Complain about low marks when their marks are higher than were predicted when they entered — or could have been predicted from the limited amount of homework they did.

—— Disparage or blame themselves without good reason.

—— Wait until the last minute to hunt for a summer job or to make plane reservations, expect someone to bail them out, and become incensed when they are refused.

—— Give up goals of importance at the first hurdle.

—— Regularly overspend their allowances.

—— Miss appointments or get there late.

—— Fail examinations because they took too long on the first question.

—— Attribute low grades to faculty carelessness or animus.

—— Berate the college administration for policies they dislike, without making any effort to do anything about it.

—— Maintain a running fire of criticism of fellow students.

—— Fail to return telephone calls.

—— Lose or fail to take care of valuable possessions.

—— Often get talked into going to a movie when they should be studying.

—— Take unnecessary chances.

—— Blame their troubles on others.

Fallacy #4 — True Reasoning Is the Key to Good Choice:
More than half a century ago, Dr. Frank Parsons of Boston advanced the following formula for the wise choice of a vocation: ". . . (1) a clear understanding of yourself, your aptitudes, abilities, interests, ambitions, resources, limitations and their causes; (2) a knowledge of the requirements and conditions of success, advantages and disadvantages, compensations, opportunities and prospects in different lines of work; (3) true reasoning on the relations of these two

groups of facts . . ." This formulation has been accepted as gospel by most practicing career counselors ever since.

Many theorists today take exception to the Parsons guidelines. They point out that people clearly do not approach career decisions in such a methodical, one-two-three fashion. Further, choices are not made solely on the basis of "true reasoning." Emotions play a large role. These theorists have yet, however, to develop a generally accepted substitute plan of use to you who are trying to make decisions and to those of us who are trying to help you.

It is obvious that your emotions will condition, and may sometimes overwhelm, your reason in your career decisions; and that you will not and cannot follow in sequence and discretely the three Parsons steps. It does not follow, however, that Parsons should be completely discredited, as some suggest. The elements of his formula continue to be useful.

"True reasoning" on the relationship between self and opportunities is only one part of the process by which you will come to conclusions, but it is certainly an important part. To allow your heart to go unguided and uncontrolled by any effort to use your head obviously can lead to trouble. As to your emotions, the critical point, I think, is to try to recognize those which inevitably sit at the decision table unbidden — for example, what you privately feel about who and what you are — so that you can deal with them effectively. And you should also try to identify those which, because you are the person you are, belong there, principally your particular "values" — be they money, or working with ideas, or challenge, or service to society, or others.

In regard to a sequential approach, while it is clear that in trying to decide on a career you will not study first yourself and then the world of work, each without reference to the other, you should be aware that these two areas need study.

Fallacy #5 — It Is Possible to Leave Nothing to Chance:
Good or bad luck will have minor impact on your career if you are thoughtful in your decisions and try to leave nothing to chance.

If you can't find in your own life history evidence to contradict this assertion, you should ask the next middle-aged or elderly man you meet about it. Successful men sometimes discount the part luck played in bringing them to the top. But if they are candid — the luckless have no trouble in being so — most will concede that chance played a consequential, even crucial role. It can be any one or several of hundreds of unexpected occurrences: an accidental encounter, a book picked up, a phrase overheard, an injury or illness, the availability of a scholarship, a turn in the economy, a blind date, a change in the weather, happening to be in the right place at the right time, the departure of a boss. Few men go through life without experiencing the sharp impact of chance on their careers. To recognize in advance that luck, always in the wings, will surely step to center stage from time to time can result in greater readiness to capitalize on the good break and roll with the bad.

Fallacy #6 — "Good" Motives Are Important:

In whatever work you undertake you should be moved primarily by a genuine desire to serve, to be constructive, to do something worthwhile, to make a contribution.

You may, in examining the reasons why you want to follow one career or another, be disturbed to discover that such are not the principal desires that move you, or if they are, that they are not unalloyed. This finding can lead to labyrinthian and, in my view, unnecessary soul searching.

Guilt feelings, prompted by a felt lack of altruism, are unwarranted for several reasons. Society applauds actions which are constructive, worthwhile, make a contribution. And it automatically ascribes good motives to such actions, whatever the truth may be. So far as social acceptance is concerned, then, you need feel no guilt about your motives if your actions are of social worth. This may not be enough, however, for you. You may be among those who want to feel that whatever they do is done for the right reasons. But there are no "right" reasons. Human beings are basically self-serving. Given alternatives, they invariably select that which promises, on balance, sooner or later, the greatest personal satisfaction. The person who is moved primarily by a desire to make money or to face challenge or to live in security is no more self-serving than the person who wants, first of all, to minister to others. And it might be added that motives are seldom unmixed. In any event, the important issue remains unchanged: what actions do the motives prompt?

While most people feel some desire to be of service to society, the great majority are driven primarily by other considerations, many of which are discussed in later chapters. If you do not feel moved beyond all else to make a contribution, you are one of a large and usually respectable company. Motives, in any event, are emotional, not intellectual responses. As such they are difficult to change. To live cheerfully, you had best learn to accept your own.

Fallacy #7 — Versatility Plus Alternatives Makes Choice Easy: *Because you are college-trained and can cope successfully with several different kinds of work, and because, being temporarily in short supply in the midst of a booming economy, you find a variety of jobs waiting or beckoning, it should be easy for you to settle on a career. And if you complain about having a hard time making up your mind, you are like that unlovable character, the "poor little rich boy."*

A person with a single competence or a single job offer may have worries, but career choice is not one of them. That problem arises, obviously, only where versatility, or the availability of alternatives, or a combination of the two are in the picture. It is this combination which confronts most of you today and it results in legitimate perplexity.

Consider the typical liberal arts student approaching graduation — and his, or her, contemporaries in business, education, engineering, science, journalism and other curricula are in much the same boat: he could enter Federal, state or local government; business has hundreds of thousands of openings each year for such graduates; he could aspire to an early commission and career in the uniformed services; the Peace Corps and VISTA may be possibilities, as may graduate school, leading to the professions or teaching or back into government and business. However, this richness of choice does not mean that it is easy to window shop deliberately before deciding. The abler undergraduates are constantly buttonholed on the sidewalk by eager recruiters bearing bags of goodies calculated to tempt them. Altogether, then, making career decisions today can be an unprecedentedly complex and anxious business.

Fallacy #8 — Career Choices Should Be Realistic:
There is a single standard called "realism" by which the excellence of your choice of a career can be judged.

"Realism" used in this context is generally intended to mean "reasonableness." It is a judgment on whether a given career decision represents a reasonable match between, on the one hand, the chooser's strengths and weaknesses and circumstances, and on the other, the opportunities available to him.

If, in making such a judgment about the decision of another, one adds the phrase "in my opinion," he is on safe ground. If he does not — he makes a mistake, for he assumes that what is reasonable in a given set of circumstances is self-evident, that his judgment should be shared by all, including the chooser. In fact, it is nothing more than opinion. No one can ever know exactly what is going on inside the mind of another, what inherited points of view, or experiences, or personal wants and needs, for instance, have a bearing on the judgments he makes. To illustrate:

A Biology major in the bottom tenth of his class insists on trying for medical school. Every consequential interest and value in his make-up would be served by a small-town practice. And he accepts the fact that he may not make it. His career counselor thinks he ought to try to become a veterinarian because they are in short supply and the standards are lower. His father, a dentist, thinks he should follow in the parental footsteps so that he will have sympathetic help if he runs into trouble. Oceanography is the advice of a professor, who foresees a coming need for trained men in this field. Each of these people would term his own view the realistic one under the circumstances, but no two are alike.

14

All but the student would agree, however, that *his* choice was unrealistic.

Or consider the English major with a brilliant record and a yen to write who has acquired a wife and child while still an undergraduate and who decides to teach at the secondary level. His faculty advisor feels he is wasting his talent, that he should go on for the PhD. His wife thinks he ought to take the higher salaried job offered him by a bank. A classmate urges him to get a newspaper job and try writing on the side. Again, three rational people have come to different but defensible conclusions as to what is realistic under the circumstances, but none correspond with his.

Fallacy #9 — Working Up a Clear-cut Plan Is the Objective: *You should set your sights on working up a well-defined, lifelong career plan, prefaced by appropriate course choices, to be implemented at graduation or, if not then, sometime thereafter.*

Once upon a time, and particularly for would-be doctors, lawyers and clergymen, and for sons entering their fathers' businesses, working up such a plan and following it, even allowing for the element of chance, was a possibility. Today such an objective rarely is, principally because accelerating change in the nature of jobs available and in the environment generally makes the future highly unpredictable. A first reason, then, for not setting your sights on such a sharply defined objective is that it is virtually impossible to attain. Only an uncertain tomorrow can be read from such facts as that 500 to 1000 new kinds of work come into being annually, while a somewhat smaller number drops out of the picture; that the country's population will double in about 50 years; and that 90 per cent of the scientists (always principal agents of change) who ever lived are alive today.

There is a second and closely related reason for not trying to set and follow a rigid course. To attempt this in any era involves early specialization, the writing off of many alternatives, and a resultant inability to take advantage of unexpected opportunities. Today such an attempt also involves the risk of early obsolescence. The sailor does not tie down the tiller in a shifting wind. The flier cuts out the automatic pilot when turbulence is ahead. Calm weather is no part of the forecast for the world of work. Retaining as much flexibility as possible is urgent. The career you look back on 50 years hence is unlikely to resemble very closely that which you may be contemplating now.

If this is the case, can anything be done to prepare for the future? Two approaches would seem appropriate. The first is to think about promising *directions,* as against specific careers. This is best done initially by eliminating from further consideration those fields or kinds of work you feel with assurance would never be satisfying. Instead of aiming at such restricted goals as banking or insurance or the United States Treasury Department, an accounting major, for instance, might decide at the outset only to write off careers in self-employment and the uniformed services, leaving open for the time being the broad fields of business, government, education, and private non-profit organizations. Further narrowing of the range of possibilities can come in good season as he learns to know himself — and the nature of these remaining alternatives — better.

The second approach might be to try to learn early how to make promising job decisions, to develop an effective approach to choice problems as they come along — again what this book is about.

Whatever the approach, no one can expect to find the perfect niche immediately. Looking for a round hole is a feasible and important enterprise for a round peg. But with thousands of jobs available and these changing shape steadily, discovering the perfect hole would be the purest of accidents — and the fit might not last.

Most people can find pleasure and profit in a number of different kinds of jobs and most jobs can be successfully performed by people of a variety of stamps. The major goal of the round peg at the start should be limited to setting a course which will reduce the chances of falling or being pushed in a square hole.

Fallacy #10 — Personality Can Change Substantially Later: *Growing maturity and experience after college can effect* *major modifications in your personality, including your interests, attitudes, values, and self-concept.*

You will certainly develop in various ways throughout your lifetime as the result of experience. But there is little likelihood that your personality, as defined above, will change dramatically after you leave college. Most people who married their spouses expecting to reform or change them in these respects would agree. The shy schoolteacher cannot become a driving executive. The man of affairs cannot easily take up the role of contemplative philosopher. The theoretically-inclined scientist will usually be uncomfortable when cast as an administrator. You will usually be making a mistake, initially and along the way, if — except out of strict necessity — you take a new job which you contemplate with distaste — more money is frequently the bait — on the theory that exposure and increasing age will bring enthusiasm, or even tolerance.

On the other hand you should give up a keenly felt aspiration only if its realization would require a drastic personality retooling. New interests can be discovered and developed. Values can be modified by added knowledge. People can think better or worse of themselves than they did at college as they learn more about others. Moderate change is inevitable, but spectacular change of innate characteristics is not.

Fallacy #11 — Leave the Decision to Tests:
Taking a battery of tests and abiding by the results is the best way to make a career decision.

It is estimated that well over 100,000,000 psychological tests — of "intelligence," achievement, aptitudes, interests, temperament, values and personality — are taken by Americans each year. And their quality is improving. But there are still very few of which the results can be considered anything but suggestive. "Testing mills," which subject the client to batteries of tests — sometimes for days — and which rely almost entirely on the results in the subsequent counseling of the client, should therefore be regarded with great suspicion.

The competent counselor considers tests as just one part of

the information gathering process he engages in with an undecided student, and a part not to be taken too seriously in many cases. He is also concerned with such matters as grades, hobbies, work history, family background and what the student says and thinks about himself. He may even conclude that tests give little promise of adding anything useful to a particular discussion and dispense with them altogether.

*   *   *

Those, then, are the major assumptions about making career decisions which, if introduced into your ponderings as you think about the future, should trigger a yellow blinker, if not a solid red light. Unfortunately, as noted earlier, there is no pat set of alternative assumptions on which you can rely. There are, however, a variety of considerations which, if used to baste your thinking, can be helpful. These are discussed in the ensuing chapters.

Chapter

2

The Traditional Measures

YOUR SATISFACTION with the work you undertake over a lifetime depends on the degree to which its content and "personality" square with your capacities and personality. The importance in the equation of your capacities — aptitudes and physical abilities and, indirectly, achievements and inheritance — has long been manifest. So also has the "interest" facet of your make-up. These factors will be discussed here. The succeeding chapter will address itself to personality and emotional considerations which have only lately been recognized as also having major bearing on job choice and satisfaction.

Since most college students are already aware in general of what their capacities and interests are (or, if not, can readily find out), you may question a chapter on this subject, however brief. I include it to stress the importance of getting as clear a reading as you can on these factors as you explore careers and because experience suggests that you may be unfamiliar with some of the aspects of these facts about yourself.

Intelligence and Scholastic Aptitude
Intelligence as such is extremely hard to measure. It has been variously defined as the ability to adjust to environment, to learn from experience, and to deal with symbols. Few tests claim to get at this capacity in its pure state, as it exists, say, in the aborigine and the Nobel Prize winner, and few people have taken the tests which make this claim. Thus they have little general usefulness today as career choice guides.

Scholastic aptitude, however, is readily measurable. Since it is intelligence-related and the only so related information readily available both to college students and to prospective employers and graduate school admissions officers, it will be the basis of this discussion. That it does not tell the whole "intelligence" story, however, should be constantly borne in mind. There are many skillful politicians, great artists, successful entrepreneurs and powerful labor leaders, for instance, who could not score well enough on a scholastic aptitude test to be admitted to the lowliest of colleges.

By this time you probably have acquired a reasonably clear idea of where you stand, relative to your peers, in scholastic aptitude. Your marks and class rank, the subjects in which you have prospered or struggled and your scores on whatever nationally used scholastic aptitude tests you have taken are all on the record.

In regard to career decisions, two questions follow. First, is your scholastic aptitude likely to change as you grow older? The answer is a firm "no." Most studies show that it remains constant from elementary school on. You will acquire more information and master new techniques as time goes on, of course, and the degree of your desire to make use of the ability you have can effect dramatic results in your performance. But your native talents as a scholar will neither improve nor decline significantly.

The second question is: What influence should your level of scholastic competence have on your career thinking? Obviously a high level is of first importance if you are thinking about further schooling. And it is also of importance in non-academic pursuits where a high premium is placed on "intelligence." Some companies, for instance, will not hire you for any job, regardless of how unrelated to scholarship it may be, if you do not stand in the top half of your class.

In most cases, so far as your qualifications from a scholastic aptitude point of view are concerned, other people will make your first post-college decision — and sometimes later ones — for you. They, not you, will decide whether or not you are likely to be able to make the grade. Interviews or formal examinations or both, reference checks and a review of your record are the precursors to acceptance in most graduate schools and employments. These investigations are seldom, of course, solely concerned with your academic talent. Graduate schools in the arts and sciences and engineering are also interested in the courses you have taken, for instance. And business and professional schools may want to know something about such aptitudes as leadership, ability to deal with figures, or manual dexterity.

Other Aptitudes

Your career-related aptitudes other than scholastic are probably also known to you, at least in general. Here your information derives from identifying which of the things you have done well — on campus, in employment and in your spare time — were done voluntarily and without tremendous effort. (Most aptitudes of consequence surface by the end of the college years.) A position on the board of the school paper, achieved through a competition and held down with ease, and chairmanship of a campus fund drive carried off successfully only because the incumbent did all the work himself, both give significant clues to aptitude. The first indicates writing talent, the second raises question about capacities for administration and leadership. (Incidentally, the ability to write and speak effectively is a competence of great importance in most jobs.) Or, with a different twist: the $2000 a student was paid one summer to tend bar at a posh summer resort tells less about his vocationally useful talents (unless bar tending is his career goal) than the $500 he earned selling pans door to door the summer before.

In addition to what the record reveals, a variety of tests are available — possibly at your college Counseling Office — such as those of mechanical aptitude, manual dexterity, clerical aptitude, aesthesic judgment and artistic ability, linguistic aptitude and musical talent.

Relating talents to jobs is ordinarily not difficult. Most job and career descriptions, whether presented orally or in writing, will directly or indirectly tell you what aptitudes are required. But here again, as with scholastic aptitude, the decision on whether you are potentially qualified will usually be made, at least early in your career, by others.

When and if you have to make your own decisions about the adequacy of your aptitudes, scholastic and otherwise, two facts are worth considering. First, your aptitudes will not change appreciably over your lifetime, though you may develop skills which have heretofore been latent. Second, in almost any kind of work you will find yourself competing with others who not only have the necessary aptitudes but are also eager beavers. It follows that you will usually make a mistake, whatever the quantities of midnight oil you are willing to burn and whatever the appeal of the job or the pressures of family or self-expectations, if you undertake work for which you have no manifest natural skill at the outset.

Occupational Interests
Again, you probably know in general which occupations interest you and which do not. It is unlikely that you would be very surprised by the results of an occupational-interest test you had taken. (Most frequently students find their leanings confirmed by such tests. This can be reassuring, especially when they disagree with their fathers about the careers they should be considering.)

A detailed discussion of fields and kinds of work of possible interest to most collegians constitutes the second half of this book. As an aside here, however, some of the general groupings of interests used by scholars in the career field are: Biological Science, Physical Science, Theoretical, People, Social Welfare, Contact, Business Detail, Concrete, Systematic, Technical, Aesthetic, Linguistic, Persuasive, Literary and Materialistic.

Most studies of occupational interests have found that they are in a state of flux up to age 15, crystallize rapidly over the next five years, change little from 20 on and at 25 are virtually fixed for life. You may acquire additional interests, especially in non-occupational areas, but your pattern of job likes and dislikes, as measured by reliable, inventory-type tests, will probably remain fixed. Research further indicates, as would be expected, that people tend to stick with the kinds of work that interest them and to leave those which do not. While it seems plausible, incidentally, there is little clear evidence that one who "whistles while he works" is likely to do a better job than one who doesn't. The only proven correlates with success are such factors as intelligence, aptitude, energy, inheritance, personality, integrity — and luck.

As noted earlier, interests do not, as far as is now known, necessarily stem from or imply matching aptitudes. There is, in fact, no generally accepted theory on their origins or, at least, on the relative influence, if any, that heredity, experience and aptitude have on them.

Physical Capacities

Most college students believe that they have limitless energy. Anyone who has observed them studying all night before examinations, or partying over a long weekend, would be inclined to agree. This ability to "sprint" is a requirement on most jobs from time to time, to meet deadlines or in emergencies, for instance. Without it you may be in early trouble after graduation since you are probably at your peak physically at college.

But sprinting ability does not necessarily imply other physical capacities which in some types of work are important. Endurance, a consistently high energy level, immunity to tension, capacity to do without rest for long periods, even muscular strength, are sometimes essential. For the successful surgeon, life is a succession of sprints, under extreme pressure, often with little chance for relaxation between. The Foreign Service officer must have the stamina to live for years in the debilitating heat or petrifying cold of the world's backwaters, much of the time perhaps working at a leisurely pace but always carrying the weight of major responsibility. The geologist employed by an oil company and the forester need rugged physiques.

Most kinds of white collar work, however, require no more than ordinary physical capacity. The warning flag in physical matters need go up only when there is something abnormal about the job's requirements or subnormal about your constitution.

23

Family Factors

Reluctant as we may be today to admit it in America, the fact is that who and what your family is may still have a bearing on how welcome you will be and your chances of success in some geographic areas, industries, companies and kinds of work where "who you are" is a factor. Your family determines who you are to a large degree — your race, color and creed, some of your values, your education, your manners and speech (hippies excepted), even your appearance (hippies again excepted). Any of these aspects of your being may, in some contexts, be either an asset or a liability, though if the latter, they are seldom today fatal to your progress once on the job, if you are highly motivated and able. Competence to do the job is increasingly becoming the key to success in a time when capable people are in short supply and the country is reaching strongly against discriminatory practices.

But we still have some way to go to complete lack of unfair discrimination. Thus, other things being equal and given a choice, you will be well advised to think in terms of fields and kinds of work where your "family factors" are either an asset or not of consequence — where this can be determined.

Achievement

The matter of your record to date, already touched on several times, is brought up again mainly for emphasis. What you have — and have not — accomplished, where you have succeeded and failed, what you have found rewarding or frustrating, interests pursued and dropped, these are guides to exploration that you will ignore to your disadvantage.

The negative aspect of the record needs special stress since it is easy to be taken in by the selected information one reveals to a possible employer or admissions officer. It may be more important, in plotting one's course, to remember — and consider the implications of — the fact that one was fired from a summer job, for example, or was not appointed to a coveted committee post, or failed to come up with a roommate in Junior year, or gave up tutoring at the "Y," than to savor one's A's or club officerships or varsity letters.

From a rapid reading of this chapter, a visitor from outer space might conclude that you as an American collegian have, at graduation, gone about as far as you can go, that, to overstate the matter, you can look for no improvement in your intelligence; your aptitudes and interests have crystallized; physically you are about to start downhill; and your chances of success have been predetermined by your family. And further, you have just been urged to look backwards, at your failures. On this evidence, you are a stagnant being, if not worse.

Nothing could be further from the truth, of course. You are just getting started and are moving into a world whose size, breadth and depth, whose opportunities for accomplishment and the variety of whose challenges no college campus can even approximate. But you are likely to start faster and go further in the working world if you know in advance what, if any, changes in yourself you can expect, as well as what you now have to offer. Such knowledge may call for unwelcome compromises with former aspirations or perhaps a raising of sights. In any case, failure to acquire accurate self-knowledge and use it can result in getting off on the wrong foot, with a resultant loss of precious time if you later change to another line of work, or, if you cannot move, a less than fully rewarding working life.

One final *caveat*. History recounts the stories of many people who made their mark in the face of serious limitations. Characteristics such as drive, dedication and ambition made the difference. While it would be clearly foolish to attempt work where the odds against you are manifestly insuperable, to give up without trying when they are merely high, and your desire is strong, would be equally foolish.

Chapter

3

Emotions and Careers

AS NOTED in earlier chapters, the commonplace, now a century or more old, that much of what men do in the name of pure reason is, in fact, influenced by their emotions, has only recently been recognized as applicable to career decision-making. It had been assumed previously, it seems, that thought and action in this particular field remained unpolluted by feelings, that "true reasoning" could hold sway. This recent finding has yet to be transformed into a practical guide for people faced with career decisions and those who would help them. Perhaps such a guide is impossible. Emotions may be too amorphous and mercurial a quantity ever to be captured in a tidy formula.

But a long step can be taken towards practical use of this finding simply by bringing it to the attention of undecided students and by describing some of the emotions they may be dealing with. Even without a tidy formula simple recognition of the situation can bring good decisions, seemingly unbidden.

You may be among those who are reluctant to accept the fact that you can't expect to be entirely rational. Or you may welcome the news, if it is news to you. It can give legitimacy to urges about which you have been feeling guilty; and it can introduce into your ponderings new factors which, far from complicating the problems of choosing, can serve to simplify them. If you are confronted with several work alternatives, all of which seem to match your aptitudes, capacities and interests, for instance, it can be helpful in making a choice to take conscious account of your feelings about such things as freedom from external control, or prestige, or the ways in which you prefer to deal with people, or what sort of role you would like to be playing before the world 15 years hence.

This chapter is divided into two parts. The first deals with who and what you think you are and would like to be — your "self-concept" — as it relates to choosing a career. The second discusses 19 "values," here defined as those idiosyncratic, emotion-rooted, human wants and needs which can be satisfied or frustrated by the job you hold.

Illustrative student case histories are used extensively. Unfortunately none of the protagonists of these stories are women since the institution I serve has yet to become coeducational. They are all true stories in the sense that the events recounted actually happened. To protect the identity of the individuals concerned, however, the names used are fictitious and, in some instances, the history is a composite of several. All the stories suffer from one major disability as "cases" in the context of this book. No one can know for 40 years or more whether or not the hero lived happily ever after, whether the decision he made was ultimately right for him. You will have to accept, on the grounds of plausibility and my assurance (based on a quarter of a century of observation), the truth of the proposition that people who understand themselves emotionally and take this understanding into consideration as they make job choices are more likely to live a happy and productive work life than those who don't.

The Self-Concept
Those who have made a study and profession of career choice agree that a powerful, perhaps the key determinant in job decisions is the self-concept — who and what one thinks one is and could be. They speak of choosing a job to "implement" one's self-concept. This is one of the non-intellectual influences, they say, which will join you at the decision table, invited or not. At each point of choice, the theory holds, you will consciously or unconsciously pick that working role which squares most closely with the picture you have of yourself. This picture may

or may not be accurate now, or feasible as to the future. If it is not and goes uncorrected, you may be headed for trouble. The story of John Crawford, although related only indirectly to career choice, is one of a shifting self-concept, whether for better or worse only time will tell.

John's craggy, six-foot frame sagged with dejection when he came in to discuss his first term grades. They averaged C-minus. He was thinking about transferring. "Better get out of here before the roof falls in."

John had been a football star, class leader, top scholar and ranking Beau Brummel at his small town high school. He had come to "believe my own press clippings," he said. On arrival at college John was teamed with a roommate who came from a more socially sophisticated background, and John soon concluded that he was looked on as a country bumpkin by his classmates. In fact, however, during the ritualized and suspicious mutual inspection which Freshmen everywhere initially engage in, he was regarded as just another classmate of room-filling but otherwise unknown dimensions.

He was cut from the football squad in late September. The big city dates his roommate had down for game weekends "psyched me out," and he admitted to having been a little ashamed of the one girl from home he brought to campus. As to the scholastic demands, he "hadn't got the hang of it."

In late fall he took to getting drunk on weekends and picking fights. At this point he did acquire a distinct image among his classmates, that of a "nice enough guy, but he always seems to have a chip on his shoulder."

The scene shifts to the winter of John's Senior year. The frame still sagged, but this time it was a comfortable sag. A good fraternity had taken him in and he was a top intramural athlete. He was dating a lot and indiscriminately as between city and country girls. Academically he was in the middle of his class and had been accepted by a graduate business school of average quality, both levels of achievement being much lower than might have been predicted from his College Board scores. "Why sweat it?" was the way he put it, reminiscing about the past four years. "I was looking for the pennant when I got here. Then I thought I'd be in the cellar. Now somewhere in the first division will do."

Your self-concept is made up of three parts, though there may be considerable overlap. The first is of who and what you think you really are as you look inwards, an appraisal vouchsafed, if at all, only to those closest to you. This appraisal may or may not be consonant with the facts. Many students, for example, recognizing that they tend to be self-serving, conclude that they are not as "nice" as others, whereas, in fact, everybody tends to be self-serving. Or a person may see himself as possessed of high but unrewarded executive competence, a Walter Mitty in a gray flannel suit, when actually he suffers from a crucial lack of decisiveness.

The second part of the picture of yourself is the one which you believe others have of you, what you think you look like physically and what impression you think your personality makes — your concept of your "stage presence" before the world. And this, too, often does not correspond with the facts.

Finally, you probably feel you could be somewhat better, or different from what you think you now are, in regard to your private self or your public self or both. This is sometimes termed the ideal self.

Since these self-concepts have a bearing on the work you will seek, whether you realize it or not, it is obviously important that you take the trouble to explore them. It is also important that you be as sure as you can that the pictures you have of yourself, inside and out, are in keeping with the facts. A conscious and conscientious effort to look at the truth dispassionately, through your own eyes or, better still, through those of someone you trust, is the only way to accomplish this. Some assurance that there is a reasonable match between self-concepts and reality is urgent because a seriously distorted view of yourself can lead to unfortunate developments. If it is exaggerated, disappointment and a sense of failure may be in store. If it is too modest, you may go through life without realizing your potential, even though possibly with good cheer if you never recognize your error.

Special attention should be paid to the concept you have of the impression you make on others. A wide discrepancy between this self-concept and the impression you actually make — let's call it your "personal style" — carries a particularly great potential for harm, depending on the kind of work you undertake. Such misconceptions are widespread — and have been for some time if Bobbie Burns's lines can be taken as evidence: "Oh wad some power the giftie gie us to see oursels as others see us . . ." Disappointment may not be the end of Al Johnson's story, but surely the red flag is up.

A Political Science major, Al looked a little like a worried heron, glasses perched half-way down a long nose, hunched shoulders, long, spindly legs. There was a kind of whining abrasiveness about him which one guessed would irritate anyone he dealt with. Nevertheless, he had a small circle of warm friends, all intellectual sophisticates, as was Al.

He wanted to talk about a career in elective politics. It was suggested that such a career usually is possible, if at all, only after one has made a mark doing something else, but that he might run for some office on campus and spend a summer in his congressman's office in Washington to see how he might fit the role. Al turned down the first idea but welcomed the second.

The congressman's administrative assistant, in a summer's-end report, said that Al had handled the clipping book and had also done some first-class research for speeches. Another intern, a "gregarious type," had been assigned to greeting constituents. Al had been strongly advised, the report said, that his interest in politics would be best served by going on for a Ph.D., to be followed by teaching and consulting.

Al came back to campus enthusiastic about the summer. He had done some routine chores and research, he said, but what he liked best was listening to proceedings from the balcony of the House and greeting visitors to the office when he had a chance. He obviously felt he had excelled in the latter capacity.

When last heard from, Al was pursuing an advanced degree in Political Science at another university — and planning to enter elective politics as soon as opportunity arose, still apparently oblivious of his probably fatal personal style limitations.

One's personal style — one's habitual ways of thinking and talking, of associating with others, of acting and reacting — is of major consequence in some professions and occupations, among them the performing arts, the ministry, courtroom law, all kinds of supervision, and, in general, wherever success depends heavily on the impression one makes on others. Since most jobs involve some dependence on others for success, however, personal style is never unimportant; a minimum capacity to get along with others is always necessary. The research scientist must work with supporting technicians, professional colleagues and superiors. The freelance writer must cultivate his sources of information and court editors and publishers. The composer can't rub musicians and conductors the wrong way. It is only, however, when one aspires to a career where particular kinds of personalities thrive and others do not that a careful assessment of what his personal style actually is is urgent.

Values

The word "values" can mean different things to different people. Our concern in the pages that follow is with those wants and needs, varying in kind and pattern among individuals, which can be satisfied or frustrated by what one does for a living. More precisely, the subjects to be explored are: what, on the job itself, may or may not be important to you; which of its features can make it pleasant or unpleasant, tolerable or intolerable; what can make it worth doing for its own sake; and what off-the-job outcomes or derivatives are important to you. The "on-the-job-off-the-job" dichotomy is used because, although you doubtless have some concern for values of both sorts, you probably tend to feel more strongly about the one or the other. In any event, these are the emotion-based bents you should try to identify and invite in to help you with your decisions.

Aside from being idiosyncratic, values have a number of things in common. First, as with occupational interests, your particular pattern cannot be predicted from your heredity, aptitudes and experience. Parental concern for and provision of material blessings need not, for instance, presage a desire for affluence in their young. Second, your values tend to remain fixed after you have reached your majority, though they can be sated — one can achieve the degree of eminence to which he aspires. Or they can be thwarted — a writer with a yen for creativity and freedom to come and go as he wishes may be forced to give up freelance writing because he lacks the necessary talent and finds he can't feed his family on rejection slips. Or again they can be modified to a degree — the pressure of competition on the job may cause a person to change his views as to what is ethical.

Third, you may find your values in conflict — a desire to be of direct service to people may run counter to a feeling that social work and most other "helping" occupations are not sufficiently prestigious. Fourth, values are emotional in character, a fact you may recognize clearly enough in others with whom you disagree but may find hard to admit with regard to your own. Finally, values are seldom discretely identifiable (though they are so presented here for the sake of orderliness) — a person may be driven by desires for money, control, challenge and pace all at once without knowing clearly which of these is predominant. The story of Ed Piwonski illumines some of these common denominators of values.

Ed was the son of a job printer who had made it the hard way after leaving school at the eighth grade. When Ed first came in for a consultation, he was all business. He had decided on hometown law as a career and simply wanted advice on what courses would best serve the purpose. He appeared to resent being asked why he had settled on the law, but then went on to say that his father thought this would give him security, a good income and, eventually, a leading place in the community. He brushed off a further question about what his own views were.

Over the next three years Ed discovered an aptitude for

languages; traveled one summer on a grant with a study group in Europe; and spent another as a counselor at a camp for handicapped children.

He came in again in the fall of his Senior year, principally to get information about the Foreign Service Officer Examination which was scheduled in the near future. Ed explained his decision largely in terms of negatives. Hometown law was out, he said. "Too cut and dried and there's a bigger world." Teaching had been urged on him by some of his professors and while it was a chance to be of direct service to society, he had turned the idea down because "teachers don't rate very high." He had been tempted briefly by an offer to join the international operations of a major oil company. The money to be made had appealed to him but "you never know when the natives will cut the pipes and the company can fire you without taking a deep breath." He summed up by saying: "A foreign service officer doesn't make much and bounces around a lot. But he has a chance to do something important at the start and he can count on his job and if he sticks with it he'll be a somebody before he's through."

Values are worth considering not only in connection with your daily work but also with your avocations — and you will be having more time for these as the average work day grows gradually shorter. You are unlikely to find work which meets your value specifications in every particular. Free-time activity can fill out the picture to the extent that it is not dictated by your job (the man who must play golf with customers), or by your family (the woods are full of green thumbs turned den mother).

Nineteen values are examined below, grouped in two categories. The first 13 are "on-the-job" values, and the last six, "off-the-job" values. A further word on the dichotomy before describing the values themselves.

In America the script generally prescribes that boy pursue girl for love and love alone. Only a cad would give consideration to her money or lack of it, social position, health and handiness around the house. When a boy — or girl — is pursuing a career, however, the same prescription does not hold, or at least some exceptions are tolerated in some quarters. You may give highest priority to "love," that is, finding work which you will enjoy for its own sake. Or you may without offense be more concerned with, say, how much money you will make, or with security, cheerfully facing the possibility that jobs which will serve these purposes may turn out to be chores. You probably tend to fall into one category or the other, as suggested earlier. There is usually overlap, however, and you can move from one to the other in the course of a lifetime. A person initially out to "make a million," for example, can make it and then move on to give expression to a hitherto latent urge towards service to society by getting into educational administration.

While you will find considerable tolerance for your values if they are other than true love for your job, you will also find a widespread belief that off-the-job-oriented people — in the sense used here — somehow are not as commendable as those who put love of their jobs first and perhaps do not serve society as well. There is really no evidence to support this belief. In any event, you probably cannot be reasoned out of your personal values and will do your best work, whatever it is, if you are not forced or persuaded to adopt uncongenial patterns.

Let us begin with 13 on-the-job values.

People

Some career counselors would make the following question a standard part of their procedure in talking with you: Are you people-oriented, or ideas-oriented, or things-oriented? They would not imply that you can or want to find a career that will match one or another of these orientations to the complete exclusion of the others, but there might be the suggestion that once you had established your preference, you could forego further consideration of your feelings about the alternatives.

Such a suggestion is unwarranted, at least so far as people-orientation is concerned. Contact with others is some part of all paying jobs. And the chances are, of course, that you will work for and with others continuously while on the job. You may, in addition, supervise others. And, even if self-employed — in creative work, the professions, and in consulting and other entrepreneurial enterprises — you will at a minimum have to deal with suppliers of the things you need and with customers for your services or goods. Thus, whatever the principal focus of your work — people, ideas or things — your preferred ways of dealing with people should be a continuing issue as you make your choices. This situation might lend itself to charting, with degree of interest in people *per se* along one axis and the various ways of dealing with people along the other. Bob Miller, Ralph Smith and Arthur Collins would appear at quite different places on such a chart.

Bob was a notably gregarious soul, a born joiner, full of conversation, one who felt isolated during his Freshman year because he had only one roommate. (He had enlisted six more by the time room drawing took place in the spring of that year.) At the end of his Junior year he was elected, without effort on his part, president of a large campus organization. Once on the job he discovered he had a talent for and thoroughly enjoyed leading — he wondered somewhat guiltily whether a more exact word might be "manipulating" — others. On the strength of this discovery he decided to amend his career thinking. Instead of teaching, which he originally had in mind, he made educational administration his first choice and planned also to look into opportunities in industry and government which might lead quickly to supervision.

Ralph, a sophomore with the makings of a competent and dedicated architect, was nevertheless uneasy about architecture as a career. The only practitioners he knew were the members of the architecture faculty and two friends of his family, both of whom worked by themselves. Neither teaching nor self-employment appealed to him. In the course of mulling the matter over he made two findings which cleared the air. First, he realized for the first time that he particularly enjoyed collaborating with other students on architectural projects and that his best work resulted from such collaboration. Second, he attended a career panel on city planning and learned that architects are badly needed all over the country as members of urban and regional development teams.

Because Arthur, our third example, had turned in a first-class record and appeared to enjoy theoretical mathematics during his first two years, and because he seemed a retiring and inarticulate person, it was a surprise when he wanted to discuss switching to English, with the eventual objective of becoming an actor. It developed that he had a good baritone voice, had joined an informal campus singing group and enjoyed performing. Also, he had attended, over the past year, all the productions of the campus dramatic society and the local repertory theatre. "It isn't that I don't like mathematics," he said. "I do. But I like to amuse people and I can't do that as a researcher locked in with a computer and a blackboard the rest of my life, which is what people say I am cut out for. I can't see any way to do both." Had he thought of teaching? He had, but as far as he could see this was "just a matter of coming into a classroom, putting a lot of figures on the board and returning to the computer." Some weeks later he was still in doubt but tending towards the teaching of math as a career aim. He had gone with a roommate to a special lecture given annually by a professor in another discipline who was renowned on campus as a showman. "Maybe there can be more to teaching than you'd think from watching these graduate assistant jerks who give the underclass math courses," Arthur decided.

The ways in which you may prefer to associate with others are many: You may prefer to dominate, help, serve, counsel, follow, control, lead, manipulate, inform, instruct, understand, divert or persuade others; or to cooperate, consult, compete or bargain with others; or to resolve differences between others. You probably will be dealing with others in more than one way at any given time and will also find the nature of your associations changing as you grow older — from being supervised to supervising, for example. If you are basically people-oriented, it is obviously urgent that you find out early what your preferred relationships are. But even if you are a things-oriented development engineer, for instance, you may have a choice between supervision, working with a team or consulting under your own shingle. And if you are an idea-oriented psychologist, you can pursue your profession as, among other ways, a teacher or researcher or advertising agency staff member.

Ideas

As a way of working life, you may prefer rumination, playing with concepts and theories and hunting for new thoughts, information and inspirations, as against dealing with other human beings or producing things and concrete results; i.e., you are ideas-oriented. This is not to say, obviously, that people who do not share your preference don't deal with ideas. A capacity to work comfortably and effectively with ideas is essential to success in all careers which are attractive to collegians. What distinguishes you from others, if you are ideas-oriented, is that you prefer thinking to doing and are relatively unconcerned with the practical applicability of what you know and learn. Michael Woods found a compromise between the two.

Michael had the problem of many young men whose families, reacting to the growing gap between what they know and what is being taught at colleges these days, question the usefulness of what their sons are learning in the context of making a living. As a Freshman, Michael took anthropology, calculus, philosophy, religion and French. At the end of the year, his parents began putting pressure on him to head in more "practical" directions. Michael himself was not unconcerned about making a comfortable living. But he was reluctant to write off the possibility of spending some part of his working life in the realm of ideas — his preference at the moment was for math. How to combine the two? While browsing in the career library one day, he came across the recruiting literature of one of the "think tanks." These are organizations, staffed largely by Ph.D.'s and post-doctoral types from many disciplines, which work on such matters as logistics, operations analysis and the propounding of questions which need answers. They work for the Military Services, urban redevelopers and private industry, among others. He also learned from a friend at graduate school that some industries allow their Ph.D.s to work on "their own" research part-time, even though it might be entirely unrelated to the firm's business. These possibilities satisfied both Michael and his parents and he went on in math.

Of the various kinds of work which can satisfy this value, truth searching — scholarship and "pure" or "blue sky," as contrasted with applied or developmental, research — is the least "polluted" with the necessity for concern with people and things. Some other kinds of work which can be rewarding, if you are one who needs time for leisurely, non-pragmatic reflection, are teaching at the college and postgraduate levels, urban planning and such creative endeavors as painting, composing music and writing fiction and poetry.

Things

You are "things-oriented," according to our construct, if your greatest satisfactions come from accomplishments that can be touched or seen, or from intangible achievements which can be measured and are of practical use. Abstract ideas may play a preliminary role and working with others may be required to effect the end result, but it is concreteness and workability in the result that things-oriented people seek. Roger Brown accidentally discovered that satisfaction of this kind of bent could be found within the field of law.

Roger was vaguely interested in the law but had been somewhat "turned off" by the dinner-table impression he had from lawyer friends of his father that the work consisted of dealing either with abstruse concepts or with people in trouble. He was something of a loner and of a highly practical turn of mind. There seemed no point in trying to find a summer job in a law firm to explore these impressions further, since the few openings available each summer are snapped up by the thousands of law students eager for experience and future employment contacts. Roger could type and got work through one of the employment agencies which specialize in providing temporary help to firms when members of their office staffs are sick or vacationing. Within a week he was farmed out to a patent attorney whose secretary would be gone for two weeks. He was fascinated by what he saw and heard. He made himself sufficiently useful and agreeable during the two weeks to be asked to stay on for the rest of the summer as a mail clerk and general helper. On his return to college he described patent law as "the kind of nuts-and-bolts-job a guy can really get his teeth into."

If you are things-oriented, you can find satisfying work in many areas. Jobs related to the end products of such industries as manufacturing, publishing, construction, mining and farming have obvious appeal to those who want tangibility in the fruits of their work. Or one can satisfy this preference as a librarian, curator or forester.

Where tangibility is not at issue, the list of possibilities is endless — all the kinds of work in all the fields which involve dealing with figures, with organizing, with planning and with operating. Only a handful of the occupations discussed in the latter half of this book are without facets which would be attractive to things-oriented people.

Inner and Outer Direction

Nobody prefers to be "led around by the nose." Most consider themselves ready and able to make their own decisions. Society reinforces independence of spirit by dubbing those who do not show it "sheep" or "conformists." These things being so, and since most college sudents have already demonstrated a propensity and capacity for running their own shows — they would not otherwise have arrived and survived at college — you might ask why a discussion of inner and outer direction is included here.

I include it because the desire to be master of one's own fate, in fact varies widely in intensity between individuals. For every person who wants unalloyed self direction, with the loneliness, the unaided decision making, the high order of initiative and, frequently, the willingness to take large risks it entails, there are thousands who will find adequate expression of their need for independence within the framework of supervision. And this is as well, since most of the jobs available today, at whatever level, are supervised to some degree. Corporation presidents, four-star generals and university presidents all work for somebody else.

Outer direction can be exercised by agencies other than human supervision. A work routine, a deadline, a commitment, the setting of a goal, the cultivation of a habit, all can give a measure of outer direction to what one does. Some people, finding that the human supervision they are getting is not enough for them, consciously or unconsciously contrive such inanimate controls over themselves. This proved to be Jack Toland's answer.

Jack's record when he came to college showed a high order of independence in his make-up. He had voluntarily spent one summer in charge of 70 American Indian children, the sole outsider on the reservation. Another summer he had worked for his father selling juke boxes on commission. He planned to run this or some other small business as a career. Shortly after arriving on campus he had taken charge of sales for the student grinder agency. Jack's marks at the end of his first term were far lower than had been predicted. "I have too much time and I fritter it away," was the way he diagnosed the problem, "At high school you had to follow a schedule all day." At the end of the year, his marks were up. It turned out that a student friend of Jack's who had been driving a school bus to make money had left college and willed the job to Jack. This meant that he now had to get up each weekday morning at six for the school-bound trip and to stop whatever he was doing each afternoon at three for the return. "Now I've got too much to do," he said — but without much conviction.

Self-employment in business, the professions, farming or the creative arts is the obvious answer for you if your need for independence is acute, providing you have the necessary competences. A high degree of, though not complete, autonomy is enjoyed by pastors, professors and some kinds of commission salesmen and by researchers and conservationists. Finally, line positions in all fields of work bring increasing independence as one moves up the ladder.

Ethics

You probably feel that you know what the ethical thing to do is in most circumstances, whether or not you always live up to your own standards. And this may lead you to brand standards differnet from your own as, on the one hand, pragmatic or reprehensible or, on the other, as idealistic or impractical. The fact is, however, that your convictions about what is right and wrong are strictly your own. No one shares them in all particulars and some may disagree with you in general.

And jobs are like people in this respect. In each, across the whole spectrum of kinds and fields of work, certain standards of conduct tend to prevail, but in no two are they exactly the same. And few are clearly higher or lower than others on any absolute scale; they are simply different. If these things are so, then the trick is to find work in which the prevailing standards match your own. Making a good match is important because, if your job is a bad misfit ethically, you will either leave or loathe it.

You may not feel you could be happy in private enterprise, where profits are always a vital consideration, for instance; or in elective politics, where readiness to compromise is essential to polling a majority of the votes; or in criminal law, where one may know one's client is guilty but be obliged to put up the best possible defense; or in public relations and sales, where the objective is to put the best possible face on things; or in the ministry where conduct above possible approach is expected. But these feelings, if you have them, do not enable you to label those who follow these callings as more or less "ethical" than you are. It is that their standards of moral rectitude are not yours and that you had best look elsewhere for a career. For you are not likely to change your ethical code substantially nor are you likely to alter those which obtain in these kinds of work so as to suit you.

And there are subtler shadings. You must be willing to play some office politics if you are to work successfully in large organizations, be they governmental, educational, professional, church or business. Or, again, if you feel dishonest whenever you have to keep to yourself reactions which would be offensive to others, or are unwilling to pay an occasional undeserved compliment, you had best stay out of such occupations as trust administration, teaching and supervision of all kinds.

Determining whether in a given occupation or industry the prevailing standards are consonant with your own is difficult without first-hand exposure. The only rule of thumb would appear to be that the greater the competition for advantage, between persons or organizations, the more relaxed the prevailing ethical standards are likely to be. One may add that in many organizations competitive pressures fluctuate from time to time, leading businesses and individuals to amend their standards somewhat, a phenomenon sometimes called "situational morality."

Direct Service to Society
The belief that what they do for a living is directly helpful to others — and by "others" they can mean anything from the people they deal with daily to humanity at large — is a matter of great consequence to some people. It may be a desire for regular, face-to-face service to others. Or it may be an urge, whatever their own daily duties, to participate in a cause which seems to them to be immediately and manifestly useful to society. It is in the latter guise, of course, that this feeling is ascribed to large numbers of your generation. For Allen Rowe this drive had both facets.

Allen's father was a well-to-do businessman widely noted for his charitable and civic good works. Allen was brought up to be concerned about those less fortunate than himself. It was made clear around the dinner table that he was expected to do something about this concern in later life, and his father's unspoken assumption was that he would, after the parental model, do it avocationally. The way of professional social workers, those "lowly, under-paid, bleeding hearts," would surely not appeal to Allen. Since Allen talked about law and business during his first two years at college and obviously relished frequent travel, sailing, country club life and other material good things that only large earnings can buy, his father had no reason to doubt the correctness of his assumption, so when Allen became involved in tutoring children in the ghetto of a city near campus in his Junior year, his father charged it off to youthful and transitory idealism. It came as a shock, then, when Allen announced in the spring that he was going to make a career of social work and had landed a summer job in the slums. He had deeply enjoyed the tutoring and had, further, for the first time gotten some measure of the magnitude of the Nation's urban poverty problems. His father was mollified to learn that he planned to go on for a Ph.D. and that top social work administrators can make $25,000 a year or even more. But the thought that his son could actually want such a career remained so preposterous to him that he didn't give up his opposition until Allen had been accepted by a graduate school of social work.

The need to be helpful to others in a face-to-face relationship can be met, of course, in all the "helping" professions, among them, in addition to social service, YMC-HA jobs, teaching, the ministry, medicine and counseling of all types, and in political and civil service work of many kinds. It can also be met for some in less obviously serving work. Selling life insurance, for instance, appeals to many principally because it involves persuading others to make provision for their families. The possibility of handsome earnings and the freedom to come and go which may also be involved can be entirely secondary considerations to such people. Similarly, causes which can reward this desire range from the obvious to the not so obvious, from population control, smog abatement, the Red Cross and the Foreign Service, for example, to the preservation of free enterprise, law enforcement and government service of all kinds.

The key word in this discussion is "direct." You probably want to feel that the work you undertake is somehow useful to others. Most people are at pains to justify what they do in this context, and most socially acceptable work is, in fact, socially serviceable. But this is not the point here. Rather, it is the possibility that your job satisfaction will depend heavily on your

belief that your work or the cause you serve is immediately helpful to others, not one or two removes away.

Immediate Results

Your reaction to your college experience can be a fairly good test
of where you stand in regard to your need to see immediate
results from your efforts. The two poles of this need can be illustrated by the frivolous comparison sometimes made between
surgeons and dermatologists. The surgeon's patients either die
or get well in jig time, so it is said; the dermatologist's never
get better or worse. At college there are long periods when you
have nothing to show for your work. The question is whether
or not you feel comfortable in this situation. Bill Spencer was
a student who wanted to know the answer to "How'm I doing?"
more often than every few months.

Bill was an Economics major, a second-rate sprinter on the
track team, sold magazines to students door-to-door in the evenings and was a member of the Investor's Club, where he was usually the first to urge the sale of a stock that wasn't performing up
to expectations. During his first three years, Bill had gone along
with his father's strong feeling that he should, when he graduated,
join the book publishing firm for which his father worked. With
this in mind, Bill took a summer job there at the end of his Junior
year. He was having second thoughts when he came back to campus in the fall and wanted to take "the tests." "Somehow, book
publishing doesn't seem to me to be where the action is, but my
father says I'm all wrong, that there's plenty of action and that,
anyway, action isn't the point." While his answer sheet for the
Strong Vocational Interest test was away being scored, Bill did
some browsing in the career library for the first time. When he
came back to discuss the test results, he opened by asking whether
they showed that retailing might fit him. "In retailing you're on
the move and you know where you are all the time." The test results were supportive. He then asked if he could have them to mail
to his father and whether openings were likely to be available in
retailing when he graduated. He could and they were. He de-
parted to do battle.

The desire to see results promptly is not necessarily that classic sign of immaturity, an unwillingness to forego immediate pleasure which predictably will impede the attainment of an important long range goal. If you are one who rebuilds his hi-fi set or starts to knit a sweater for her boy friend on the eve of a crucial exam, you probably have some growing up to do. If, on the other hand, you spend frequent evenings over the year on the set or the sweater, then possibly you are one of those who become frustrated by not knowing how they are doing often enough to suit them, a feeling which can be experienced by some people of manifest maturity.

Nor is concern for immediate results necessarily evidence that you are temperamentally impatient, so far as that word signifies chronic dissatisfaction with the progress you or others are making. Accountancy is a rewarding profession for people who value frequent evidence of accomplishment, but patience is one hallmark of those who practice it.

Neither is ambition or lack of it related to this desire. Banking, not a business in many of its aspects which gives one frequent chances to see what he has produced, harbors a fair share of the country's ambitious young people. Conversely, the Nation's 2000-odd public employment offices are staffed largely by employment interviewers and unemployment insurance claims takers who enjoy their work because it gives them an opportunity to produce concrete results daily, not because it is apt to lead to fame and fortune.

Jobs which can offer you frequent evidence of personal accomplishment are growing fewer. Machines are taking over many of the kinds of work which once provided rewards for those who have a concern for immediate results. And as employing units, particularly in education, business and government, grow larger, teams and committees are increasingly the action takers. If you are strongly immediate-results-oriented, you may in the future have to look more and more to your hobbies and other avocations to achieve satisfaction in this respect.

Some kinds of work which can bring a measure of this satisfaction, beyond those mentioned above, come readily to mind:

the creative arts; jobs connected directly with the production of goods and services; line as opposed to staff work; jobs involving direct service to others; real estate brokerage; journalism, and conservation work.

Although not strictly to the point, it might also be noted that people vary in their tolerance for waiting to reach their eventual career goals. Many, for example, have given up ambitions to become senior bank officers, or Army generals, or psychiatrists, or architects, because of the foreseeably long road to the top. If you are in great haste to reach the summit, however, it is perhaps well to remember that the shorter the road, the tougher the grade and the more the hairpin turns where a mistake or bad luck or a lack of outstanding competence can untrack you and send you tumbling.

Pace

The securities trader on a stock exchange floor paced by the chattering ticker tape, and the certified public accountant deliberately working over a company's books at the end of the fiscal year are, if they enjoy their work, constituted quite differently. Each would probably find the other's work unbearable for long.

Tastes in pace cover a broad spectrum. And its pace is a facet of any job you hold that you are likely to be particularly aware of. "The atmosphere is relaxed," or "You're on the go all the time" are typical and frequently heard remarks made by people describing their work. Because of the intensity of feeling you will probably have about the pace of your job, you may find yourself trying to revamp it if it is unsatisfactory. You may, for instance, invite or create new demands on your time, or conversely, try to eliminate or delegate responsibilities. Or you may simply increase or reduce the "busy-work," which on most jobs is of flexible quantity.

A desire to be on the go has no necessary relationship to a capacity for hard work. It may be simply a preferred mode of working. The person who elects the hectic life of a business executive does not work harder than the one who chooses to burn the midnight oil as a scholar. (If you are not one who naturally pursues his business "on the double," however, you had best keep it to yourself when you first go to work in any organization. There is one company president, for instance, who will never hire a man who smokes a pipe.) Carl Johnson learned something about the varieties of pace simply by walking across the street.

Carl was an electrical engineer. The summer of his Junior year he got a job with a company in the highly competitive packaging machinery business. His story on his return to college went something like this: "Doing what comes naturally one day, I was reading a technical journal at my desk and this young engineer came up and said, 'You'd better put that down or you won't last long here. No reading on company time is the rule.' I got talking with this guy after work and he was really excited about the company, to my surprise. 'A real lively outfit. The pressure's on all the time.' And it sure was! Several weeks later I went over to lunch with a friend of mine who worked for a company across the street which was on cost-plus government contracts. He was scathing about my company. 'They keep people jumping over there just to watch them jump. And this no reading bit. No wonder the president is always landing on his development staff about reinventing the wheel.' I took these remarks back to my engineer friend. His reaction, equally acid, was, 'You know, you have to sight the guys over there by a post to be sure they're actually moving.' "

The pace on a given job is related both to the kind of organization one works for and the nature of one's work. As to the first, the key factor is the organization's need to compete for survival and growth. With exceptions, the work pace in governmental and educational settings is markedly slower than that in private enterprise and self-employment. Within private enterprise, by the same token, the pace is likely to be faster in the consumer goods field, for instance, than in utilities. As to the nature of the work, people in the financial, research, systems and procedures and planning ends of any organization, for example, move in a more measured manner than those in general management, sales, public relations, production and labor relations.

Challenge

"Challenge," used interchangeably or coupled with "opportunity," is the most overworked word in the lexicon of the business concerns and other organizations which try to attract you to their employ. Their advertising and recruiters imply that problems of major moment, whose resolution will shake the world, keep you on your toes and bring you quick fame and fortune, will face you from the outset. They assume that you and all your friends want "challenge."

The implication, in the first place, is groundless in most cases. A few (the number is increasing) concerns will, in fact, turn you loose, early in your career, to sink or swim, selling on commission, or in a supervisory job or other clearly responsible work. And if you have an advanced degree, especially in science or engineering, you may be confronted with important unsolved problems soon after arrival. But in most organizations, the only challenge (Webster's New Collegiate Dictionary defines the word, among other things, as "an invitation to engage in a contest") you can expect as a newcomer is competition with other newcomers in the mastery of a lot of new information, on the one hand, and for recognition by the boss, on the other. There is nothing surprising or reprehensible about this situation. In many lines of work the skills and knowledge necessary to tackle problems of any importance can only be acquired through an apprenticeship. Futher, many employers want considerable time to appraise new employees before taking the real risks of handling them real responsibility. The only issue is the hoodwinkery involved in describing such break-in periods as being "challenging."

The assumption that all of you want challenge in your careers is correct in the sense that few of you would admit to not wanting it. But the fact is that many of you will fare more cheerfully and successfully in the world of work if you pursue paths that are relatively free of "contests." For challenge represents not only the opportunity to succeed but also the possibility of failure. There can be no contest where the outcome is foreordained. One who welcomes and thrives on challenge in any real sense is a willing risk taker and must in addition be highly competitive, decisive, self-confident and a compulsive worker; employment where the rule is "up or out" does not scare him. This is not a description of the average collegian. You can get some bearing on the genuineness of your own desire for real challenge by assessing your habitual approach to contests of whatever kind. If you frequently incline to caution, your taste for challenge is doubtful. This does not mean that high places will be out of reach, however. The less trying obstacle courses generally ascend, if more slowly. The combination of a good mind, good sense and hard work brings "opportunity" in most settings. Frank Nichols is a case in point.

Frank was business manager of the campus newspaper. He had reached this position both because he had been a bear for work in his underclass years and because, later on, he had come up with a number of imaginative schemes — special editions, contests and advertising gimmicks — which brought the paper's profits to new highs. In the fall of his Senior year he was approached by the man who had edited the paper several years earlier and who was planning to launch a new nation-wide periodical. Would he run the business side of the new venture? The salary would be modest at the start but if the magazine went over there was no telling how bright the future might be. Frank had no other job leads, no interest in going to graduate school and no immediate need for a substantial income. After several months of soul-searching, however, he turned down the offer. "It's all very well to experiment with a paper on campus. What have you got to lose? The college will bail you out if you pull a boo-boo. But this other deal — it'll be two years at least before the returns are in. So I'm in clover if it goes over. But if it doesn't I'm back where I started with two years of my life wasted and a failure on my record. I think I'll look around for a job with one of the big weekly magazines or a small city daily."

Creativity
People who have "creative" talent in marketable forms have no problems in expressing their urges to be creative. They design

buildings, paint, dance, sing, act, sculpt, compose, write, decorate interiors and make pots. With or without marketable talent, however, most people feel the yen to create in some degree. In Jim Craig, for instance, it flamed but was damped, at least temporarily, by second thoughts.

Jim discovered poetry as a Sophomore. He had entered college in the business curriculum but had become disenchanted and had switched to liberal arts. Looking ahead, he had been considering law, the priesthood, and teaching, each interest inspired by warm regard for a man he knew in the field. Then came poetry and all else was forgotten. He frequented the bohemian quarter of a near-by city. He sat at the feet of the leading *avant-garde* poets and the editors of little magazines, and wrote for the campus literary periodical. However, first-hand the knowledge of how young poets live, acquired in his travels, considerably lessened his dedication to the muse. He was used to comfort. In the fall of his Senior year he made a point of taking the Graduate Record Examination in English and did some inquiring about the more conventional writing professions. He remained determined to write. In the end he decided to enlist in the Army and thus give himself three more years to mull the matter over.

Your urge to create can always be expressed, no matter how limited your aptitude and how little your job apparently calls for creativity. If you are an office manager, for example, you can work up a new procedural handbook or set up a new filing system. Above the minimum level which can be satisfied by such activity, however, the need to be creative must be supported by talent of some kind, if it is not to be thwarted. Fortunately, there are many aptitudes and skills other than those normally dubbed "creative" which can be employed creatively. Those of the scientist and the engineer can be so used, not only in research but also in application and development work. City planning calls for the creative application of a dozen different competences. Reporting and editing and even headline writing and make-up on a newspaper can be creative. And so with public relations and advertising and the drafting of legislation and trust instruments.

Precision vs. Tolerance of Ambiguity

Some people, engineers, actuaries, comptrollers, computer scientists and airline pilots among them, place high value on precision, logic, a methodical approach to problems, mastery of subject matter and categorical evidence. Others can cheerfully rely in intuition, can make decisions easily without having all the facts, are undisturbed when they have to fly by the seat of their pants; such people gravitate into psychiatry, social work, advertising and politics. Most people fall somewhere between these two extremes. The aspirations of Tom Bliss seemed to be out of keeping with his location along the spectrum.

Meticulous in manner and dress, Tom was majoring in Experimental Psychology with the intention of going into research until, one day, he decided out of the blue to try the advertising business. He had been fascinated by a book about subliminal selling. Tom had not investigated the world of work in general, which was surprising in one who was known in his department as a thorough researcher. He brushed aside the suggestion that further inquiry about the advertising business might be useful. While he did not say so directly, it appeared that he feared this might be upsetting. During the Senior recruiting season, he was interviewed by all the representatives of advertising agencies who came to campus. One made this confidential appraisal: "We could well use him in research. Sharp mind. But he wants to be an account executive. With his apparent inflexibility, he wouldn't last a week in the advertising game in anything but research or accounting."

Tom's story points up an aspect of tolerance for ambiguity which makes it, perhaps, unique among the values we have been discussing. Finding work which matches your feelings in this area can be more than a matter of your happiness on the job. It can mean the difference between success and mediocrity, or even disaster. An automotive engineer must add to his skill a deep visceral concern for precision if he is to avoid slips which could send tens of thousands of cars back to dealers for replacement of faulty steering linkages, for instance. Conversely, a newspaper reporter who cannot bring himself to write his story until every last fact is in hand will miss press deadlines and soon be out of a job. A few people, lawyers turned legislators, for example, can work both sides of the street. But if you are like most people, your tolerance for ambiguity, be it great or small, covers only a small segment of the spectrum.

Control

A wish for independence, discussed earlier, may be satisfied simply by the absence of direction from or dependence on others in your decision-making — as the doctor who elects to hang out his own shingle as against teaming up with others in a clinic or serving on a hospital staff. Or it may go a step further, to become a desire for authority. Ben Wilson's choice was based on this kind of desire.

Ben, a marketing major, was a class officer, advertising manager of the Senior yearbook and, as a guard, the playmaker on the basketball team. With this extracurricular record and top-quarter academic standing, he was courted by perhaps a dozen company recruiters. Those less sophisticated in identifying young men's feelings, who stressed pay or fringe benefits or plant location to Ben, were soon decided against. As spring rolled around, three companies were left in the field — a textile concern, an insurance company and a public utility. The first offered him the independence of commission selling early in his career and a next step into sales management. The insurance representative said that for a considerable period, while he learned the ropes in the home office, Ben could not hope for a supervisory job. But, he pointed out that one way in which the company cultivated good relations with its community was to nominate employees to serve as leaders in such activities as the Community Fund Drive. Ben could, if he wished, receive such a nomination immediately. The public utility, however, got Ben. Within a month after he joined them, they promised, he would be in sole charge of a half a dozen semi-skilled employees in one of their outlying offices.

Control is usually acquired through direct supervision over

others, If you have this yen, you should usually choose line, as contrasted with staff jobs in any organization. But there are jobs calling for little or no direct supervisory responsibility which, nevertheless, can give you a measure of control. The budget director in any large organization, exercising the power of the purse, can have influence far beyond the handful of people who report to him. The political boss, perhaps invisible in the shadow of the candidate for office, often runs the show. And in many organizations, employees from the executive vice president on down are well-advised to clear their plans with the youthful assistant to the president, a staff officer, before making a move.

Authority, obviously, seldom comes unearned. To acquire it one must have, beyond the urge, the ability to persuade those he would boss (people he wants to hire or lead) or those who can give him control (his supervisors) of his fitness for it. And this generally takes self-confidence, competitiveness and decisiveness, together with the ability to work easily with others, to plan, to organize and to follow up. Without these qualities in liberal measure, a strong desire for control is likely to be frustrated.

Variety

Most entry-level jobs in all fields are relatively routine and repetitive compared, at least, with college work. You will usually have to serve an apprenticeship, whatever your goals, in order to acquire the skill and knowledge necessary to reach them. But you surely want a career which will have variety eventually. The issue, looking ahead, is not, then, between routine and variety but what kind of variety appeals to you. An analogy might illustrate at least one major difference between people in their needs for variety. Some want to drive the straight highway of growing competence in a specialty and expect to find the kind of variety they need in the scenery along the way. Others like traffic, turning corners and shifting gears constantly. Ted Sawyer was one who liked traffic.

Ted was not well known on campus. He was an average student, dabbled in intramural athletics, wrote an occasional piece for the paper and ran the student parking agency. Undistinguished as this record apparently was, Ted was among the students most sought after by recruiters seeking future general managers (the most "trafficky" of occupations) in the winter of his Senior year. His résumé told the story. Off campus, Ted had a part interest in a restaurant and worked on the counter at night. He was a force to be reckoned with in the local Chamber of Commerce, although only half the age of most of its members. He sold articles to leading magazines. He had, one summer, been a key member of a congressman's campaign staff. Another summer he had organized a tour agency in Austria. Ted did not warm to any of the several handsome offers he received. The recruiters all stressed the shortness of the road to general management from the entry jobs they had open, but Ted was skeptical. He finally decided to go on to graduate business school, although more schooling didn't strongly appeal to him. The decision was based on the fact that, more and more, companies are putting the men they hire from graduate business schools to work as management auditors, assigned to review company operations and procedures from top to bottom and to make recommendations for change to top management. Ted felt that this was the fastest route by which he could reach the kind of variety which appealed to him.

All the professions offer you choices in kinds of variety. As a doctor you can do research or specialize in orthopedics or cancer surgery, for instance, or you can become an internist or family doctor, the latter-day equivalent of the general practitioner, who has practically died out with the rapid growth of medical knowledge. As a lawyer you can take all kinds of cases or can concentrate on, for example, maritime or labor law. Architects can take on whatever jobs come to hand or go into city planning, on the one hand, or concentrate on, say, public school or office design, on the other. In education, you can choose teaching, administration, scholarship, research or combinations of these. Engineers and scientists, as they move up, can elect to continue in essentially loner staff work as researchers or development experts, or they can take on supervision. (This option is a fairly recent development, incidentally. Previously, to reach the top in pay and recognition, an engineer or scientist had to became an administrator, at least part time. Employers eventually discovered that this requirement was resulting in the loss of good research and development people and the creation of poor supervisors.)

Outside the professions, the same kinds of choices are available in many lines of work. As a salesman, you can handle a variety of products or services, or only one, finding the variety you need in the latter event in the diversity of your customers. The reporter is basically a wordsmith and fact-finder but in a single week may cover everything from a crime to a concert. Personnel work may include wage and salary administration, training and recruiting, management development, employee relations and union contract negotiation, or you can specialize in one of these fields.

Perhaps the most varied of all work in the "traffic" sense is top-level general management in all fields of work. Unless you start out with a business of your own, however, you can't become such a generalist until you have first mastered most of the special competences included in your general management portfolio-to-be, or are at least able to understand and evaluate the recommendations of those who have.

We turn now to off-the-job values.

Money

You may want to "make a pile," or "just be comfortably off," or perhaps, "couldn't care less about money." These attitudes about money and the many shadings between them are all tenable. You should stick to your own unless and until you feel like changing it, regardless of any adverse reaction you may get from others. Your feelings about what standard of material well-being would be satisfactory, whatever their sources, are probably deeprooted and thus to be disregarded only for far more compelling reasons than what someone else thinks — excepting possibly your wife and children, of which more later. Your only concern about your goals as to money should be that you have a clear idea of how many dollars it will take to meet them.

There is only one way to find out. That is to learn what order of income is necessary to support a given standard of living. Your own is the obvious place to start. A conducted tour through your family's book of accounts can be most illuminating. Many parents, however, are reluctant to reveal the details of their finances to anyone, even their grown sons or daughters. If this is the situation, the next best approach is to ask members of the older generation you know well how much they estimate it costs people with whom you are both familiar to live — the couple who have set up housekeeping in a bohemian quarter pad, neighbors, families who travel a lot, families with varying numbers of children in school and college.

If you want to take the trouble, also, it is possible to know what many people make. These are people in government employment, in the Military Services, in public education and the officers of corporations, all of whose salaries are matters of public record. (Benchmark figures for 1967 appear in Appendix A.) A caution here, however. Millions of families have non-apparent income from securities or other sources, and more than one person in a given family may be working, unbeknown to you. On the other hand, families may also have non-apparent commitments, institutionalized relatives or costly savings programs, for instance. That a person is a "GS-15" in the Federal Service with an official salary of, say, $18,000, does not necessarily mean that this is what his family actually has to live on in the course of a year.

Finally, there are available at many bookstores helpful publications on what money buys, some from the Federal Bureau of Labor Statistics, and often couched in terms of percentages — on the average, for instance, families of four spend 20 per cent of their incomes for rent or the equivalent, and 23 per cent for food.

There are two twists to the matter of money which are often overlooked. First, where you live and whom you associate with off the job have a lot to do with what constitutes a little or a lot. It costs the professor in a small college town, for example, far less than it does his contemporary, a bank trust officer, living in a big city suburb, to maintain a comfortable home, to entertain appropriately and, often, to educate his children adequately.

Further, the professor pays no commuter fares, may lunch at home and can often find recreation at his doorstep.

Second, being unconcerned about money, if you happen to be, is all very well while you are single. Your style of living is nobody's business but your own. But if and when you marry, the feelings of others whom you cannot disregard come into play. You may find a wife who will gladly or, at least uncomplainingly, take in washing or cheerfully forego night courses, travel and entertaining because you can't afford these things. But no child is happy in penury. Your unconcern for keeping up with the grown-up Joneses may be shared by your wife, but your offspring, when Christmas comes, are not likely to "care less" if their stockings don't bulge like those of the little Joneses.

Security

Unless you have an independent income, or wouldn't mind living on relief, or can subsist on grubs and berries, you can't be entirely unconcerned about the steadiness of your future employment. A need for some security of person and family is common to all. Above a minimum level, however, people vary widely in the stress they place on this aspect of their jobs. For some it comes close to being the dominant consideration as, for example, it was for Fred Wheeler.

As an R.O.T.C. "scholar," Fred owed the Army several years of active duty after graduation and was also thinking, without great enthusiasm, of making the Military Service his career. His academic interests lay in international affairs. He had a number of other alternatives available to him after he had served his hitch, including offers from several business concerns and government agencies. But his responses were guarded. Fred's father was a securities salesman whose personal volatility had meant a life of feast or famine for the family. Fred felt that the all-important consideration in evaluating alternative careers was the security offered, and he made no bones about it. "I may not be able to do exactly what I want to, but one thing is certain. My kids and wife aren't going to go through the same thing we did." His plan when he graduated was to serve a summer internship in the United States Information Agency, in part to learn at first hand just how secure the foreign service-type appointments offered by the USIA to permanent employees were, then to go into uniform and, after that, to make a final decision.

No organization could long survive if it guaranteed all its employees their jobs. Something must be accomplished and personnel who cannot or will not contribute must go, wherever they work. On the other hand, employers are universally concerned with providing as much security as circumstances permit, knowing that this is always a factor of at least some consequence to present and prospective employees.

Job security is greatest in the civil service at all governmental levels; in the Military Service; in education; and, among businesses, in utilities, banking and insurance (except sales). The basic reasons differ. Civil service laws are primarily designed to protect employees from political pressures in the performance of their jobs and to limit patronage appointments. They have the effect, in addition, of assuring civil servants that their jobs are secure short of gross incompetence or misconduct. The same level of security obtains in the Military Services, but here it is because the special training and experience necessary for effective performance cannot be found elsewhere, once a person has been in for several years. Teachers' jobs are protected to more or less degree, depending on where they teach and their positions, so that they will feel free to think, write and speak their own thoughts without regard to the views of their superiors. Education administrators in general also have this protection. As between businesses, security increases as the intensity of competition for survival decreases. It should be noted in regard to government and education, however, that many top-level administrators are not covered by civil service laws or academic tenure and are as vulnerable as their colleagues in comparable positions in business, in some cases even more so.

Several other considerations bearing on job security are worth mentioning. One is competence. The abler you are, the less you need fear loss of your job and the more easily you can land another. Another is the demand for particular talents. Security will be no problem for you if your skill is in short supply. Another is the state of the economy. The general level of concern for security among all who work for a living rises and falls with the unemployment rate. And another is the matter of age. Your concern for security will probably jump sharply when you pass 40. Thereafter you will be at an increasing disadvantage in competition for jobs with younger people. Finally, if you make security a top priority in choosing your work, you will usually progress more slowly than you otherwise would.

The Job Setting
Where they live with their families, how much they are away from home, how they get back and forth from work, how often they have to pull up stakes, what the office is like — these are considerations which are of importance to most people to at least some degree. Some are so "wrapped up in their work" for its own sake, or for the off-the-job rewards it brings them, that they pay scant attention to the environment. For others one or more of these "setting" factors are of overriding importance in determining how happy they are likely to be with their jobs.

The geographical location of the job is highly important to many. They may feel strongly about returning to or remaining on their native heaths. Or they may want to be in a place with particular characteristics, where it is warm, or where there is near-by skiing, for example, or in suburbia or a small town. Or again they can be strongly moved to settle down and dig in roots, to become permanent members of a community, regardless of geographic location. This latter "nesting" urge is likely to have strong family supoprt. Most mothers and children prefer to stay put. Jim Allen was one who wanted to go home, regardless.

Jim came to college planning to go to law school in his home state and then to return to his hometown to practice, run for office and "shake things up around there." As time passed, his accumulating academic record made it clear that he would not get into the state law school. Further, in his Junior year, two young lawyers hung out their shingles in the town where he lived. Going into business at home didn't appeal to Jim nor did teaching in the local schools. He had about resigned himself to the teaching alternative, however, rather than not to go home, when, during the Christmas recess of his Senior year, he got into conversation with the life insurance salesman who dealt with his father. The salesman was planning to leave the area within a year or two and thought Jim could be trained in time to replace him. The home office of the insurance company was approached with the proposition and turned out to be enthusiastic, and Jim began his study of the insurance business in his spare time in the month remaining before graduation.

The Foreign Service, the Military Service, college teaching and the ministry (both in the early years) and large multi-divisional corporations are no places for you if you prefer to be immobile. Concerns whose facilities are not dispersed, most government employment, the professions and some educational settings are better fits for "homesteaders."

Where you live in relation to where you work may also be of great concern to you. In a bygone era breadwinners generally walked to work. They had lunch at home or could get there if the pump broke down or the cows got through the fence. Such proximity of work and home is rare today but the desire to approach it as closely as possible can be strong. On the other hand, you may prefer to commute a fairly long distance. It gives time to read the paper or think going in (many a good idea has been introduced in a metropolitan office by the phrase, "It occurred to me on the way to work . . .") and to "unwind" on the way home. If you will not commute and also dislike apartment living, you will find the job pickings increasingly slim. It is estimated that 90 per cent of all Americans will be living — and the bread-winners working — in cities by the turn of the century, as against 70 per cent today.

Travel on the job itself is another classification which may be of importance to you in one way or another. You may want none or a little, or you may prefer to be on the road frequently. Here again, if you much prefer to be home nights, there is little comfort for you in the prospects. As transportation and communications speed up and organizations grow larger and spread out, a willingness to travel extensively will become more and more a requirement for consideration for worthwhile jobs in all fields.

Finally — and this matter possibly belongs in the on-the-job category — you may have strong feelings about your work place itself. Many men will willingly sacrifice possible higher earnings for an office window from which they can see the seasons come and go, for instance. Privacy-minded engineers may turn down an otherwise attractive offer because they would be required to sit in a "bull pen" with only their drafting boards and a potted plant separating them from their colleagues. And strong feelings about status symbols may come into play, not always unreasonably. Middle-management executives have been known to decide against an offer after noting that the office they would occupy is remote from those of the company's officers, or finding that they will not be able to choose the pictures to be hung on their office walls. More than concern for the trappings themselves may be at work in such situations. They can often tell one more about where he will actually stand in the management pecking order of a company with which he is negotiating than all the words he hears during interviews.

Prestige

The value least likely to be acknowledged by its possessor — and most possess it in some degree — is the desire for prestige. All of us need the respect of some others. We can't be happy without the regard of our families and working colleagues, at least. For many, however, the need for the esteem of others goes beyond those close to them and can be a powerful motivating force. It is confessed to reluctantly, in spite of the fact that by definition it can only be attained by being someone or doing something estimable. And this reluctance comes about because the desire for esteem appears to be the opposite of humility, a principal virtue in the Judaeo-Christian ethic. How can a man openly seek the admiration of others — or even admit the desire to himself — in a society that preaches that virtue should be its own reward.

Jack Scranton was one who faced up to his desire for prestige and seemingly came up with a long long-range solution.

Jack had a great interest in things mechanical. He had spent a number of summers working with an uncle who operated a small machine shop and he tinkered with his motorcycle almost compulsively. He wanted help in deciding what to major in. A test he took as part of the exploration indicated, with emphasis, that his interests were very close to those of airline pilots and, to a lesser extent, to those of engineers and architects. At first he liked the pilot idea — he had always had a hankering to fly. But as time went on he found himself gravitating towards architecture. After some soul-searching, he sheepishly admitted that he didn't feel that pilots have the prestige that architects do and that he guessed he did care about prestige. Some time later he returned to say that he had it all worked out. Pilots have long breaks between flying assignments. He would major in architecture and go on for the necessary graduate work and apprenticeship. Then he would train as a commercial pilot. And then he would practice architecture between flights. For the moment, at least, he was undeterred by the thought that he would be graying at the temples by the time he achieved his goals.

The degree of prestige you will have will be determined, in the first instance, by your occupation and, on occasion, by the organization you are affiliated with, if any, and your position in its hierarchy. With this information about you, one personally unacquainted with you can make a tentative, personal judgment as to the esteem you should be accorded. Prestige also can be earned over time by accomplishment, whatever one does for a living.

The first requirement, if you are prestige-conscious, is to choose an occupation, within the limitations of your ability and opportunities, which seems to you adequately prestigious. Accomplishment can, of course, come only with time. Studies suggest that doctors, lawyers, top-level business executives and advertising men, chemists, bankers, creative artists and college professors head the collegiate prestige list. But this is a consensus only.

Seldom will two people rank occupations in the same order. The important thing is to be guided by your own feelings.

Circumstances may make it impossible to shoot for the top of your list, as also may lack of ability or interest. In this case avocations can provide a measure of satisfaction. Many whose jobs will never meet their needs for the esteem of others have secured the wide respect they wanted by excelling at such hobbies as book or stamp collecting, or at sports or games, or by leading charitable or fraternal or cultural or civic endeavors, or by undertaking part-time public office, or by playing an active role in political organizations.

Power

The urge to wield power over men and events off-the-job is strong in some people. It is an extension of the desire for control discussed earlier. It may be without specific objectives, simply a yen to be one of those in a community or political party or profession or industry who "calls the turn." Or power may be wanted for a definite purpose, as by the person who seeks public office because of the capacity it will give him to right certain wrongs he sees about him. In Warren Rothman's case it was not particularized.

"You know, what I sometimes dream of doing is being a state trooper and arresting a man who turns out to be a big wheel and having him try to threaten me and I just stand there smiling while I write out the ticket." Warren looked embarrassed when he'd heard what he said. "I guess that's childish," he added. He had planned for years to be an accountant, but increasingly, in the past year or two, he had felt that something would be missing. He knew he would enjoy the work itself but, "Somehow, nobody around pays much attention to accountants." To further explore what accounting had to offer, he found a summer job with a nationally known accounting firm. The president, he learned, was the confidant of a number of top industrialists across the country, and high up in organization politics in his state. That shed a different light on what a career in accounting could lead to and Warren decided to stick with his original plan.

Power, in the sense in which it is used here, can be had from three principal sources. Position is one. The top executives in private enterprise and non-profit organizations, the heads of departments of government, and elected officials, for example, all have power simply because they are where they are. Money is the second. A millionaire will always be listened to, if not followed, by those who would like his help — companies needing capital, charitable, cultural, civic and educational institutions, and politicians, among others. The ability to persuade others, whether or not supported by intelligence, is the third. Great thinkers who are widely read, advisers to men in high posts, clergymen, editorial writers and dynamic public speakers are cases in point.

If those things are true, it follows that power comes to no one early and unearned, except through the inheritance of money or possession of charisma. If you have a yen for power, the best you can do right now is set off in a promising direction.

Freedom to Come and Go

Your college work pattern probably fits your needs if you are one who places high value on being able to make up your own mind about when you will labor and when you will play. There are few clocks on campus that must be punched without fail. The emphasis is on performance. Such was Joe Pool's need for freedom, however, that even college gave him claustrophobia.

Whatever may have been Joe's natural desire to be able to come and go as he wished, it was probably reinforced by his upbringing. The themes in his home were: "Hard work and long hours are good for you; The more it hurts, the more good it does you; Timeliness is next to Godliness." Joe still felt regimented at college, although he enjoyed his major, which was journalism, and writing sports for the college news bureau. He took to cutting classes more and more frequently. Then he failed to get several papers in on time. Then he slept through an exam. And then he had a meeting with the Dean who invited him to leave college for a year or two. He was secretly delighted and promptly found a job as a cub reporter. A year later he was back, somewhat chastened. "Reporting fences a man in even more than college," he said. The experience had not turned him from journalism as a career but it had shown him that freelancing was that branch of the occupation which would meet his needs. It had further shown him that he still had a lot to learn before he could hope to make a go of it, and that kept him on the reservation through graduation.

People who need this sort of freedom may or may not have, in addition, an urge to be independent in other respects, or to face challenge, or to be creative. Providing they do not have to be at certain places at certain hours, they may well be quite content with close supervision, or with repetitive activity, or with little opportunity for self-expression. Security may be of consequence to them or it may not. And it is not necessarily a matter of wanting more time than others have to pursue avocations or putter or relax or play golf. Such people often work longer hours in total than their nine-to-five colleagues. But they want to be able to take a day off to go fishing or antiqueing when the spirit moves them.

Selling on commission — as do life insurance underwriters, real estate brokers, investment salesmen and manufacturers' representatives, for instance — is the kind of work most readily available to you if you are this kind of person. Professional fund raising in some settings is another occupation which calls for relatively little clock-punching. Many scholars and researchers are free to make their own hours. Field representation for publishers, foundations and such government agencies as the Geological Survey and the Wages and Hours Division are other appropriate pursuits. Solo practice in the professions offers considerable freedom as to one's hours. And finally, running a business of one's own should obviously be cited, but with reservations. In theory, if you elect this route, you wholly control your own time. In practice, however, at least early in your career, you will probably find yourself working not only the regular day but long night and weekend hours to boot.

*   *   *

So much for emotions and careers. Many of the values cited

above may be relevant to your thinking about the future, or perhaps only a few are. And there may well be emotion-based considerations of consequence to you which we haven't touched on. However the point is that, since career choice is not a purely logical exercise for anyone, it may help towards arriving at the best possible decision, if you try to identify and take into account the various emotional tugs and pulls which will inevitably influence your thinking. Some ways of identifying them, if they are not already apparent — and of learning more about what the world of work has to offer you — are discussed in the next chapter.

Chapter

4

Ways and Means

IN WHAT HAS GONE BEFORE, those of your characteristics which have a bearing on career choice — your intelligence, aptitudes, physique, family background, interests, achievements, self-concept and values — have regularly been related to specific kinds and fields of work. The second half of the book, "The Choices," in describing kinds and fields of work, relates each back, explicitly or implicitly, to these characteristics. The intent is to set forth and interconnect the elements which are basic to exploring careers.

I offer you only, however, a primer or guidebook, not an encyclopedia. Help in exploring is available from a variety of other sources. Some of these have been touched on already and will be discussed below only to the extent that there is something to add. Others will be noted for the first time.

The Home

In the chapter on "Fallacies," it was stated that your parents' values are never exactly, or perhaps may not even generally be like yours. What you were brought up to believe, however, is perhaps the single most important influence on your values, for your parents have done all they can, directly and indirectly, to instill their own beliefs in you. You may, of course, accept the teachings of your home or you may repudiate them — perhaps even term them "phony" — as the result of differences in personality and your own experiences with life.

Whether you tend to agree or disagree, a careful comparison of your parents views and your own can be revealing. Apparent agreement may turn out to be a thoughtless going along and thus may not reflect your actual feelings. A man can reflexively follow his father into business, for example, and then later discover that teaching is where he would be happiest. On the other hand, disagreements can appear to be sharper than they actually are (and can lead to unwise decisions) because they surface during the sometimes emotion-charged period when you are declaring your independence of your family. Sons and daughters have been known to over-react to family preoccupation with security and money, for instance, by embarking on careers involving more risk and less financial promise than they really want.

What Others Say

It has been suggested — perhaps unnecessarily — that you take advice about what your decisions should be, from whatever quarter, with a grain of salt. What others know about themselves and about their own work, however, can be a valuable source of information for you.

Such information, except in a sketchy form, is not often readily volunteered. But most people like to talk about themselves in depth to a sincerely interested questioner. It becomes, then, a matter of asking probing questions of many people, of parents and other relatives, of chance acquaintances on planes and trains and buses, of other students, of faculty members, of company recruiters when they visit the campus, of career panel members, of anyone, in fact, who comes to hand.

"What do you do and do you like your work?" usually isn't enough. Rather you might ask: "What does your day's work consist of and in what surroundings?"; "You say it's 'rewarding' ('boring', 'exciting', 'varied') ; what are the rewards you have in mind?"; "What sort of people thrive in work like yours and what sort doesn't?"; "What are the reasons people fail or succeed in it?"; "What do you particularly like and dislike about the job?"; "How did you happen to get into this line of work; what appealed to you; has it turned out to be what you expected and why?"

From such probing — not being content with, "I'm a salesman

and it keeps me on the jump" — you may learn something new about a given kind of work of possible interest and also about the values of others possibly relevant to you. A professor may comment offhand that he enjoys the teaching facet of his work and the freedom to come and go that he has. A few more questions and you may get new insights into the conflict he feels between his own desire to concentrate on teaching and institutional pressure to put research first, or vice versa, a problem which confronts many college professors. And a few more may produce such surprising information as that, in the first decade or so, college teaching can be a highly competitive profession as young men vie for recognition and tenure; that the promotional ground rules are very hazy; and that some senior professors make $35,000 or more a year.

Or starting with the impression that directors of research are all good gray men who sit all day with their feet on their desks, smoking pipes and contemplating the ceiling, you would discover to your surprise, by asking the right questions, that most such men are on the run most of the time, holding conferences, traveling to distant meetings, consulting with project leaders and inspecting facilities.

In regard to the values of others, while they will never be exactly like yours, learning "what makes others tick" can produce new self-understanding. In this connection, if you are one of the many who aspire to follow in the footsteps of someone you've admired at a distance, it is obviously important that you find out "what makes him tick" and establish a reasonable similarity between the two of you on this score before setting forth.

Reading

Most of what needs to be said about career reading materials — other than stressing the importance of reading them — is covered by this caution: Keep the author's aim in mind.

Career publications whose sole purpose is to supply accurate information come from three principal sources: the United States Department of Labor and some state Departments of Labor; certain publishers of staff-written books, pamphlets and periodicals which make career literature a specialty; and a handful of student-operated organizations which put out magazines and special editions of campus newspapers written and edited by undergraduates. A selected list of such publications appears in Appendix C.

Material from the first two sources is written by men who are professional researchers and writers on careers. Their only aim is to be accurate, objective and, within the limitations of space, complete. The articles produced by students have the same aim — which they achieve with varying success — and are frequently more entertaining to read than those of the professionals.

All other publications, overtly or not, are written to "sell" you on the careers dealt with and are colored by the biases of their authors. Some can be very helpful, but they should be read with this in mind. Among such material are articles and books about their work by successful men and women; brochures published by trade associations; career literature handed out by individual government agencies; and the recruiting publications of private concerns who try to attract collegians to their employ. Biographies and autobiographies are not career publications in the sense the term is used here, but can also be useful sources of information.

In assessing how seriously to take a given publication, several additional criteria can also be used. One is the date of publication. Anything over two or three years old is not likely to be an accurate guide for today. Job content, salaries and training requirements change so rapidly that career descriptions become obsolete quickly. Another is whether the account includes comments on the job's possibly undesirable features. No work is one long picnic. And a third is the incidence of adjectives calculated to stir interest, among the more frequently used being "challenging," "rewarding," "stimulating" and "opportunity-filled." The more these occur, the less reliable the material.

Fantasy

One does not often hear collegians talking about their dreams, by day or night, when they cast them in work-related roles which they think others would find ridiculous, as, for instance, doing something heroic. Nevertheless, dreams with career implications are common and should not be ignored. You have little opportunity during your college years to try out jobs. Your subconscious may through dreams on occasion give you worthwhile insights into your values. Repeated dreams of eminence, for instance, may point to a need for prestige which you had not recognized. Repetitive dreams of fear in competitive situations may be a caution light for one who has been thinking that he would like highly challenging work.

Work Experience

First-hand experience can't be matched as a means of exploring careers. The problems are that the time available for such try-outs is limited and that most jobs, on and off campus, which will expose you to a situation that you would face later on in permanent employment are usually available only when you are an upperclassman. There are, of course, exceptions to the latter limitation, among them commission selling, camp counseling, social service work and entrepreneurial ventures such as setting up a summer lawn- and garden-maintenance business or becoming a Good Humor man.

There is no apparent remedy, however, for the situation in general. It is a matter of making the best of it. If you can't land a summer internship-type job in government or business or teaching or other sorts of definite "career exposure" work or find campus employments that approximate the kinds of work you have in mind, you can, in lowly positions, learn a lot about the work of those who employ you by keeping your eyes open.

Placement and Career Guidance Services

Virtually all colleges maintain such services. Their basic functions are to provide students with information and counseling on jobs and careers, to conduct annual recruiting programs during which representatives of business concerns and other organizations seeking collegians for permanent employment come to campus to interview and to arrange for student interviews with graduate school admissions officers. Without exception they maintain extensive files of company and government recruiting material, pamphlets on interviewing techniques, and some career literature.

In recent years the scope of these services has been broadening. Many colleges are setting up extensive libraries which contain, in addition to recruiting literature, current, comprehensive, objectively written — and even audio-visual — material on careers; information on summer work and study opportunities at home and abroad; graduate school catalogues; and information on student military obligations and alternatives. They sometimes run "career day" programs, bringing men in various occupations to campus to talk to students. And more and more placement officers have graduate training in counseling or guidance. With this latter development has come increased use of tests, greater depth in the counseling offered and more research activity.

A career counselor need not have an advanced degree to be first rate, however. Many placement officers with bachelor's degrees or less are, as the result of experience and native talent, better counselors than some of their more highly trained colleagues. It depends a lot on the person. Some indicators of counseling competence are given below.

Counseling and Testing

Most campuses offer counseling services distinct from the placement service. Such services are concerned with students' emotional, personal and academic "hang-ups" as well as, in many cases, general career-choice-related problems. They try to help students through confidential interviews and testing and can be more or less effective, depending on the nature of the student's problem and his willingness to talk about it in depth. Their staffs are sometimes regarded by undergraduates, erroneously, as "headshrinkers," of use only to the emotionally disturbed or to weaklings who want a shoulder to cry on. Whatever the reputation of this service on your campus may be, if you have a bothersome problem, it will cost you nothing to pay a visit and find out if help is to be had.

Off campus there is a growing number of private, fee-charging career counseling agencies, some affiliated with non-profit organizations such as the YMCA, the YMHA and universities, some profit-making ventures. In addition, many of the 2000-odd State Public Employment Service offices across the country have trained counselors on their staffs.

Some of the private agencies have been checked out and certified as competent by the American Board on Counseling Services, and are listed in the biennially revised *Directory of Approved Counseling Agencies,* available in the counseling office on most campuses. Those which are not so listed may or may not be reliable. They are less likely to be if they go in for heavy self-promotion, ask for a down payment on the fee, offer guarantees of any sort, emphasize résumé writing and job placement, or lay great store on lengthy written reports based on test findings and full of psychological jargon.

As to testing, counselors often use a variety of tests in their work with students. It is worth repeating that with few exceptions, tests not administered and interpreted to the student by an expert are likely to be useless or worse. To describe these tests in detail would take several volumes. The point, if you want counseling, is to put yourself in the hands of a professional who knows his trade, including testing, not to attempt to acquire his expertness.

There are, however, a number of useful indicators of whether or not you are, in fact, in the hands of an expert so far as career counseling goes. A good counselor does more listening than talking, asks questions, avoids giving advice on the decisions to be made, seldom renders judgments on right and wrong, never pushes you towards one career or another, is concerned more with what you think and feel than with recounting his own experience and parading his expertness, and lets you conduct the discussion at your own pace and by your own routes, no matter how circuitous. He seldom uses psychological jargon. Discreet to a fault, he will pass on nothing of what you say to others, parents, college officials or anyone else, without your agreement. He does not become emotionally involved himself in your problem. He has at his fingertips, or otherwise readily available, the information you need, and on his bookshelf four basic books: *Man In a World of Work, Appraising Vocational Fitness,* the current editions of the *Occupational Outlook Handbook* and the *College Placement Annual.* (See Appendix C for further information on the latter two, which are published for students.)

Such a counselor considers tests only one aspect of the counseling process, possibly not even a necessary one in some circumstances. He seldom starts off with tests, in any case, and he uses them later only when you and he agree that they might produce new information or clear up doubts or stimulate thought. He is at pains to explain the strengths and weaknesses of any test before giving it to you and when interpreting its results to you. In appraising your situation, he never relies entirely on test findings, realizing that psychological testing has not yet progressed, in many areas, beyond the "tealeaf" stage in its ability to predict and measure.

Within these bounds there is room for considerable variation in counseling "styles." Some counselors are more articulate or directive or test-oriented than others, for instance. However, the competence of any career counselor who departs sharply from the above bill of particulars is open to serious question.

*   *   *

Someone once pointed out that one cannot choose what one does not know. So far as careers are concerned, the statement might be amended to say that one cannot choose wisely, except by accident, without knowing both about himself and about his alternatives. What has been written in this first half of the book is principally concerned with trying to help you know yourself better. What follows, the second half, describes most of the alternatives you have to choose from.

Part II
What the Choices Are

Introduction

This second section contains information on most facets of the world of work of possible interest to collegians. Ignorance and misapprehensions — which limit choice, in effect, to a handful of questionable stereotypes — won't necessarily lead to mistakes, of course, nor will comprehensive knowledge guarantee instant sagacity in making decisions. But, here as elsewhere, the odds for making promising choices are affected by the amount and accuracy of the information on alternatives the chooser has at his command.

Most of the section is composed of thumbnail descriptions of the six basic "fields" of work — Education, Government, Profit-making Enterprises, Self-Employment, Private Non-profit Organizations, the Military Services — and of 62 kinds of work which between them occupy the vast majority of college graduates today and will continue to do so in the forseeable future. The six "field" formulation is an adaptation of the official government ten "industry" categorization, and was devised in the interests of greater clarity for the purposes of this book. In regard to the "kinds" of work, while only 62 of the hundreds of possibilities have been selected for specific discussion, many others are mentioned in the descriptions and elsewhere in the book. References to them all can be located through the index.

Why the distinction between "fields" and "kinds"? To be knowledgeable about a given job, one must know not only what the occupant does during the workday, the "kind" of work, but also the setting in which he does it, the "field" of work. There can be substantial differences in the nature of the jobs of mechanical engineers, for instance, depending on whether they are employed by state highway departments, manufacturing companies, school systems, the Army, or themselves. Reversing the coin, since each field employs many different kinds of workers, knowing that a man is in government, or education, or a private non-profit organization, say, is only a start at learning what he actually does. In any of the six fields he could be anything from a financial expert to a psychologist. And even such a two-dimensional picture may still be inexact. A psychologist could be doing research or he could be counseling in either education or private enterprise, for example. All of this, it should be stressed, particularly in the light of the high rate of mobility of today's workers, refers to the nature of jobs, not to individuals who hold them. The incumbent of a job at any given moment may be progressing through a "field" career, a lifelong civil servant, for instance, who takes on a succession of different kinds of work. Or he could be wed to one kind of work, law, for example, but be moving from field to field. Or he might be doing both. Or, of course, he could be standing pat, the man and the job synonymous.

The chart on pages 82-83 cross-lists kinds and fields of work. (Careers which Liberal Arts graduates can pursue with little or no more supplementary "pre-vocational" training than is required for those in other undergraduate disciplines are indicated by a dagger.) Disagreement between individuals about the location of some of the dots is inevitable since definitions of the kinds and fields of work differ. But this is beside the point. The point is that the chart, if studied, will assure the reader that, in general, he has not overlooked any important alternative, a problem which most frequently results from the usually erroneous assumption that a given kind of work can be found in one field only, or that, in a given field, the kinds of work to be found are highly limited.

Following the chart is a section entitled "Matching Up Your Values and Careers: A Self-administered Appraisal." This provides the reader with a pencil-and-paper means of determining roughly which of the kinds of work described are likely to satisfy or to frustrate his or her particular values.

In thinking about work descriptions, wherever you find them, there are a number of generalities which should be kept in mind.

Nationally and internationally, population continues to grow at a rapid — some feel a disastrous — rate. Among other things, this means increasing demand for most goods and public and private services. It also means that most of the country's and world's major problems are constantly becoming more acute. People who want to concern themselves as careerists with either of these predictable developments will be in heavy demand.

Again in the matter of population, the low birth rates of the Depression 1930s in this country have resulted in a critical shortage today—and this will continue for some years to come—of men and women in early middle age, the age which normally supplies all fields of work with their "middle-management" people. Able collegians, therefore, can look for far more rapid advancement over the next few years than was possible 10 or 15 years ago, as employers in all fields attempt to fill their middle-management ranks.

Because this is an age of exploding technology, the world of work is unprecedentedly kaleidoscopic, many jobs becoming obsolete, many others being newly established and many changing in content each year. Further, work in general — including administrative and managerial jobs — is becoming increasingly complex, and the more routine and repetitive occupations are disappearing (it is estimated that automation is eliminating 35,000 jobs each week). The implications in terms of career exploration of these facts are four: People will need more and more formal training to land the jobs of their choice in the first place; they will have to study constantly during their careers to keep up with "the state of the art"; they should develop and maintain as broad an assortment of competences as possible in order to be able to take advantage of new opportunities or to shift direction easily if the skills learned originally become obsolete; and finally, published job descriptions may not reflect the current facts, either as to the content of a given kind of work or the jobs available — anything more than two years old should be checked on this score.

Although the "not-for-profit" sector of the economy (meaning in this context government, education and non-profit enterprises) is spawning additional jobs far faster than is the profit-making sector, the latter field still employs the great majority of people. Since deaths, retirements and transfers-out, as well as growing total employment, determine opportunity for newcomers in all fields, the profit-making sector will continue for many years to come to provide far more openings, from top to bottom, than all the other fields combined.

Changing jobs after getting started is not, by definition, a bad thing, in spite of the older generation's tendency to pontificate about the virtues of perseverance. Moreover, the mobility of America's workforce is, in fact, one of its greatest strengths. It is only when job-hopping results from an unnecessarily uninformed choice, when information which would have prevented the mistake was readily available but went unsought, that the waste of time and energy involved, for both the individual and his employer, becomes inexcusable. (Incidentally, it is easier to land a new job if one remains on the old one while hunting.)

In conclusion, a word about the work descriptions themselves. In composing them I relied primarily on materials prepared by professional researchers and writers on careers. Some of the best and most readily available of these materials are listed in Appendix C for those who want more detail than this book presents. In addition, I have drawn from a variety of publications too numerous to cite individually, countless conversations, "career panels" by the score and first-hand exposure over the years to all six of the fields of work and a dozen of 62 kinds of work described in this part of the book.

The factual sections of each description — and job title alone, so far as "prestige" is concerned — will for the most part suggest the personal values the particular kind of work is likely to satisfy or frustrate. Each includes, in addition, a section entitled "Values" or "For People Who:," designed to note "value" aspects, excepting "ethics," of the work which may not be apparent from the facts about it. Ethics will not be mentioned at all. The ethical content of a given job, important a consideration as it is, simply cannot be clearly identified, nor would it be susceptible to definition if it could.

Finally, salaries are discussed in terms of comparisons rather than dollar amounts, and the reader is referred to Appendix A for 1967-68 benchmark figures. Changes take place today so rapidly — increases in pay for most kinds of work range from 3 to 7 per cent annually — that figures become obsolete overnight. On the other hand, relationships in pay between, for instance, fields of work, kinds of work, fields of academic study and places of work tend to remain constant. Appendix A includes as a point of departure the Federal government's pay schedule, the Military Services pay scale, current offers by business to collegians with various academic backgrounds and various degree levels and figures on teaching salaries from kindergarten to university levels, all as of this writing.

THE 62 KINDS OF WORK

Fields of Work

as students who think in terms of career "Fields" commonly describe their interests.

CAPITALS show the six general Fields of Work which comprehend all the others and which are described on the preceding chapter pages indicated.

(Columns marked † indicate careers which Liberal Arts graduates can pursue with little or no more supplementary "pre-vocational training" than is required of those from other undergraduate disciplines.)

Field of Work (Page)	Accountant (122) †	Actuary (123) †	Advertising Worker (125) †	Architect (126) †	Artist — Creative and Performing (128) †	Bank Worker (129) †	Buyer (131)	Chiropractor (133)	City Planner and Related (134) †	Computer Scientist (Programer)‡ (136) †	Conservation Worker (137) †	Counselor (139) †	Criminologist and related (141) †	Curator (142)	Dentist (143)	Dietician (144)	Education Worker (Non-teaching) (146) †	Engineer (149)	Environmental Health Specialist (Sanitarian) (151)	Foreign Language Worker (152) †	Fund Raiser (153) †	General Manager (Executive, Administrator) (155)	Home Economist (158)	Humanist (159) †	Industrial Designer (161) †
Advertising	*		*						*											*		*	*	*	*
Airlines	*		*	*					*								*		*	*		*	*		*
Banking	*		*						*								*			*		*			
Business	*	*	*	*	*	*	*	*	*	*	*	*	*				*		*		*	*	*	*	*
Communications	*		*						*								*	*	*	*		*			*
EDUCATION (92)	*		*	*	*	*		*	*	*	*	*	*	*	*	*	*	*	*	*	*	*	*	*	*
Farming	*		*								*			*			*			*			*	*	
Finance	*	*	*			*			*											*	*	*			
Foundations	*			*					*					*			*	*		*	*	*		*	
GOVERNMENT (97)	*	*	*	*		*	*	*	*	*	*	*	*	*	*	*	*	*	*	*		*	*	*	
Industry	*	*	*	*			*		*	*	*	*	*				*		*	*	*	*			*
Insurance	*	*	*	*					*		*			*			*			*					
International Work	*		*	*	*	*			*	*	*			*			*	*		*	*	*	*	*	*
Journalism	*		*		*															*		*	*	*	*
Manufacturing	*		*						*	*			*			*			*			*	*	*	
MILITARY SERVICE (115)	*	*	*	*			*		*	*		*	*		*	*	*	*	*		*				*
Motion Pictures	*		*	*	*												*		*	*		*			
PRIVATE NON-PROFIT (114)	*	*		*	*	*			*	*	*	*		*			*	*	*	*	*	*	*	*	*
PROFITMAKING (100)	*	*	*	*	*	*	*	*	*	*	*	*	*	*	*	*			*		*	*	*	*	*
Politics	*		*						*												*	*			
Publishing	*		*		*				*								*			*		*	*		
Radio - TV	*		*	*	*				*								*	*		*	*	*	*		
Recreation	*		*	*	*		*		*		*		*				*			*			*	*	
Retailing	*		*	*		*			*								*	*				*	*		*
SELF-EMPLOYMENT (109)	*	*	*	*	*		*	*	*	*	*	*	*		*			*		*	*	*	*	*	*
Urban Redevelopment	*		*						*	*	*	*	*				*	*	*	*	*	*			*
Utilities	*		*	*					*	*								*				*	*		
Writing, Editing		*		*					*								*	*		*	*	*		*	

† Careers which Liberal Arts graduates can pursue with little or no more supplementary "pre-vocational training" than is required of those from other undergraduate disciplines.

(Specializations Within These Kinds are Mentioned in the Text)

162 Insurance Worker †	164 Interior Decorator-Designer	165 International Worker †	168 Labor Relations Worker †	170 Landscape Architect	172 Lawyer †	174 Librarian †	175 Marketing Analyst and Related †	177 Mathematician, Statistician	178 Medical Technologist and Related	115 Military Services Officer	179 Minister, Priest, Rabbi †	181 Nurse (Registered) †	183 Operations Research Worker	184 Optometrist	185 Personnel Worker †	187 Pharmacist	188 Physician and Osteopath	190 Pilot (Civilian) †	191 Podiatrist (Chiropodist)	193 Production Manager †	194 Public Relations Worker †	196 Purchasing Agent †	197 Radio-TV Worker †	199 Recreation Worker †	200 Sales Worker †	203 Scientist, Natural	206 Scientist, Social	209 Secretary †	210 Securities Worker †	212 Social Worker †	213 Systems Analyst	215 Teacher, Professor †	217 Therapist and Related †	219 Traffic Worker (Industrial) †	220 Veterinarian	222 Writer, Editor †
	*	*			*	*	*	*							*						*	*	*		*		*	*			*					*
	*	*	*	*	*	*	*	*				*	*		*		*	*			*	*			*		*	*			*			*		*
		*			*	*	*	*				*			*						*	*			*		*	*	*		*					*
*	*	*	*	*	*	*	*	*	*			*	*	*	*	*	*	*	*	*	*	*	*	*	*	*	*	*	*		*	*	*	*	*	*
		*	*		*	*	*	*					*		*						*	*	*		*	*	*	*			*					*
*	*	*	*	*	*	*	*	*	*		*	*	*	*	*	*	*	*	*		*	*	*	*		*	*	*	*	*	*	*	*	*	*	*
		*			*	*	*	*							*			*		*	*	*			*	*	*	*						*	*	*
*		*			*	*	*	*					*		*						*	*			*		*	*	*		*					*
		*			*	*		*			*				*		*				*	*	*			*	*	*		*						*
*	*	*	*	*	*	*	*	*	*		*	*	*	*	*	*	*	*	*	*	*	*	*	*		*	*	*	*	*	*	*	*	*	*	*
*	*	*	*	*	*	*	*	*	*			*	*	*	*	*	*	*	*	*	*	*	*	*	*	*	*	*	*		*	*		*	*	*
*		*			*	*	*	*				*	*		*		*				*	*			*		*	*	*		*					*
*		*	*	*	*	*	*	*	*		*	*	*		*		*	*		*	*	*	*	*	*	*	*	*	*	*	*	*		*	*	*
		*			*	*					*						*	*			*		*			*	*	*								*
		*	*		*	*	*	*	*			*	*	*	*	*	*		*	*	*	*		*	*	*	*	*	*		*	*		*		*
*		*		*	*	*		*		*	*	*	*	*	*	*	*	*	*	*	*	*	*	*	*	*	*	*			*	*	*	*	*	*
	*	*	*	*	*	*	*					*			*		*	*			*	*	*		*			*						*		*
*		*	*	*	*	*		*	*		*	*	*	*	*	*	*		*		*	*	*	*		*	*	*		*		*	*		*	*
*	*	*	*	*	*	*	*	*	*			*	*	*	*	*	*	*	*	*	*	*	*	*	*	*	*	*	*	*	*	*	*	*	*	*
		*			*	*	*	*							*						*		*					*								*
		*			*	*	*	*							*					*	*	*			*		*	*			*			*		*
	*	*			*	*	*	*							*						*	*	*		*	*	*	*						*		*
	*	*		*	*	*	*	*							*			*			*	*		*	*		*	*		*	*		*	*		*
	*	*	*	*	*	*	*	*					*	*	*	*	*				*	*	*	*	*		*	*			*	*		*		*
*	*	*	*	*	*	*	*	*			*	*	*	*	*	*	*	*	*		*	*	*		*	*	*	*	*		*			*	*	*
	*	*	*	*	*	*		*				*	*		*		*				*	*		*		*	*	*		*	*					*
		*	*	*	*	*	*	*				*	*		*		*			*	*	*	*		*	*	*	*	*		*			*		*
		*	*		*	*					*										*		*			*	*	*				*				*

Matching Up Your Values
and Career Possibilities

(A Self-administered Appraisal)

THE CHART at the end of this chapter (Pages 90-91) indicates for each of the 62 kinds of work the values discussed earlier which that particular employment will *generally* and *notably* satisfy. It is included to provide you with a tool which, if you use it as suggested below, will assure you that you have not overlooked potential "fits" and will help focus your further reading on the jobs most relevant to you.

Two categories of jobs are, presumably, "most relevant" to you. In the first are those which square closely with your personal pattern of values and, in addition, with your interests, personality, aptitudes, abilities, family background and present level of training and capacity for further training, in effect, the "traditional measures" discusssed in Chapter 2, Part I. Use of the suggested procedure will flag such jobs so far as values are concerned, producing for you a list of potential "fits" which you will then want to winnow, before turning to the job descriptions, by testing it against the traditional measures.

The second category of "relevant" jobs are those which, from what you know of them, have some appeal for you. You will find most of them among the 62 listed on the chart and you may want to put a check mark beside them now, as a first step. They warrant further consideration, of course, if they also turn out to fall into the first category. If they do not, you may, nevertheless, want to investigate further, for two reasons. First, you may want to find out what your misapprehensions about them are. Second, while *in general* they are not likely to satisfy your value pattern *notably,* you may find that in certain atypical settings they might do very nicely and thus that they should not be written off summarily as possibilities.

A few additional considerations before turning to the procedure:

1. Six of the values discussed earlier — ethics, money, power, prestige, setting and variety — are not included among those listed on the chart. This is because they cannot be treated meaningfully in this sort of categorical, systematic framework. They should, however, be kept in mind, together with the traditional measures, when the time comes to winnow the list which the chart produces for you.

2. There can be one or more of three reasons why a given value is not ascribed to a given job on the chart. First, the value is not likely to be generally and notably satisfied by that job. Second, the value is likely to be actually frustrated by that job — one who likes to be racing around all the time would find library work inhibiting, for instance. And third — law being a case in point — the occupation is pursued in so many and such diverse ways that it cannot be said that it would generally and notably satisfy the value.

3. The values ascribed are those which obtain when the job is pursued as an *employee.* The values which come into play when one elects self-employment are described on pages 109-114.

4. You are entirely at liberty, of course, to quarrel with the values I've ascribed, in general and particular. But before you reach conclusions based on your disagreements, be sure that you know how I have defined the value (I mean no more nor less than what I have said in the earlier section describing it), and that you are not judging from a questionable stereotype or from impressions derived from knowledge of the job as performed in an exceptional setting. And — a related matter — if your scores surprise you, high or low, you may want to reconsider your own value pattern, the one you have applied to the chart, as well as those it sets forth.

EXAMPLE

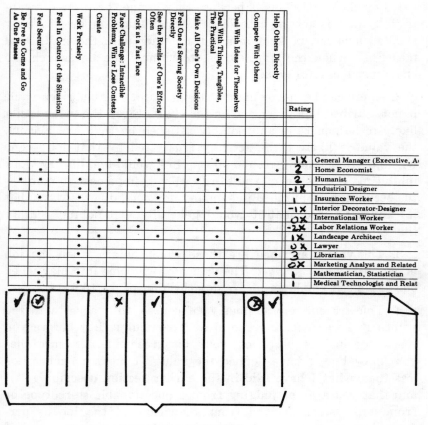

Be Free to Come and Go As One Pleases	Feel Secure	Feel In Control of the Situation	Work Precisely	Create	Face Challenge: Intractible Problems, Win or Lose Contests	Work at a Fast Pace	See the Results of One's Efforts Often	Feel One Is Serving Society Directly	Make All One's Own Decisions	Deal With Things, Tangibles, The Practical	Deal With Ideas for Themselves	Compete With Others	Help Others Directly	Rating	
		*			*	*	*			*				-1 X	General Manager (Executive, A...
	*		*				*			*			*	2	Home Economist
*	*		*					*		*	*			2	Humanist
		*	*				*			*		*		▸1 X	Industrial Designer
	*		*				*							1	Insurance Worker
			*			*	*			*				-1 X	Interior Decorator-Designer
														0 X	International Worker
		*			*	*						*		-2 X	Labor Relations Worker
*		*	*				*			*				1 X	Landscape Architect
		*												0 X	Lawyer
	*		*					*		*			*	3	Librarian
			*							*				0 X	Marketing Analyst and Related
	*		*							*				1	Mathematician, Statistician
	*		*				*			*				1	Medical Technologist and Relat...

<u>YOUR</u> VALUE PATTERN

To put the chart to use, look at the Example given on the opposite page and proceed as follows:

1. Draw short lines down from and perpendicular to the edge of a blank piece of paper at the same intervals as those between the values listed.

2. Pencil in a "V" in the spaces opposite those values which you feel are important to you, and an "X" opposite any values to which you have a negative reaction.

3. Circle the "V" where you feel this is an all-important consideration, that you would be unwilling to undertake any career which would not satisfy this value. Circle the "X" where you would be unwilling to take a job which virtually required the presence of the particular value in yourself.

4. Slide your paper down the chart from job to job, inserting in pencil in the blank space to the left of each job listed, a figure representing the total of "V's" which match dots on the chart *minus* "X's" which match dots. If, of course, there is no dot to match a *circled* "V," the job in question should be tentatively stricken from consideration. The same is true if there is a dot to match a *circled* "X."

This procedure will produce higher and lower (some even minus) scores, the former attached in general — but with exceptions — to those kinds of work which are likely to be a good fit for you from the point of view of values, the latter to those which are not.

To illustrate, let's see what can be learned about possible good and bad fits for the self-rater posted in the Example.

First of all he (or she) checked "industrial designer" and "insurance worker" as having immediate appeal and has so indicated by putting a checkmark to the right of each.

He then indicated on his sheet of paper that he would like to find a career in which he could be directly helpful to others, under no circumstances would require that he enjoy competing with others, would give him a feeling of making some sort of direct contribution to society, would not require that he work at a frantic pace, would assure him of security on his job and would give him considerable freedom to come and go as he pleased.

Moving his sheet down from job to job, he finds that "general manager," "industrial designer," "interior decorator-designer," "international worker," "labor relations worker," "landscape architect," "lawyer" and "market analyst" are apparently out of the question (he has so indicated with an "X") because none of them generally and notably offer job security and, in two cases, put a considerable premium on an urge to compete with others, in addition.

At this point, however, we need to take another look. In the first place, did he really mean the circles. Whether or not, he checked "industrial designer" as having appeal. Perhaps in an atypical setting it might be non-competitive and provide the job security and other satisfactions he wants. He should keep it on the list of possibilities for the time being, pending further investigation. Also, if "lawyer" and "international worker" have any appeal, they should not be scratched — for the same reason and for an additional one, i.e., such is the variety within each of these kinds of work that it cannot be said that they will generally and notably satisfy many, if any, values — note that there is only one dot for "lawyer" and none for "international worker." Thus high scores are impossible in both cases but, under certain circumstances, either might provide a reasonable fit. As to the other kinds of work he has marked with an "X" or on which he has a low score, it is probably safe to eliminate them from further consideration.

Our rater's scores are comparatively high on "librarian," "home economist" and "humanist" and these should be listed for further investigation unless there are compelling reasons to the contrary. Incidentally, this rater's value pattern produces "3s" or higher, weighed against all 62 kinds of work, for "conservation worker," "counselor," criminologist," "education worker (non-teaching)," "fund raiser," "minister, priest, rabbi," "social worker," "teacher-professor," "therapist" and "veterinarian" — in addition to "librarian."

As to the "middle" group of kinds of work, between relatively high and relatively low as to score, probably only "insurance worker," which he checked as having appeal, is worth his continued interest.

By applying this procedure to the entire list of 62 kinds of work, you will divide it into two categories, those kinds of work which are likely to (or might possibly) fit your pattern of values and those which are not. The next step is to eliminate from the "likelies" and possibilities those which clearly wouldn't fit you when the traditional measures and the six uncharted values discussed above are taken into consideration. This will leave you with a list of kinds of work worth serious additional exploration, an exploration which can be initiated by selective reading from the descriptions of fields and kinds of work which follow.

THE 62 KINDS OF WORK

JOB VALUES

Some human wants and needs — differing in strength and pattern from individual to individual — which a job can satisfy or frustrate.

JOB VALUES	Rating	Accountant †	Actuary †	Advertising Worker †	Architect †	Artist — Creative and Performing	Bank Worker †	Buyer †	Chiropractor	City Planner and Related †	Computer Scientist (Programer)	Conservation Worker †	Counselor †	Criminologist and related †	Curator †	Dentist	Dietician	Education Worker (Non-teaching) †	Engineer	Environmental Health Specialist (Sanitarian)	Foreign Language Worker	Fund Raiser †	General Manager (Executive, Administrator) †	Home Economist	Humanist †	Industrial Designer
Help Others Directly							*		*				*	*		*									*	
Compete With Others				*				*																		*
Deal With Ideas for Themselves					*						*														*	
Deal With Things, Tangibles, The Practical		*	*		*		*	*	*	*	*	*				*	*	*	*	*			*	*		*
Make All One's Own Decisions					*	*																			*	
Feel One Is Serving Society Directly										*		*	*	*				*				*		*		
See the Results of One's Efforts Often		*	*	*	*		*			*		*			*	*		*					*	*		*
Work at a Fast Pace				*				*															*			
Face Challenge: Intractible Problems, Win or Lose Contests										*			*	*						*			*	*		
Create				*	*	*									*	*	*								*	*
Work Precisely		*	*		*			*		*				*	*	*	*		*		*				*	*
Feel In Control of the Situation														*						*			*			
Feel Secure		*	*				*			*	*	*	*	*	*	*	*	*	*	*	*	*			*	*
Be Free to Come and Go As One Pleases					*	*						*						*						*	*	

† Careers which Liberal Arts graduates can pursue with little or no more supplementary "pre-vocational training" than is required of those from other undergraduate disciplines.

(Specializations Within These Kinds are Mentioned in the Text)

Insurance Worker · Interior Decorator-Designer · International Worker · Labor Relations Worker · Landscape Architect · Lawyer · Librarian · Marketing Analyst and Related · Mathematician, Statistician · Medical Technologist and Related · Military Services Officer · Minister, Priest, Rabbi · Nurse (Registered) · Operations Research Worker · Optometrist · Personnel Worker · Pharmacist · Physician and Osteopath · Pilot (Civilian) · Podiatrist (Chiropodist) · Production Manager · Public Relations Worker · Purchasing Agent · Radio-TV Worker · Recreation Worker · Sales Worker · Scientist, Natural · Scientist, Social · Secretary · Securities Worker · Social Worker · Systems Analyst · Teacher, Professor · Therapist and Related · Traffic Worker (Industrial) · Veterinarian · Writer, Editor

The Six Fields of Work

EDUCATION

To go into "EDUCATION" is to enter the service of that 30-odd per cent of the nation's population, most of them under 25, involved in formal learning. Teaching is far and away the principal — and often is thought of as the only — kind of work in this field. The full education team of over 3,200,000 includes, however, close to half a million people otherwise engaged. Most occupations, in fact — among them a majority of the "business" occupations, all the professions, and research in many disciplines — are to be found in the academic setting. In addition, a number of non-teaching jobs are peculiar to education, in particular academic and student services administrative positions. All these kinds of work are discussed among the occupational descriptions which conclude this book. This chapter is concerned primarily with education as a field of work, its dimensions, facets and future. It also touches on the several values which all jobs in education can usually satisfy and one it will always frustrate.

Dimensions, Facets, Future
Some 59,000,000 Americans, moving towards the completion of some unit of study, are enrolled today in schools, colleges and universities. Additional hundreds of thousands are taking courses for self-improvement or pleasure. Of the "degree-bound," 38,000,000 are in the elementary grades, 14,000,000 in secondary schools, and the remaining 7,000,000 in institutions of higher education, including universities, two- and four-year liberal arts

colleges, teachers colleges, technical and professional colleges and institutes, and the military academies. The vast majority of these students are served by public institutions, five out of six at the elementary level, nine out of ten at the secondary, and two out of three in higher education. The latter proportion is up, incidentally, from one out of two in the past decade. Only a third of the close to 3,000 institutions in higher education, however, are publicly controlled.

This picture is not static. By the mid-1970s enrollments will have increased by some 7 per cent to 63,000,000. The mix, however, will be different. Elementary students will number slightly *fewer* than they do today, the result of the recently declining birthrate. On the other hand, the secondary school and higher education populations will each be larger by 2,000,000. The ratios between those attending public and private institutions will remain about the same except in higher education. There the public colleges and universities will gain ground. This is due to two factors: the proliferation of two-year colleges, which are springing up by the score annually and now number over 900, almost all publicly controlled, will account for perhaps 3,000,000 students by 1975 and, as private institutions try to hold the line, the forced expansion of state universities and "multiversities."

About 2,700,000 teachers and some 500,000 administrators and others in supporting roles serve these vast and increasing numbers of learners. They are not distributed proportionately among the various categories of students, mainly because teacher-pupil ratios differ markedly between categories. In private elementary schools (six out of seven are parochial) each teacher faces, on the average, 33 pupils; in public elementary schools, 26; in public secondary, 21; in private secondary, 18; and in colleges and universities, 13. Among the latter institutions, the proportion of staff to students is highest in universities and lowest in junior colleges, with four-year colleges in between.

Four hundred thousand new jobs, for teachers, administrators and researchers, will be created by growing enrollments in the next seven years, all, of course, at the secondary and higher-education levels. But this by no means tells the whole story about opportunities over that period. Half of those presently in education will retire, die, or move into other fields of work during that time and will have to be replaced. Over-all, some 1,800,000 openings for newcomers to education will be available, more than 250,000 a year — and this trend is likely to continue well into the foreseeable future. Taking into consideration the numbers to be replaced, pupil-teacher ratios, and growth in enrollment, if any, the largest number of openings between now and 1975 will be in elementary education, followed in order by secondary education and higher education. Private institutions will offer about 12 per cent of the openings through the secondary level and 30 per cent beyond.

Turning to opportunities in terms of subjects taught — and they are proliferating rapidly as new fields take shape and old ones are subdivided or merged — information is available only in higher education. Here students seeking a bachelor's degree in the social sciences, humanities, education, business, and related subjects, now about 75 per cent of the total, appear to be increasing their lead slightly over candidates for the comparable degree in the natural sciences, engineering, and related disciplines. In terms of individual subjects, striking increases proportionately are expected in the social sciences themselves, in English and journalism, in mathematics and statistics, and in the biological sciences. Equally striking are the anticipated decreases in engineering and in the health professions. It should be stressed, however, that all this is a matter of ratios. In no consequential category will the actual numbers receiving degrees drop over the next seven years.

At the advanced degree levels the trend picture as between the "social" and "natural" sciences is reversed. The latter, which now occupy about a quarter of those headed for a master's degree and half of those pursuing the doctorate, are expected to make sharp advances at the expense of the former, with engineering leading the way. Oddly enough, a dramatic drop in the percentage of students seeking post-graduate degrees in education itself will account almost single-handedly for the "social science's" loss of position. But even here the actual numbers receiving degrees will increase slightly.

Values

Of the personal values discussed earlier, four — the desire to serve society, the urge to make a lot of money, security, and, just possibly, pace — have relevance to most jobs in education.

As suggested by the use of the word "service" in the sentence which opens this chapter, the field of education offers to all who enter it an opportunity to satisfy the desire to be of obvious service. This may be through direct, daily help to others as a teacher, librarian, counselor, director of a language laboratory, chaplain, coach, director of student aid, or therapist. Or it may be in terms of working for a "serving" cause, albeit at one or more removes from those served, in curriculum development, for instance, or in fund raising, purchasing, property management, experimenting with teaching machines or programed learning or educational TV, or doing research on the learning process. Whatever one does, education is clearly a socially serving work setting.

As to money, education is a field where there are no incomes in six figures, whether one teaches, administers or does research, and precious few even close to $50,000 a year. Thus it is no place for one who sets high store on a handsome income. Starting salaries have increased sharply in recent years and in some cases are competitive with those in other fields. And money goes further in the education environment than elsewhere, as a rule. Keeping up with the Joneses here, in modes of entertainment and standards of dress, for example, is generally less expensive than keeping up with them outside the academic community. And fringe benefits are comparable to those in other fields. But the fact that virtually all educational institutions, public and private, are non-profit and chronically under-financed means that salary increases, while they can be counted on, are small, and the ceiling, often set by law, comes relatively soon into view. (See Appendix A for 1967-68 benchmark figures.)

As to the security offered, jobs in education generally rate at the top, along with those in government and the Military Services. This situation results in part from education's need, in competing for manpower, to compensate for its salary disadvantages; in part from the critical importance of assuring teachers freedom of expression; and in part from the lack of clear and accepted standards for determining who is doing a good job and who isn't. The last problem too frequently means, incidentally, that time-servers and superior performers are rewarded equally. Among those who teach, up through the secondary school level, virtually automatic annual contract renewals are the rule. In higher education, up to the associate professor level, the contract is often for three years — but there is nothing automatic about renewal. This is, perhaps, the most highly competitive and insecure segment of the teaching profession. Once one makes it to associate professor, however, he acquires "tenure," which all but guarantees him his job until retirement.

Among administrators and other non-teaching personnel, the jobs of those in the Federal Office and the state departments of education are generally secured by Civil Service laws and regulations. The security of the rest, while not as firmly nailed down by law and custom, is nevertheless similar to that of civil servants and teachers.

Finally, the matter of the pace of the work. It is impossible to maintain that a relatively leisurely address to the matters in hand is characteristic of all jobs in education. Up-the-line administrators, classroom teachers in overcrowded schools, and professors who take on heavy consulting or textbook writing or committee commitments would, with others, take violent exception to such a contention. Nevertheless, in no other field of work are most of the "plants" shut down for some three months each year. To this extent, and for those whose principal work is directly with students — the great majority — education is certainly a less hurried work environment than any other.

Beyond service to society, money, security and, possibly, pace, all of the personal values discussed earlier can be satisfied (or may be frustrated) somewhere in the field of education.

GOVERNMENT
(Excepting Education and Military Service)

Somewhere in government — Federal, interstate, state, county, or municipal (local) — there is a good living to be had in whatever kind of work, with few exceptions, a person wants to do. *The Federal Career Directory* lists some 200 different kinds of white-collar jobs in 80 departments and agencies, for students majoring in 76 disciplines. To a lesser degree, the story is the same at the lower government levels. Most of these jobs are common to one or more of the other fields of work but some are peculiar to the public service, for instance, those in the Foreign Service, city management, air traffic control, environmental health, legal prosecution, law enforcement, taxation, elective politics and the judiciary.

What follows applies only to jobs in the executive branch of government. Elective and judicial positions are not covered because they do not constitute careers for which one can specifically prepare or at which one can earn a living from the outset. Neither can be entered, as a rule, until one has won his spurs in some other kind of work.

The Dimensions
Some 8,000,000 Americans, exclusive of those in public education and the Military Services, hold government jobs, roughly one out of nine who work. The Federal government employs about a third of them and, contrary to common belief, only one out of nine of these works in Washington. About 250,000 Federal employees, for instance, are based in California, and over 100,000 in foreign lands. The great majority of the country's remaining 5,000,000-odd civil servants are employed by state, county and local governments. Though growing rapidly, interstate agencies still account for only a handful.

Except at the Federal level, where new hiring has leveled off, government employment will increase rapidly into the foreseeable future. Government is a service-to-people field and people in America are not only doubling in number every 50 years or so (presently declining birthrate notwithstanding), but are also demanding more services per head. Far and away the greatest number of opportunities will, of course, be at non-Federal levels, but the Federal government, though not growing, will still have to recruit hundreds of thousands of workers each year, including some 25,000 collegians, to replace employees who have died, retired, or gone elsewhere.

Government salaries are approaching those offered in other fields, including business and industry, so far as what one can expect at the start and can hope to make up to a decade or so out of college. One Federal agency, for instance, virtually guarantees an able, energetic liberal arts bachelor's degree holder, starting at about $7000, total earnings over three years of $30,000, and it will throw in the cost of tuition and books at a local university if he chooses to undertake formal study on his own time.

But the government careerist's top salary is set by law. At the Federal level this ceiling is at a figure equivalent to the salaries of upper-middle managers in business. Appointive jobs at all government levels, jobs to be had without working one's way up through the ranks, pay subsantially more on occasion, however. This is particularly true at the state and local levels, in the case of city managers and municipal and state department heads, for example.

Values and the Way of Life

Except that everywhere there is a ceiling on earnings — this is not a field for one who wants to make a million — government somewhere can offer a job which will fit every possible pattern of personal values. Public service in general, however, does have a number of prevailing characteristics of significance to one who is thinking about it in the context of his values.

The first which comes to mind is the high order of job security enjoyed by most government workers. Under civil service and merit system laws and regulations (instituted to reduce political pressures in governmental decision making) a person's job is safe unless he errs catastrophically or the budget of his agency is cut. This latter eventuality hardly warrants mention in this era of plateaued or expanding governmental spending. In any event, only the newcomer needs to worry about appropriation cuts. As he gains seniority, he acquires rights to comparable jobs held by those junior to him, if his own is eliminated.

As to pace, in the top jobs, as well as at all job levels when new programs are being set in motion, in emergencies, and when the concern is with one or another of society's great intractable problems — slums, pollution, crime, for example — the government worker is often under heavy pressure and must move at a frantic clip. But for most, much of the time, at home and abroad, the pace is likely to be more leisurely than that which prevails in profit-making enterprise and self-employment, perhaps even than in education and the Military Services. The reasons are clear. Government agencies are not continuously competing in the marketplace for survival. No periodic profit-and-loss statements are involved. Thus, the pressures for efficiency are normally mild and only sporadically intense. In addition, since government workers enjoy a high order of job security they are not easily pushed.

This does not mean that most government workers are timeservers. On the contrary, those in the middle and upper echelons, at least, are usually highly dedicated, self-starting hard workers. Nor does it mean that internal competition does not exist. Within government departments, infighting — for promotion and recognition among individuals, as well as among agencies for jurisdiction over new programs — is every bit as rugged as it is elsewhere.

On another count, government is by definition public service. As such, it can, in all its facets, be rewarding to those who need to feel that what they are doing is helpful to others. And many of its jobs give the incumbents the opportunity to see at first hand the impact of each day's work.

Generally speaking, government officials carry broader responsibility, travel more, are more in the public eye, deal with less routine work, and are more dependent on appearances for success than people at the same pay level in business. In the latter regard, the civil servant must look busy. His personal conduct must be above reproach. Taxpayers and legislators, his employers, lean heavily on this not always accurate measure of performance, since there are few more definitive ones available.

The worker in a large government agency, to remain cheerful, usually must be willing to wait for promotion and greater challenge — the wheels often grind slowly; must be tolerant of red tape and buck-passing; and must be flexible — change is an inevitable condition of life where ultimate decisions are made by legislatures. It should be noted, however, that except for change, he would be confronted with the same problems in organizations of comparable size in other fields. An organization's size, not its field, determines the amount of bureaucracy it harbors.

Finally, most civil servants can count on staying put geographically. At the Federal level most jobs — and opportunities for promotion — are in Washington and large regional installations; at the state level, in the state capitals; and at the local level, within the county or city limits.

PROFIT-MAKING ENTERPRISES

In spite of the omnipresence of profit-making enterprises in America, collegians know less and have more misconceptions about them as a career field than perhaps any of the other five. The picture that "profit-making enterprise" — or its synonyms in common parlance, "business," "industry" and the "profit-making sector" — conjures up in their minds is often so far from being a likeness as to be unrecognizable. As a result, many who would thrive in business look elsewhere, and many others for whom it probably would be a bad fit give too little consideration to alternatives.

The effort here will be to describe the nature of the business world in general as a place to work, whether as a junior accountant or company president. The presentation will be as objective as I can make it, but will surely be faulted as biased in one direction or another by many. Like the proverbial elephant being touched by the blind men, business is perceived quite differently by different people. And many are prompted by their perceptions to become ardent defenders or sharp critics of the beast. Thus, no matter how balanced any presentation may be, it will be found unduly flattering or improperly derogatory by partisans, depending on their positions pro or con.

In order, the sections which follow touch on the dimensions of the profit-making sector; how it works; the differences in working environment as between small and large companies; how to identify progressive concerns; and personal values as related to a profit-oriented setting.

A final word. Self-employment, though in its many faces basically profit-oriented, is a way of working life quite different from being employed by others in business, and will, therefore, be treated in the following chapter as a distinguishable field of work.

Dimensions of the Profit-making Sector

4,000,000 Enterprises   The country contains 4,000,000-plus profit-making enterprises that can be divided into two categories — those which produce and sell tangibles, from apples to bicycles to skyscrapers, and those which sell services, from hairdos to vacations to million-dollar loans. These enterprises are also described as belonging to one or another industry or type of business (the words will be used interchangeably). There are many and varying lists of industries. That used by the Federal government distinguishes between some 1,000, those in the profit-making sector being divided into eight broad divisions. These divisions are: Agriculture-Forestry-Fisheries; Mining; Contract Construction; Manufacturing (20 sub-categories and 200 distinguishable industries) ; Transportation-Communications and Electrical-Gas-Sanitary Services; Wholesale and Retail Trade; Finance-Insurance-Real Estate; Other Services (which includes Recreation and Amusement, Lodging, Personal, Business, Medical, Educational and Legal Services, Motion Pictures, and Private Household).

Among the sources of information on individual concerns in these divisions — by name, industry, size, management, etc. — are The *College Placement Annual* (2100 listed) ; Dun and Bradstreet's Reference Book; Poor's Register of Corporations, Directors and Executives; Standard and Poor's Corporation Records; *Fortune* magazine's annual list, "500 Largest U. S. Industrial Corporations"; local and state industrial directories; membership lists of Chambers of Commerce and Manufacturers' Associations; the Small Business Administration, whose headquarters are in Washington, D. C.; the financial pages of newspapers; and state Public Employment Service offices.

The Size of Individual Businesses While it is true that the trend today in the profit-making sector — as in education and government — is toward bigger organizations, the giant firms still account for only a fraction of the country's total work force. Exact employment figures are impossible to come by, but indicative is the fact that, in terms of total sales, the 500 largest industrial firms and the 50 largest concerns in each of the banking, utility, transportation, insurance, and retail-wholesale fields employ between them only about a quarter of all Americans who work for a living. Put another way, most workers are — and will continue to be into the foreseeable future — employed by the country's 4,000,000-odd smaller enterprises. There are, thus, ample alternatives to working for the giants.

Growth Profit-making enterprises employ a large majority of the country's 75,000,000 workers. The number so employed is growing but more slowly than is the case in other fields of work, particularly state and local government. This situation results in large part from the fact that business can increasingly produce more goods and services with fewer workers. Within the business sector, concerns providing services and the construction industry are growing fastest, followed by wholesale-retail trade, and finance, insurance and real estate. Employment in manufacturing, transportation, and public utilities is expanding relatively slowly, and in mining and agriculture it is declining.

Growth rate is not, however, necessarily the prime consideration in weighing the opportunities for newcomers, as noted earlier. Total numbers currently employed by a given industry — or in a field of work or company within an industry — may have more bearing, due to the openings created by predictable deaths, retirements and transfers-out. Manufacturing, for example, which employs close to 20,000,000 people, will have far more openings, up and down the line, for years to come than will the far faster growing construction industry with total employment of only 5,000,000. Similarly, the profit-making sector as a whole whose growth is relatively slow, will provide more opportunity than all other fields of work combined, for some time to come.

Dynamism The profit-making sector can be, though it often isn't, a lively place to work, due to omnipresent competitive pressures, technical advances and in some quarters, its growing sense of social responsibility. Competition is nothing new. The technological explosion, relatively at least, is. The potential excitement is not limited to such "glamour" fields as electronic data processing, transportation, communications, atomic energy and aerospace. Business is pushing out the frontiers in many less visible areas. The cryogenic industry, for instance, is approaching the billion-dollar mark in sales as it finds new ways of applying temperatures in the minus 200-459 degree range to the solution of problems in such diverse fields as medicine and electric power generation. The picture is similar in such areas as educational aids, bio-medical devices, oceanography and pollution control, and there is the growing number of "think tanks" whose post-doctoral employees of all disciplines not only seek answers to difficult questions but also propound questions that need answers. In regard to social responsibility, profit-making enterprise is increasingly involving itself, on its own or in cooperation with government, in communications, slum housing, the exploration of space and the retraining and employment of the underprivileged, among other areas.

25,000 Kinds of Work The great majority of the 25,000-odd kinds of work performed in America, from accounting to zoology, are to be found in the profit-making sector. Included are most of those of interest to college graduates, among them 57 of the 62 dealt with in this book.

Salaries Business's previous long lead over other fields of work in the salaries paid, from top to bottom, has recently narrowed at the beginner level. But the traditional gap remains from the middle-management level on up. At the top levels such extras as stock options, profit sharing, liberal expense allowances and bonuses can put the businessman's actual income out of sight relative to all fields except self-employment.

Promotion There is at present — and for a number of years, there will be — an acute shortage of men and women in early middle age, the vintage which normally supplies business as well as other fields with its "middle managers" in all kinds of work. This shortage results from the low birthrate of the Depression 1930s. Young men and women entering business today thus have an unprecedented opportunity to move rapidly from their apprenticeships to positions of substantial responsibility.

How the Profit-making Sector Works

Profits To survive, business concerns obviously must take in more money than it costs to produce the goods or render the services they offer for sale and to pay for such relatively fixed costs as taxes and insurance. This is not an optional matter. These profits are needed to undertake the research and the upgrading of equipment and processes essential to remaining competitive. In addition, the owners of a business, or the stockholders, must be compensated in one way or another for the risk they take in giving it the use of their money. Further, capital is needed for daily operations and for growth. And finally, profits may be used for such other purposes — more or less optional depending on one's point of view — as contributions to nonprofit-making organizations and payments under bonus and profit-sharing plans.

The success of a business is usually judged by the amount and consistency over time of its profits. But competition — or government regulation — assure that exorbitant profits will rarely be made. It has been estimated that the average profit for all businesses is on the order of 3 to 4 per cent of sales.

Share of the Market In a few industries, notably the utilities, businesses are granted a monopoly since the public has determined that this will provide better service at lower cost than would a competitive situation. Elsewhere, competition is relied on to effect this end. Most businesses are thus engaged in a constant struggle with others like them for the dollars available to buy the particular goods or services they deal in — their share of the market. They rise or fall, depending on what happens to that share. Two things follow: First, the customer calls the tune as to what is produced; business must be acutely sensitive to what he wants, and must continually strive to anticipate (and, if possible, increase) his wants of the future; second, since it must produce at a price that is competitive, business is concerned, beyond all other fields of work except self-employment, with the efficient use of its animate and inanimate resources.

The Stockholder The managers of business, except for the tiny and dwindling fraction who own all or a large part of the enterprises they manage, are the employees of those who own business, the stockholders. Thus managers must reflect in their decisions the views of their stockholders. If they go counter to these views, say in the matter of how much risk to take, at best the concern's stock will drop and capital will be hard to come by as the stockholders take their money elsewhere. At worst, the managers will lose their jobs.

Social Responsibility In reply to its critics business has long pointed out such obvious facts as that its taxes and those of its employees support most of the services, including the public schools, provided by government; that its productivity has brought America the highest standard of living in world history; that it provides most of the jobs available; that the country's security rests on its might; and that private educational institutions and most charitable and cultural endeavors rely heavily on its contributions. It has added to its defensive arsenal of late the fact of a growingly active interest in social problems hitherto left largely to government, education and non-profit organizations. Pollution control, slum redevelopment and the training of the underprivileged are among the fields it is entering.

Some of this new activity — the proportion is much debated — is stimulated by a new and genuine social consciousness, as public problems become more complex, intractable and urgent, and some is a matter of pure self-interest. Business can continue to ignore these problems only at the risk of mounting public criticism, criticism likely to be expressed eventually in more regulation of business and in the forcing of its participation in social endeavors. Further, some individual businesses are becoming involved principally to enhance their competitive positions within their industries. The Rotarians have a phrase for it: "He profits most who serves the best." Whatever the motivation, however, no business will long survive if it puts expenditures for good causes ahead of making a reasonable profit.

Bureaucracy Business as a field of work is probably no more or less bureaucratic than other fields. Bureaucracy is principally related to an organization's size. Big organizations must secure and digest increasingly voluminous and complex information, must plan systematically and must coordinate and control many different activities. To accomplish these ends they must be elaborately structured, work must be compartmentalized, responsibilities must be sharply defined, and the decision-making machinery must be intricate. In consequence, regardless of the field of work, human nature being what it is, there will inevitably be some buck-passing, red tape, infighting, jockeying for position and visibility, make-work, pressures for conformity, undue emphasis on personality, endless committee meetings and the other symptoms of bureaucracy.

Mobility Readiness to make a move, geographically or occupationally, is frequently vital to making progress in business. In large, multidivisional concerns the promotional path often consists of a succession of assignments to increasingly important jobs in branches located in widely separated places. Further, top general management comes only to those who have welcomed the opportunity to perform in a variety of capacities. And those well up the ladder often find that the fastest way to get further ahead is to seek — or accept — a better job with another company. In this connection, the number of executive recruitment firms, who serve their client companies by locating for them in other companies the executives they need, has grown prodigiously in recent years.

Working for Small and Large Companies

As one moves towards the ends of the spectrum of numbers employed by individual businesses, differences in the working environment as between the large and small become increasingly distinguishable. At the far ends, these differences may be of kind. Formal training programs for newcomers, for instance, are universal in companies employing 10,000 or more but virtually non-existent in those with payrolls of 50 or less. But for the most part the differences are in degree only. It might be noted that some of them exist as between large and small organizations in other fields of work, such as government and education, and between the headquarters and branches of large firms.

In general, the following things are true of smaller concerns, as against larger ones.

—The lower the salaries from bottom to top, the fewer the "fringe" benefits and the less the formality of the salary structure. Total incomes at the top, however, may approximate those in large concerns, particularly if top management receives a large share of the profits over and above salary.

—The greater the part each employee plays in the total operation. This means that he is more visible to his supervision, and, thus, that his mistakes and successes are more quickly spotted. This also means that rewards and punishments are prompter and more dramatic, and that, if he is competent, an individual will have a larger hand sooner in making decisions with company-wide impact. It should be noted here, however, that a big decision in a small company may involve $1,000 while a little decision in a big one may involve $10,000 or more.

—The greater the chance that membership in or the goodwill of a small group, often the family which owns the enterprise, will play a disproportionate part in promotion. It will surely affect the chances of acquiring a share of the ownership.

—The greater the possibility of rapid company growth or sudden failure and, thus, the greater the chance of quick, personal success or abrupt unemployment.

—The greater the variety of the work at the outset and along the way and the less the opportunity to learn one skill thoroughly through specialization. The variety may, of course, include chores like buying office supplies and driving the company truck, which in larger concerns are assigned to unskilled and semi-skilled labor.

—The less the sophistication in the planning for executive development and the less the likelihood that the company will encourage and pay for off-the-job formal, job-related study.

—The fewer the openings up the promotional ladder.

—The fewer the experts and specialists within the company on whom one may (or must) call for help in solving problems.

—The less the possibility of having to move from place to place to move up.

—The less the bureaucracy.

—The greater the opportunity to see frequently the results of one's own efforts.

—The longer and more irregular the required hours on the job.

—The more authoritarian, arbitrary and "intuitive" the top management.

Identifying Progressive Companies

Whatever one's preferences in such matters as kind of work, company size, industry and location, one will, assuming he has some freedom of choice, want to join the soundest and most progressive concern which will hire him. Suggested below are some ways of evaluating companies on these scores.

Much data on publicly owned companies is readily available in annual reports, the financial pages of newspapers and business magazines. One will probably have to visit the offices of a stockbroker or investment counselor or banker, however, to see such more useful material as the newsletters of banks and investment houses, the reports of investment advisory services, and various compendia of an analytical nature.

The best sources of information from your point of view, however, may be informal, oral ones. Among these, if they will express opinions, are the personnel in State Public Employment Service offices (2000 of them across the land), college placement officers, bankers, stockbrokers, investment counselors, the executive secretaries of local and state Chamber of Commerce and trade associations, real estate brokers, computer salesmen (progressive companies buy computers as soon as they can), and employees of companies themselves.

Finally, you can apply to what you read and hear the criteria used by professional evaluators. Among them are: How professional, energetic and farsighted is the company's management; how much money is being spent on research and development; how fast and steadily are sales growing; how much attention does the company pay to internal manpower planning and development; how stiff is the competition within the industry; what is the earnings record; does the company have raw material problems; is its share of the market growing or declining; on what does the business's future prospects depend — population growth, growing urbanization, the general state of the economy, scientific and engineering research, government contracts or other government action, customer tastes, constant innovation; and how diversified are its products or services.

Values

So numerous and varied are the facets of business that it can provide a rewarding work setting for any person, whatever his values, with one important proviso. He must be in agreement with his employer's inevitable expectation that, regardless of what he does, he wants to and will make a contribution, direct or indirect, long- or short-range, to the company's profitability. This is not to say that the impact of his daily work on how much money is being made need be an omnipresent consideration for every employee. But this is management's ultimate measure, as it has to be. Its tests of performance are ultimately pragmatic, dollars-and-cents ones: Does the idea have practical application so far as the balance sheet is concerned? Is the work useful in terms of making a profit? A person who strongly objects to being so judged will have rough sledding in a business environment.

SELF-EMPLOYMENT

It is possible in America to be one's own boss in a large variety of occupations. And many people think longingly of the freedom from taking direction from others, from the danger of being fired, from mandatory retirement and from necessary limits on what can be earned, all advantages thought to go with self-employment. Yet only about a tenth of all who work for a living work for themselves, and the proportion is diminishing. Some see in this small and declining fraction evidence that Americans are losing their traditional spirit of independence. Perhaps, but it is surely true that, as a practical matter, it becomes increasingly hard in most occupations to succeed as an independent. Three of the four necessary ingredients, hard work, good luck and good judgment, are presumably in no shorter supply today than they have been over the centuries. But the fourth, adequate competence, gets harder and harder to come by. As knowledge expands geometrically, the skills and processes by which society serves itself become ever more complex and thus ever more difficult for an individual to master. And mastery may not be enough. In a growing number of fields things can be done most efficiently by organizations manned by specialists. Efficiency is of the essence, since everyone in self-employment must compete in the marketplace for customers for the goods or services he offers.

Self-employment nevertheless remains an open option for most collegians. A discussion of its parameters, of the ingredients essential to success, and of the personal values it can satisfy or will usually frustrate follows.

The Parameters
Some 8,000,000 Americans run their own shows. Half of them are professional people practicing, singly or as partners, "under their own shingles." Included are not only those in such traditional professions as medicine, law, architecture, engineering, dentistry and accounting, but many who have elected to go it alone in occupations more usually found in an organizational setting. Personnel experts become private placement agents or executive recruiters (the number of the latter has grown from a dozen to 900 in the past decade) ; experienced buyers set up shop to serve small concerns which cannot afford full-time specialists;

executives go into management consulting; reporters turn into syndicated columnists or public relations counselors; college development directors become fund-raising consultants. In fact, only in those kinds of work peculiar to government (law enforcement and the Foreign Service, for instance), education (academic administration) and the military is it impossible to undertake solo practice.

Another quarter of the self-employed are independent farmers. The number of these is shrinking steadily as this is a field in which, in particular, size of organization and specialization breed efficiency. Most of the remaining quarter of the 8,000,000 run small businesses, typically retail establishments such as restaurants, motels, groceries, museums, filling stations and consumer goods stores, though some are producers of goods. The rest who go it alone include creative people and those who, like the cleaning woman and bootblack, have no choice because they lack marketable skills. Commission salesmen are not included since most are controlled to some extent by the concerns for which they sell.

The Ingredients of Success

Though no longer sufficient to assure it, hard work and good luck are still essential to success in self-employment. On the first score, while it is true that many established independents have, or appear to have, more leisure than their contemporaries on a payroll, it's a safe bet that on the way up they had less. One estimate is that people who run their own shows spend a day more a week on the job than those who don't. In the matter of luck, the self-employed person is highly vulnerable to adverse developments beyond his control. He is usually rooted physically, maintains no branch operations elsewhere, and offers a limited variety of goods or services for sale. He has thus little room for manoeuvre if changes in the economy or public taste, unexpected competition, amendments to laws affecting his occupation, his mistakes, even the routing of a new super highway, jeopardize his earnings. And there is, too, the matter of personal health. The Blue Cross may pay the medical bills but who will mind the store while he is out sick?

Hard work and the right breaks, however, are only the start. A high order of competence is essential to earning an independent livelihood. The professional depends on his reputation for expertness in his field. He will prosper or fail depending on what those he has served say about him to those he would like to serve. The business entrepreneur, in addition, must be knowledgeable in the many areas — finance, marketing, production, supervision, legal requirements, quality control, insurance, pricing and the nature of the competition, among them — which in combination determine the quality and price of what he sells. (More details on what is involved in going into business for oneself are available from the Small Business Administration, Washington, D. C., which, incidentally, states that each day in America 1000 new businesses are started, 900 change hands, and 930 discontinue; that there is one chance in five that a new business will stay in the same hands for ten years or more; and that lack of business know-how accounts for 90 per cent of the failures.)

Both the professional and the businessman have another problem. What constitutes competence today may not meet the test tomorrow. In a time of rapid change, both must be continuously at pains to keep up with "the state of the art."

But even with hard work, luck and competence, one cannot be sure of making a go of it. These three must be presided over by that nebulous characteristic called good judgment. When should one take a chance and when play it safe? When should advice be sought and how much weight should be given to advice received? How far should one go in pressing for a bargain? When is one getting out of his depth? Even, does one have the competence and psychological make-up to succeed alone? Good judgment is important anywhere, but in self-employment it must be of a high order and consistent. With the freedom to make one's own decisions and enjoy all their fruits, if they are wise ones, goes responsibility for making them with no one to set one right or to pick up the pieces, if they are not.

The collegian tempted to strike out on his own can assess his chances of success readily in regard to two of the four determinants. Hard work is a matter of energy level and ambition and competence, of aptitude and training. Luck, the third factor, is beyond his control, though competence and good judgment can affects its impact. As to the fourth, good judgment, his past record may give clues. And one can assume that degree of competence — not necessarily length of experience — will have a bearing, in the sense that knowledge of alternatives is the first condition to good decision making.

But these are relatively weak reeds to rely on. The best way to make an assessment, short of taking the plunge, is to find a job with a successful independent in one's area of interest, as employee or associate or heir apparent. Here one can try out his judgment directly or vicariously without risking disaster from his inevitable early mistakes. Even this, however, cannot be a definitive test. No one really knows until he has tried it, how his judgment will stand up in the lonely, unprotected, pressureful setting of self-employment, where the welfare not only of himself but of his family, his clients, his creditors and, often, his employees is at stake.

Values
The values that running one's own show can satisfy or will usually frustrate are implicit from what has gone before. Self-employment is for those to whom independence and control of the environment, pace (at least early in the game), and challenge (in the sense that economic survival is a clear, present and continuing issue), are important; who have a high tolerance for uncertainty; who enjoy seeing the results of their efforts frequently; who prefer to put-down roots geographically (which is not to say, however, that extensive travel and prolonged absences from home may not be involved as, for example, in the case of some consultants) ; and who cherish the freedom to come and go as they please (whether they exercise it or not).

Along with profit-making enterprise among the six fields of work, self-employment presents the opportunity to make a lot of money. But usually it is eventual opportunity only. Becoming established, gaining a reputation and attracting a sufficiency of customers can take a long time. Most of the self-employed face a hand-to-mouth existence at first, perhaps even a protracted period of being in debt as they struggle to liquidate loans for education and the costs of equipment, furnishings, inventory or other essentials to their full functioning. And it is perhaps important to note that in many areas self-employed professionals have average earnings only slightly larger than those who work for others. Many independent businessmen actually make less than their peers in age and training who draw salaries.

The one value sure to be frustrated in self-employment, until one has become thoroughly established in his field, is a desire for job security beyond what one's own efforts can assure. Otherwise, whatever one's pattern of values, being one's own boss can yield satisfaction in one context or another.

PRIVATE NON-PROFIT ORGANIZATIONS
(Except Educational Institutions)

Unlike the other five fields of work, people seldom elect to enter the private non-profit organization field specifically. Rather, they find themselves in it — if this aspect of where they are ever occurs to them — because they are attracted by one or another of the many and varied organizations or areas of interest in the field. It may, therefore, seem to be stretching things to lump them together, to describe as a "field" a conglomeration of organizations whose only obvious common denominator is that they are private and make no profits. There is one practical and one value-oriented reason for so doing. These increasingly numerous organizations must be included somewhere in any discussion of career alternatives which pretends to completeness. More important, however, is the fact that as a group they are, almost by definition, "cause-oriented" and thus a place to start for the many who are looking for work which gives them a sense of being of direct service to society.

The Dimensions

What follows is only a brief survey of the field. The diversity within it and the lack of systematic information about it permit nothing more here. No one knows how many private, non-profit organizations there are, but that they can be counted in the tens of thousands is indicated by such facts as that there are at least 300 distinguishable religious and 200 labor organizations in the country, that 170 separate educational associations belong to the American Council on Education, that virtually every city of the country has at least one private hospital, one YMCA and YMHA and one Boy Scout headquarters and that it takes a fat book to list all the foundations.

The concerns of these organizations are numerous, highly diverse and frequently are not confined to this country. Health, youth, labor, religion and education are indicated above. Others are charity, safety, research, the promotion of professional and business cooperation, politics, social service, fraternal ties, good government, civil liberties, population control, the granting of money for worthwhile projects, peace, educational TV, cultural affairs, urban and regional development, the provision of employment for the aged or handicapped, international affairs, the counseling and guidance of individuals, travel, recreation, natural resources, history and insurance.

Many of these organizations operate with unpaid citizen boards and a few full-time workers, professional and clerical. Some, in particular the large foundations, business and professional associations and political organizations, are looking for people who have already made their mark in other fields of work. But many are substantial bureaucracies which recruit at the college level and offer excellent long-range opportunities. And there is every evidence that their needs for collegians are growing fast.

Values

As pointed out above, private non-profit organizations provide rewarding work for those who want to be of service to others in one way or another, directly or indirectly. Only one other value, the desire to make money, is relevant to them as a group. They have virtually nothing to offer one who is concerned about high earnings. In fact, since most subsist on voluntary contributions, the pay is likely to be lower than in any other field.

THE MILITARY SERVICES

One of the principal crosses the Military Services have to bear in their competition with other fields of work for college-trained careerists is an overabundance of people who consider themselves authorities and aren't. "After all," tens of millions of Americans now otherwise employed can truthfully say, "I was on the payroll, wore the uniform, saw it from the inside. I should know." The fact is, however, that most of these sometime soldiers, sailors, airmen, or marines are unreliable witnesses. They are rarely objective — most joined up as a matter of necessity and got out as soon as they could. They rarely have a comprehensive view of the Services — most non-career men work in a limited area both as to duties and geographically. Most of them saw service only in time of war — and professional military men in America have been engaged in actual fighting only 20 per cent of their time in this century. And they are usually talking about how things were 15 or more years ago — the Services today are quite different in many respects from what they were in World War II and during Korea. In sum, military service as a voluntarily undertaken, lifelong career, though it includes some aspects with which erstwhile soldiers are familiar, cannot often be accurately described by them. In fact, few outside it can speak with authority, for except in time of war, the uniform is usually out of sight, in domestic camps, posts, reservations, garrisons, forts, bases and yards, afloat on the high seas, or stationed abroad.

What follows attempts an objective, up-to-date and comprehensive description of the Services as career possibilities — within limits. In confines itself to commissioned officers, that 8th of all who wear the uniform (and that 12th of all on the Defense Department payroll — one out of three are civilians) whose jobs are of interest to collegians considering a Service career. In the interests of brevity and because their similarities in terms of the careers they offer are greater than their differences, no distinction is made between the Service branches: Army, Navy, Air Force, Marines, and Coast Guard; or the specialties: administration, medicine and other professions, flying, supply-quartermaster-transportation-logistics, ordnance-maintenance-repair, signal corps-communications-electronics, engineering, and research and development and other technical specialties. And it does not touch on opportunities for women, these being too few to warrant coverage here.

Four matters are discussed: types of careers, entry and promotion for what we will call the "regular" officer, the way of life, and values. Because a description of military service as a career field must basically be an account of its unique profession, this section doubles as both a field of work and kind of work description.

Types of Careers

The Military Services offer incoming officers four career patterns, essentially. The distinctions are based on what a man wants to do in uniform and how long he wants to stay. He can elect to become a regular officer, one whose basic orientation at all levels is towards command of troops. Or, if specifically trained or interested in so becoming, he can concentrate exclusively on one of the specialties mentioned above. Whatever his choice — and he need not make the decision immediately — he can become either a one- or a two-career man. He can stay in the Service throughout his life, providing he is not "selected out" because of relative incompetence; or he can retire after 20 years or so and undertake a civilian career. The large number who exercise this option is suggested by the fact that the average age of Service retirees in a recent year was 45.

Within the Services, the more a man specializes, the more likely it is that his skills will have a civilian market if he elects the two-career path. The regular officer, from training in many fields (though often concentrating in one) which may or may not have civilian equivalents, often acquires a competence which is peculiar to the Military. Thus he may have trouble in finding civilian employment, at least until as a senior field grade officer his work becomes comparable to that of top executives in other fields. In any event, those who go the two-career route must usually find paying work when they take off their uniforms, since retirement pay is modest.

Entry and Promotion of the Regular Officer

The career officer corps has long since ceased to be a "club" with members drawn largely from and completely dominated by graduates of the several Service academies. In a recent non-war year, only 5 per cent of the newly commissioned officers in all the Services were academy graduates, the balance being made up largely of graduates of Reserve Officer Training Programs and, to a lesser extent, Officer Candidate Schools. Direct appointments of doctors, lawyers and other professionals accounted for the rest. Again, in a recent year, only a quarter of the regular officers in the Army prepared at West Point.

An "academy coloration," however, increasingly asserts itself as one moves up the ladder of rank. But studies suggest that this is not necessarily because, as is commonly believed, promotion preference goes to those who "wear the ring." Success as a regular officer seems to be correlated far more closely with commitment to the Services as a career and, most important, the amount of post-college formal training, both specifically military and general, a man has undergone. In both respects, academy graduates outdistance their R.O.T.C. and O.C.S. colleagues.

This matter of advanced training warrants special comment. The officer who wants to remain in the Service must take advance training from time to time. His only choice is the kind of training to pursue. A special sophistication is required which cannot be learned in the college years or on the job. This is true whether he is dealing with weaponry, the administration of Service personnel spread all over the globe, intelligence, the nationals of other countries or troops in the field.

Movement into positions of great responsibility, for the direction of others or for a function, comes fast in the Services. Training programs are just long enough to develop minimum skills. Extended "internships" beyond that point are rare. Once launched, the regular officer's promotions will depend, up through "middle management," on perhaps the most methodical and objective performance rating system to be found in the world of work.

The number of positions at the top, for senior field grade and general officers, is set by law and is comparable, in terms of percentage of total employees, to that in industry. Thus deaths, retirements and promotions in the echelon immediately above him, as in other fields, will affect an officer's progress as he nears the highest ranks. And it is at these levels that "selection out" of the less able takes the biggest toll.

Finally, opportunities for promotion are, of course, affected by whether or not the nation is at war. Whereas in government, business and education a person can look for upward progress at a pace consonant with his ability, in the Services, so long as wars come and go, the career officer may go through periods of breakneck promotion or stagnation largely unrelated to his competence.

The Way of Life

Rotation is, perhaps, the most striking feature of the regular officer's life. Through most of his career he is on the move from station to station, sometimes stopping for only a year, seldom for more than four. His assignments, in time of peace, run the gamut from executive or staff or teaching work similar to that in civilian life, to troop or ship command or diplomatic service in remote, uncomfortable and even dangerous outposts.

The constant movement within the officer corps colors the leadership an officer exercises and receives. Authority, except in combat, is considerably more institutionalized, leadership less personalized, than in any other field. Rank *per se* and highly structured organization are counted on to a larger extent to keep the wheels rolling, as must necessarily be so where today's commander is gone tomorrow and tomorrow's the day after. This obviously means more authoritarianism, more emphasis on discipline (in combat, obedience must be reflexive), more uniformity in the way leadership is exercised.

The constant movement also has an impact on the officer's social life. It is a factor in the strong sense of belongingness which characterizes the professional officer corps, an atmosphere which has, however, been considerably modified in recent years by the increasingly close working relationships necessary between officers and civilians, especially in scientific, business and educational matters. On another score and somewhat surprisingly, frequent changes of station and this sense of belongingness stimulate, rather than inhibit, participation by officers and their families in the civic affairs of the communities where they are stationed. A recent study found officers generally more active in such affairs than their opposite numbers in the business community.

Values

A cheerful life in Military Service depends, in the first instance, on one's acceptance, at least, of its purpose. There is no question, of course, that officers as a group are basically specialists in violence, preparing for action most hope they will never have to take. Within that frame of reference, it should be noted that the preparation is increasingly in terms of being ready, not to fight an all-out war for national survival, but to use the minimum force necessary to accomplish a variety of policing and surveillance assignments around the world. Whatever the purpose, there is no challenge to George Washington's view that "To be prepared for war is one of the most effectual means of preserving peace."

Beyond acceptance of the military purpose, there are two personal values that the Services throughout can satisfy, and perhaps four that it will usually frustrate. A desire for control can always be met to at least some degree. An officer's rank automatically bestows on him at least some authority over those of lower rank. Second, a career officer, granted reasonable competence, enjoys a high degree of job, if not rank, security, well into middle age.

On the other side of the coin are the facts that no one ever got rich on his Service pay; that the Services are no place for one who wants to settle down early in life; that one who treasures a high degree of independence in general and, on his job, freedom to come and go as he chooses, will not find the uniform a comfortable fit; and that, if playing with ideas without concern for their practicality is a man's bent, the Services, like business, have little to offer him.

In these respects, the Military Services in general will or will not have appeal, depending on how strongly a man feels about them. As to all the other personal values, however, today's many-faceted Military establishment offers, in one place or another, the possibility of their satisfaction.

62 Kinds of Work[*]

ACCOUNTANT

The Work   An accountant does all or some of the following: gives an employer or client an accurate picture of where he has been and informed estimates of where he might go so far as dollars are concerned; maintains accounts, prepares tax returns, makes up budgets, audits, makes analyses for predictive or explanatory purposes, estimates costs, prepares profit and loss statements and balance sheets and devises systems to control such things as inventories; increasingly uses computers in work; must know applicable laws and regulations. In some instances, extensive travel is involved. He may be a teacher in a business school.

Numbers and Prospects   About 500,000, of whom 10 per cent are women (this percentage is increasing fast) and 100,000 are Certified Public Accountants; prospects excellent and tied to growth of economy; increasing use of computers balanced by increasing interest in ascertaining the dollar facts of the past and in refining estimates of prospective costs.

Where Employed   Half as members of the financial management teams of business enterprises; a third as proprietors of independent consulting firms or employees of such firms; remainder employed by educational insitutions, government, the Military Services and private non-profit organizations.

Preparation   Beginning positions still possible for those with only correspondence school or two years of post-high school training

---

* 61 described here; the 62nd, Regular Officer, is described on Pages 115-121.

but increasing emphasis on Bachelor's and even Master's degrees; accounting majors in high demand but people with unrelated majors welcome if they have analytical minds, agreeable personalities and capacity to master the subject matter, especially data processing. To become a Certified Public Accountant passing of a test is required everywhere and in half the states there are additional requirements such as a four-year college degree or several years of apprenticeship or both; over 90 per cent of CPA's have Bachelor's degrees.

Advancement In all fields through normal channels; in business this is a specialty that can lead to the top.

Salaries At levels, varying with level of degree attained, seniority, experience, responsibility carried and field and place of employment, paid persons in other fields with the same type of schooling; one can reach upper-middle-management levels without taking on added responsibilities for unrelated kinds of work; independents can have incomes in six figures. (See Appendix A for 1967-68 benchmark figures.)

For People Who Like work which requires precision, orderliness, careful planning; who have a systematic approach and an analytical point of view; who enjoy dealing with people as business associates and, at the upper levels, as employees and potential customers; who want to work at a measured pace and to see the results of their efforts in concrete terms often, and who put high value on job security. Values associated with self-employment in accountancy are discussed on pages 109-114.

For More Information, see Appendix C or write The American Institute of Certified Public Accountants, 666 Fifth Avenue, New York, New York 10019.

ACTUARY

The Work The application of mathematical techniques to determine for insurance programs the "odds" for and against contingencies which will cost individuals money, in regard to death, sickness, accidents, unemployment, natural disasters, fire, old age, theft and others; makes much use of data processing; involves constant research on developments which affect these contingencies and sensitivity to public needs for, financial ability to pay for, and tastes in, insurance. An actuary may teach, or conduct operations research.

Number and Prospects About 3000 fully qualified; very few of them women, due to rigorous requirements for full qualification. Prospects excellent with the tremendous growth of public interest in insurance of all kinds and the impact on the "odds" of such things as new medical findings, economic fluctuations, such technological developments as faster highways and safer cars and changes in public taste and capacity to pay and continuing competion from other forms of investment.

Where Employed Two thirds by private life and health insurance companies (concentrated in the largest — many smaller ones use consultants) ; 20 per cent independent consultants or employed by such consultants; remainder work for government agencies, private non-profit organizations and the Military Services; more than half work in Connecticut, Massachusetts, New York and Illinois.

Preparation Tightly controlled by professional actuarial societies; includes four years of college preferably with a major in mathematics, statistics, economics or like field, and the passing of up to ten progressively difficult examinations, to be taken as one feels ready (five or more years is usually required) and, in addition, in some cases an extended apprenticeship. While a license is not needed to practice, membership in one or another of the professional societies to all intents and purposes is. Fully qualified actuary sometimes thought of as a Ph.D. in financial field.

Advancement Based on examinations and acquisition of experience. Once fully qualified, through normal channels, which often in insurance companies can lead all the way to the top.

Salaries At start, well above the levels, which vary with level of degree attained and field and place of employment, paid persons otherwise employed with same type of schooling; increases depend on passing actuarial examinations, each of which is worth $500-$1000 in salary increase; one can reach upper-middle-management levels without taking on added repsonsibilities for unrelated kinds of work. Some top executives (who started as actuaries) and independent consultants earn in six figures. (See Appendix A for some relevant 1967-68 figures.)

For People Who Enjoy working with figures; value precision and at the same time can live with the necessity of making guesses about the future on far from categoric evidence — decisions on which millions of dollars may depend; who want to see the results of their work often, prefer to deal with others in a business-like setting, want job security and a moderate work pace, and are undisturbed by relative anonymity. Values associated with self-employment as an actuary are discussed on pages 109-114.

For More Information, see Appendix C, or write The Society of Actuaries, 208 South LaSalle Street, Chicago, Illinois 60604.

ADVERTISING WORKER

The Work Preparation and "broadcasting" of appeals to the general public or to a special public to buy or think well of products, ideas, services, institutions or persons. Worker may be an artist, writer, photographer, actor, model, film expert, producer, psychologist, researcher, administrator, salesman, economist, layout expert, media director or analyst, buyer, designer or typographic expert, or a combination of two or more of these, or a coordinator and director, called in advertising agencies an "account executive," responsible for bringing together the skills required to produce an advertisement.

Numbers and Prospects About 130,000 full time and another 200,000 from time to time; substantial number of women employed, especially in some of the specialties. Prospects good, tied to population and business growth and to continued sharp competition in the profit-making sector; employment may fluctuate dramatically in general and in particular concerns and product and service fields due to the fickleness of public taste, economic ups and downs, new products, new media, new ideas and the large role that personal predilection and intuition play in decision making.

Where Employed About a third in advertising agencies, independent enterprises which sell their services to organizations with goods, ideas or services to sell; remainder in the advertising departments of organizations which create and place their own advertisements, or with the various media selling time and space to advertisers, or as specialists in one or more areas relevant to advertising who sell their services for a fee. Agencies concentrated in New York, Chicago, Detroit and Los Angeles.

Preparation Varies with specialty; no set requirements for one interested in a top generalist-type position, but increasingly a college degree with a major in advertising, or one of the relevant liberal arts, journalism, business administration or marketing is preferred; some employers even looking for Master's level training. Many people enter advertising from other kinds of work, particularly journalism. A flair for using English and generating ideas important.

Advancement Few set routes, except in specialties; generally depends on competence, energy, ability to deal effectively with others and luck.

Salaries At start, at levels, which vary with level of degree attained and field and place of employment, paid persons otherwise engaged with same type of schooling; from there on, aside from specialists, usually depend mcre on ability, experience, hard work, effectiveness in human relations and good luck than on seniority and pre-set salary scales; top earnings among the highest in the country. (See Appendix A for some 1967-68 figures.)

For People Who Enjoy a frequently frantic pace; have a high tolerance for ambiguity; have a strong creative bent; like dealing with people as competitors or potential customers or business colleagues; want to see the results of their efforts frequently (so far as the actual advertisement is concerned) and can live with the uncertainty of not knowing immediately whether they have been effective; are relatively unconcerned about job security; and have an answer satisfactory to themselves to the charge they will frequently hear that advertising people are "hucksters." Values associated with self-employment in advertising are discussed on pages 109-114.

For More Information, see Appendix C or write The Advertising Federation of America, 655 Madison Ave., New York 10021.

ARCHITECT

The Work Designing and overseeing the construction of buildings and appurtenances thereto; increasingly is concerned with housing developments, industrial plants, office buildings, transportation terminals, shopping centers and city and regional planning, as against private residences, once a principal activity. Requires not only creativity but the skills of the engineer and draftsman, expert knowledge of materials, soils, water tables and climate; familiarity with relevant regulations and laws; business sense, capacity to supervise others, and ability to both form and to follow the tastes of clients. In long-range environmental planning an architect must be something of a social scientist and philosopher. May be generalist or specialist even to such details as furniture design, interior decoration or lighting; may teach or write; many "moonlight" (the urban planner, for instance, who teaches or designs residences and home alterations in the evenings).

Numbers and Prospects Aboout 32,000, of whom 3 per cent are women; the prospects are excellent, witness one prediction to the effect that there will be more building in America between now and the end of the century than in all the country's previous history; involved is the growth of population, of congestion, of the complexities of construction and of concern that buildings be pleasing to the eye as well as functional.

Where Employed About half are self-employed, alone or in partnership; most of the rest work for architectural, construction, business and real estate concerns; a growing number are employed by governments at all levels, particularly as members or leaders of urban and regional planning and development teams.

Preparation Normally five years, if vocational concentration begins early; increasing emphasis on broad, liberal arts background as necessary foundation; this is leading more and more to six and even seven-year curricula, capped by a Master of Fine Arts as the entry level degree. Following degree, three years of apprenticeship with registered architect normally required before one can take the state registration examinations necessary to independent practice. Some Ph.D.'s granted.

Advancement   Sooner or later into independent practice, or if continuously employed by others, through routes common to persons in other professions.

Salaries.   Usually meager for an extended period if one opts for the private sector either as employee or in self-employment; in government comparable to those paid professionals in other fields with like training; successful private practitioners have incomes which compare favorably with these earned at the top in other professions; the earnings of independents result from fees of from 6 to 12 per cent of the cost of the construction. (See Appendix A for additional information.)

For People Who   Have strong creative bent and talent to go with it; like to deal with tangibles and see the results of their work frequently but can also live, on occasion, with uncertainty and protracted waiting; enjoy working with people as leader, persuader, supervisor and cooperator; like precision, on the one hand, and the challenge of tackling nebulous and difficult problems on the other; have no strong urge for job security; and want the freedom to come and go as they please. Values associated with self-employment as an architect are discussed on pages 109-114.

For More Information, Appendix C or write The American Institute of Architects, 1735 New York Avenue, N.W., Washington, D.C. 20004.

ARTIST — CREATIVE AND PERFORMING

A categorical description of the work of people who make their living primarily as artists, creative or performing, is unnecessary here because most aspects of their work are well known. They cannot make a living over a lifetime— as painters, sculptors, writers, singers, actors, dancers, composers, musicians, potters, photographers, etc. — unless their works are widely seen or read or they are personally widely seen or heard— and generally appreciated. This public exposure usually brings with it common knowledge about other aspects of their work.

Even if this were not so, it would be a mistake to suggest the possibility of a career as an arist to any collegian who hasn't already thought of it. Interest in such a career almost invariably goes hand in hand with talent. The problem is not the chance that anyone with the requisite combination of talent, capacity for hard work and willingness, in most cases, to undertake the rigorous training required and to wait for success, will overlook the possibility, but that many without these qualifications consider it one.

These paragraphs are included, then, principally to assume that the book's discussion of kinds of work of possible interest to collegions is reasonably comprehensive.

BANK WORKER

The Work   Only those jobs peculiar to banking will be discussed here. The work of other bank employees, and they are many, whose duties — general management, financial, public relations, advertising, personnel, purchasing, and so on — are common to business generally is described elsewhere. Incidentally, in banking such jobs may have deceptive titles. A bank's "cashier," for instance, is a senior officer whose role is basically that of controller.

Mortgage Loan or Credit Officer   Examines and evaluates applications for loans and lines of credit, with authority to approve up to the level warranted by the seniority of his posision; handles foreclosures; follows loan markets; develops loan prospects; negotiates and draws contracts in his area of interest. (To be found also, to a minor extent, in insurance and, as the principal occupation, in the personal finance industry. "Credit" — and collections — managers in business and industry determine what the terms will be where the customer does not pay cash and follow up overdue accounts.)

Trust Officer   Handles private, corporate and probate trusts and estates in the charge of his bank; drafts and checks trust instruments; prepares trust tax returns; evaluates assets in trusts and invests them or advises on their investment; collects trust earnings. (To be found also in investment counseling houses.)

Foreign Exchange Trader   Deals with bank's overseas interests; evaluates foreign currencies; studies overseas monetary trends; is responsible for overseas transactions; may travel extensively or live abroad for periods.

Securities Trader Conducts bank's stock and bond transactions; advises bank and those whose money the bank has in charge on their investments. (See also "Securities Worker" job description.)

Where Employed One-half in 28,000 commercial banks and their branches (usually nearby) ; remainder in 800 mutual saving banks and their branches, the 12 Federal Reserve banks (government institutions which "bank" for private banks), and foreign exchange firms.

Numbers and Prospects Close to 800,000 persons are employed in banks half of them women, 150,000 of them "officers" (of whom more than 15,000 are women) ; concentrated in the East and in large banks. Considerable growth expected as population increases, branch banking expands and new sevices are instituted. Data processing will eliminate more and more routine jobs and increase proportion of administrators and the technically skilled.

Preparation Liberal or business Bachelor's degree virtually a requirement with, however, no insistence on banking-related course work; some bigger banks looking for Masters of Business Administration or law school graduates. Larger banks encourage and pay for evening study towards advanced degrees, or conduct internal training courses of from six months to two years; American Institute offers formal course work at its headquarters or on the premises of member banks.

Advancement To junior officership — almost one-fifth of all bank workers are "officers" — usually takes five years and it may be "up or out" to this level. Once there, employee has equivalent of "tenure" in education; thereafter progress is typically steady and gradual with, relative to the sharply competitive industries, fewer opportunities to take dramatic strides and less liability to dramatic falls. Retirements will open up many senior positions in next few years.

Salaries In private, profit-making banking, somewhat below the levels, varying with level of degree attained, seniority, experience, responsibility carried and place of employment, paid persons in most other kinds of business with the same type of schooling;

fringe benefits relatively high. In government, bank salaries are on same level as those of comparably prepared people in other kinds of work. One can reach middle-management levels in either without taking on responsibility for more than one banking specialty; earnings of top officers in banks equal to those in other kinds of business; knowledge and judgment acquired in banking jobs can lead to unusually successful investment of one's own funds. (See Appendix A for 1967-68 benchmark figures.)

For People Who Like working with figures and facts; deal easily and tactfully with others in a serving relationship; enjoy being "in the know" about business and government developments within the community, small or large, served by their bank; set considerable story by job security; enjoy community activity (which banks usually encourage) ; are discreet; find no problems in the necessity for adhering to fairly strict standards in appearance and manners; are in no rush to get to the top; and like a moderate work pace.

For More Information, See Appendix C or write the American Bankers Association, 12 East 36th Street, New York, New York 10016, or The National Association of Bank Women, Inc., 60 East 42nd Street, New York, New York 10017.

BUYER

The Work Buying from manufacturers and wholesalers for resale the goods which fill the shelves and counters of the country's 1.5 million retail stores. A buyer may concentrate on buying or may also have responsibility for the sale of what is bought. Must be familiar with employer's sales policy (high-volume, low mark-up, for instance), an expert on the goods to be bought, and a good judge of the current and prospective tastes of retail customers (three-quarters of whom are women) ; may also influence consumer taste; frequently travels to trade shows and manufacturers' plants; may have irregular hours; is concerned with such related matters as inventories and merchandising activity.

Number and Prospects About 70,000 full time, of whom half are women; rapid increase in numbers likely (even with increase in centralized buying) if, as is predicted, retailing, already the country's largest industry, continues its recent fast growth.

Where Employed   By independent retail stores and retail chains; or may be self-employed, serving a number of stores, usually from a big city base.

Preparation   Greatest emphasis is on personal qualifications; college degree not now essential to entry but becoming more important; employers flexible as to college course work but technical training may be required by the nature of the goods to be bought. Knowledge of data processing in connection with inventory control and buying trend analysis useful.

Advancement   Normally from counter sales to stockroom to assistant buyer to buyer. Some large stores run quickly "cadet" or "college board" training programs for personnel just-out-of college. Many top retail executives started as buyers and moved up through merchandising; self-employment is another way to rise; results rather than seniority or age are principal determinants of success.

Salaries   At levels, varying with level of degree attained, seniority, experience, responsibility carried and field and place of employment, paid persons otherwise engaged with same type of schooling. One can reach middle-management levels without taking on added responsibilities for unrelated kinds of work. Buyers receive discounts on purchases in the stores they serve; independent buyers can have handsome earnings. (See Appendix A for 1967-68 benchmark figures.)

For People Who   Are self-reliant and relatively unconcerned about security; can take pressure and a fast pace; are venturesome and can live cheerfully with uncertainty; work well with many kinds of people; are competitive and like to bargain; and put a high premium on dealing with things and on seeing the results of their efforts promptly. Values associated with self-employment as a buyer are discussed on pages 109-114.

For More Information, See Appendix C or write Association of Buying Officers, 100 West 31st Street, New York, New York 10001.

CHIROPRACTOR

The Work Para-medical work which rests on the theory that diseases of the nervous system account for many illnesses, and involves manipulation of the body, particularly the spine, in attempting cure. Also employs light, heat, water, diet, x-ray and exercise therapy. Drugs or surgery are not employed. Is typically done in an office setting with regular hours. A chiropractor may teach either full time or while conducting a practice.

Numbers and Prospects About 24,000 practicing of whom 10 per cent are women; considered growing field for women. Opportunities expected to be substantial for the well trained, provided public acceptance becomes increasingly widespread.

Where Employed Great majority in private practice; 45 per cent in states of California, Missouri, New York, Ohio and Texas; some in teaching and doing research in chiropractic schools.

Preparation Usually four post-high school years at chiropractic school which stresses relevant scientific disciplines; some states require one or two years of preliminary non-specialized college education; most states require passing of an examination for a license to practice.

Advancement Normally from assistant or junior partner to an experienced practitioner, to private practice, alone or in partnership.

Salaries For the few employed by others, at levels, varying with seniority, experience, degree of responsibility carried and field and place of employment, paid persons with four-year liberal arts degrees; in private practice, one can reach upper-middle management levels; community acceptance of the discipline has important bearing. (See Appendix A for 1967-68 benchmark figures.)

For People Who Have an interest in medical practice but lack the talent, time or funds to pursue a full medical degree; enjoy working with people in a serving relationship; like a moderate work pace; and can face the scepticism of the public and the hostility or non-acceptance of the medical profession where it exists. Values associated with self-employment as a chiropractor are discussed on pages 109-114.

For More Information, see Appendix C references or write The American Chiropractic Association, American Building, 2200 Grand Avenue, P.O. Box 1535, Des Moines, Iowa 50306.

CITY (Urban, Regional) PLANNER (Developer, Redeveloper)
The Work The planning of new communities or the replanning of urban communities or larger inhabited areas to make them both as functional and as aesthetically attractive as feasible. Planners are concerned with buildings, streets, utilities, transportation, safety, zoning, recreation, health, education, culture, pollution, relocation, demolition and other tangible and intangible factors affecting how and where people live and work. There is particular current emphasis on elimination of slums, creating new communities in hitherto empty spaces and, particularly in regard to larger geographic areas, working out long-range land use plans. This involves membership in or leadership of a team which brings to bear on the planning problem the skills (and often conflicting viewpoints) of the engineer, lawyer, economist, anthropologist, political scientist, social worker, architect, demographer, educator, sociologist, artist, public health worker, tax expert, builder and environmental scientist. Work may be full time in an office or, frequently "in the field," researching, fact-finding, or supervising. Much out-of-hours time may be spent conferring with and attempting to get support from interested government and private persons and groups. Insufficient funds, politics and public inertia and conservatism are often stumbling blocks. Worker may have considerable authority and influence or very little, depending on setting; may teach.

Numbers and Prospects Some 6000 full time; considered a growing field for women; openings expected to increase far faster than supply of qualified people as population grows, and as rapid migration of people from the country into the cities and from the cities to suburbs continues; as government concern and available funds grow; as private enterprise ($1,000,000,000 pledged by insurance companies recently) goes into urban redevelopment; and as complexity of solutions increases.

Where Employed Three-quarters by Federal, state, regional and local governments or combinations of these governmental entities; ratio of two planners to 50,000 urban population typical; remainder largely part- or fulltime independent consultants (many of whom work fulltime for government and moonlight); a few teach or do research in colleges and universities.

Preparation Still in flux. Bachelor's degree, preferably in a relevant discipline is essential to entry; some senior planners think further training should be taken on-the-job; growing emphasis, however, on post-graduate schooling of from one to three years, either in city planning specifically or in a relevant discipline.

Advancement From entry-level employee doing drafting, field censuses or other repetitive specialized jobs, to broader responsibilities and eventual supervision; from small planning organizations to larger ones, as specialist or supervisor; into private practice.

Salaries At levels, varying with level of degree attained, seniority, experience, responsibility carried and field and place of employment, paid persons otherwise engaged with same type of schooling; one can reach upper-middle management levels without taking on added responsibilities for unrelated kinds of work; independent consultants can have handsome earnings. (See Appendix A for 1967-68 bench mark figures.)

For People Who Want to be involved in an obviously urgent social undertaking; enjoy challenge in the sense of tackling often nearly insuperable problems; (in government jobs) want job security; like selling ideas; can tolerate uncertainty, frequent frustration and compromise (implementation of plans requires consensus from taxpayers, politicians and, often, many special interest groups with conflicting views). Who can work cooperatively with a variety of specialists; enjoy dealing with details and tangibles; and are a combination of idealist and pragmatist, able to move easily from the imaginative and abstract concept to the concrete and feasible proposal. Values associated with self-employment in this work are discussed on pages 109-114.

For More Information, see Appendix C or write The American

Institute of Planners, 917 15th Street, N.W., Washington, D.C. 20005.

COMPUTER SCIENTIST (PROGRAMER)

The Work Is concentrated in the "hardware" (electronic data storing and processing machinery) aspect of the use of computers; ("software" — though the dividing line isn't clear — generally refers to development of problems and programs for machine implementation or solution and is discussed further on under "SYSTEM ANALYST"). Programs and problems in fields as varied as marketing, teaching, inventory or production control, weather prediction, missile guidance, law, payroll accounting, football opposition scouting and archaeology are put-into "languages" suitable for a particular machine by the programer who then feeds information into machine; debugs the operation and participates in evaluating the results. Must study constantly to maintain familiarity with successive "new generations" of computers.

Numbers and Prospects Estimates run as high as 120,000, working with perhaps 55,000 computers, including a large but undetermined number of women; prospects excellent, since "hardware" industry is growing by 20 per cent a year, and the new applications which are continuously being introduced more than offset the growing capacity of the increasingly sophisticated machinery.

Where Employed In most large organizations in all six fields of work where computers can reduce paperwork and information analysis and processing which would otherwise have to be done by hand, or can control processes more effectively than other means; in small organizations whose business is research and analysis, independent or for others; and in independent or organization-affiliated (attached to a university, for instance) service centers whose capacities are shared by or assigned to many different users.

Preparation Two years of intensive post-high school special training a minimum; amount required goes all the way from there to the postdoctoral level in some cases; no preferred pattern yet established. People who have specialized in engineering, mathematics, statistics, the physical sciences and, of course, programing, are in heavy demand at all levels. Training on specific machines as they are introduced, either on the job or at the manufacturer's plant is a continuing necessity. Most scholars and researchers in most fields and many in administrative, production and other kinds of work have a speaking acquaintance with computer capabilities, if not operation.

Advancement Through growing expertness in special areas; to administration of large installations; into systems and operations analysis.

Salaries Because of great demand, somewhat above levels, which vary with level of degree attained, seniority, experience, responsibility carried and field and place of employment, paid persons otherwise engaged with same type of schooling; one can reach middle management levels without taking on added responsibilities for unrelated kinds of work. (See Appendix A for 1967-68 benchmark figures.)

For People Who Thrive on the necessity for great precision in their work; like to deal with things and to know how they are doing frequently; want some opportunity to exercise imagination; enjoy a deliberate, patient, persevering kind of pace; prefer associating with others as business colleagues; and value high job security.

For More Information, see Appendix C or write to The Association for Computing Machinery, 211 East 43rd Street, New York, New York 10017.

CONSERVATION WORKER

The Work The application of specialized knowledge of one or several of the many relevant disciplines to the protection, development and management of the country's soil, forests, wildlife, rangelands and water. A conservation worker is concerned with assuring that natural resources will not be exhausted, destroyed or damaged and that future needs for them, economic, recreational and aesthetic, will be met. He may concentrate in such areas as maintaining wild animal and fish populations, fire or flood or pest control, air and water purity, soil erosion or the planning of recreation areas; may be a soil conservationist (the only profession whose members work virtually exclusively in this field), forester, range manager, biologist, engineer, geologist, chemist, planner, economist, naturalist, photographer or flier; may or may not spend most of his time in the open; may teach.

Numbers and Prospects Some 25,000 foresters (not all, however, engaged full time in conservation-related activity) ; about 3,500 range managers; otherwise, no figures available. Few women are employed because of the rugged nature of the work. Prospects excellent as population continues to grow and open space to dwindle; as people have more and more time for recreation and travel, and as the demand for products derived from wood, water and soil put an increasing demand on available resources.

Where Employed Particularly by government agencies in connection with government-owned parks, forests, national monuments and recreation areas; some teach in schools of forestry and elsewhere; some are employed by private concerns whose products or services (paper or recreation, say) depend on the continuing availability of certain natural resources; a few work for non-profit organizations devoted to stimulating public interest in natural resource preservation, or are independent consultants.

Preparation Four to five post-high school years, including intense vocational specialization, for foresters, soil conservationists and range managers; in other areas of conservation, what is usual in other fields; advanced degrees are important for those who aspire to teaching, research and high level management.

Advancement From professional practice as an employee into management or independent consulting. If one teaches or does research, up the usual ladders.

Salaries At levels, varying with level of degree attained, seniority, experience, responsibility carried and field and place of employment, paid persons otherwise engaged with same type of schooling; one can reach middle-management levels without taking on added responsibilities for unrelated kinds of work. (See Appendix A for 1967-68 benchmark figures.)

For People Who Want to feel their work is of direct service to society; enjoy considerable freedom to come and go; like work-

ing in the open; want to deal with tangibles but can wait for
results; enjoy dealing with others as persuader (required in
many conservationist roles) ; value job security. Values associated
with self-employment as a conservation worker are discussed on
pages 109-114.
For More Information, see Appendix C or write The Forest Service, U.S. Department of Agriculture, Washington, D.C. 20250.

COUNSELOR

The Work Helping students at all levels (and in some cases
adults) resolve educational, vocational, personal and emotional
problems; or helping the physically or emotionally handicapped
to overcome their difficulties and to take up as normal a life as
possible; or assisting people in making career decisions or in seeking a job. A few counselors specialize in marriage and "life adjustment" counseling. In any area a counselor must have the
capacity to understand each client's personal world, knowledge of
all the resources available to help him, some training in the psychology of personality, knowledge of relevant tests, and the ability
to diagnose and refer appropriately problems which can be better
handled by others. He spends most of his time talking to and
working with clients, with their relatives and friends, and frequently with uninvolved individuals (potential employers and
school and college admissions officers, for instance) who are in a
position to be helpful; may also teach and do research.
Numbers and Prospects About 45,000 elementary and secondary
school counselors, of whom 25,000 work full time and the rest
part time and about one third of whom are women; some 6000
vocational (employment) counselors, 4500 of whom are in public
employment service offices and 1500 in private non-profit or commercial agencies and one half of whom are women; about 6700
rehabiliation counselors, three quarters of whom are in state
and local government agencies and the rest scattered, and one
fifth of whom are women; unknown number in the other settings
noted below.
Where Employed Principally in public schools and colleges; also
in the 2000 state public employment service offices and in state and

local public institutions such as hospitals, clinics and prisons; some for such Federal agencies as the Veterans Administration, Office of Economic Opportunity and Peace Corps; a few are employed by private non-profit agencies, sheltered workshops, labor unions and insurance companies; a few practice independently for profit.

Preparation   Minimum four-year Bachelor's degree majoring in a relevant discipline plus some experience for vocational counselors, but growing emphasis on at least 15 post-college credits in the career guidance field; rehabilitation counselors usually must have Master's degree in the rehabilitation area and in some states must pass an examination to practice in public agencies; school counselors normally required to have Master's degree in counseling or guidance and to have taught for two or three years in the public school system; in other settings, requirements vary, going as high as a Ph.D. in counseling or clinical psychology for practice on some college campuses and in some profit-making organizations and non-profit private centers and agencies.

Advancement   Unless one elects to go into administration of broader functions (education or welfare administration or employment office management, for instance) which is perfectly possible, top jobs involve only supervision of a relative handful of subordinates in the same specialty; for the highly trained, possibility of independent practice.

Salaries   At levels, varying with level of degree attained, seniority, experience, responsibility carried and field and place of employment, paid persons with same type of schooling; one can reach lower-middle management levels without taking on added responsibilities for unrelated kinds of work. (See Appendix A for 1968-68 benchmark figures).

For People Who   Like to deal with people in a helping relationtion and also as professional colleagues; have enough of the crusader in them to be willing to press uninvolved persons who could be helpful (potential employers, for instance) ; who are comfortable in work where all the relevant facts are seldom available; who like to see frequent results from their efforts but, at the same time, can tolerate slow progress; who enjoy the challenge of facing sometimes apparently insuperable problems, can remain emotionally uninvolved in the troubles of others, want to feel they are being of immediate service to society, and set high store by job security. Values associated with self-employment as a counsellor are discussed on pages 109-114.

For More Information see Appendix C or write The American Personnel and Guidance Association, 1605 New Hampshire Avenue, N.W., Washington, D. C. 20009.

CRIMINOLOGIST AND RELATED

The Work May involve one or more of the following activities: investigation of crimes and the causes of crime, law enforcement, crime prevention, study of laws applicable to crime, punishment, laboratory research, administration of penal and correctional institutions, rehabilitation of criminals, and probation and parole work.

Numbers and Prospects Except that the Federal government employs 20,000 in investigative and enforcement work (the Federal Bureau of Investigation accounts for less than 7000 of these, a score of other departments and agencies for the rest) no figures are available; very few women are involved; prospects excellent as the incidence of and concern about crime across the nation continues to increase.

Where Employed By government at all levels, with concentrations in larger population centers; a few in private detective agencies and large companies.

Preparation Above the policeman level, a Bachelor's degree in criminology or in such related subjects as the physical or biological sciences, sociology, psychology and education with heavy reliance on on-the-job training; for top jobs Master's and doctoral level degrees in criminology and corrections or in law or medicine are increasingly required; for some employments such as the FBI, there may be additional requirements as to physical size, age, success in examinations and particular course work such as accounting.

Advancement From staff membership to supervision and administration.

Salaries At levels, varying with level of degree attained, experience, seniority, responsibility carried and field and place of employment, paid persons otherwise employed with same type of schooling. (See Appendix A for 1967-68 benchmark figures.)

For People Who Want to feel they are being of direct service to society and helpful to others, directly or indirectly; who like work which requires precision and an analytical approach and the challenge of dealing with situations where the answers are often not apparent and very difficult to ascertain; who enjoy a feeling of being in charge and have considerable concern for job security.

For More Information, write The American Association of Criminology, Inc., 141 First Parish Road, Scituate Harbor, Maine 02066.

CURATOR

The Work The supervision of a collection of valuable objects, large or small, of broad or narrow scope, belonging to a museum in such fields as art, archeology, history, natural history, science, industry, commerce, children's interests, handcrafts or the way of life of a great man; involves caring for collection and purchasing items to supplement it (often necessitating extensive travel), arranging exhibits, writing and giving talks about it, doing research in connection with it and soliciting funds to support it; collections may be housed indoors or exhibited outdoors.

Numbers and Prospects No estimate of numbers available but many women are involved; prospects are good. It is estimated that a new museum is opened every three days.

Where Employed In the country's more than 500 museums, sponsored by government, private non-profit organizations, educational institutions, business and entrepreneurs.

Preparation Meticulous training in one's field of interest, often up through graduate degrees; a few graduate schools offer specific courses. "Curator" is considered synonymous with "expert."

Advancement From assistant posts to responsibility for small collections and thence into broader responsibilities and eventually direction of an entire museum.

Salaries No definitive figures available but probably at levels, varying with the level of degree attained, experience, seniority, responsibility carried and field and place of employment, paid persons otherwise employed with liberal arts schooling. (See Appendix A for 1967-68 benchmark figures.)

For People Who Like to be precise in their work; prefer to deal with others as professional colleagues and, on occasion, as servants; want to be creative to a degree, but in connection with tangibles; and prefer a measured pace and considerable job security.

For More Information, write The American Society of Museums, Smithsonian Institution, Washington, D.C.

DENTIST

The Work Extracts, fills and cleans teeth; fits and installs false teeth; straightens crooked teeth; performs surgery on jaw and mouth; treats diseases of gums and mouth; is familiar with X-ray, laboratory and oral surgery techniques and procedures; work involves constant standing and requires great dexterity and sharp eyesight; most dentists are generalists; orthodontistry (straightening teeth) largest of the specialties; may teach.

Numbers and Prospects Over 100,000 practicing, very few of whom are women. The need is likely to increase faster than supply, because of population growth, the country's growing affluence and health consciousness (public and private), and expansion of health insurance plans; proportion of specialists likely to increase; fluoride, by saving more teeth to be worked on, will not reduce need for dentists.

Where employed Ninety per cent in private practice; most of rest are officers in Armed Services; a few are in public health services, hospitals, school systems, dental schools as teachers, and laboratories; concentrated in cities and populous states (one-third in New York, California, Pennsylvania and Illinois); a serious shortage in smaller communities.

Preparation At least two years (increasingly three are required) of pre-dental college work, concentrated in science and mathematics, for eligibility to take the usually required Dental Aptitude Test; dexterity and good spatial judgment and eyesight among things tested; four years of dental school (two of study, two of practice) required for licensing as general practitioner, and up to three additional years as specialist. Most dental schools are competitive.

Advancement   Depends on skill and abilty to command confidence of patients. By opening new practice, buying established practice or joining an established dentist. Through normal routes when in the employe of an institution, the Armed Services, etc. Advancement also possible by becoming specialist.

Salaries   For those employed by others, at slightly lower levels, varying with seniority, experience, responsibilities carried and field and place of employment, than those paid physicians; one can reach upper-middle management levels without taking on added responsibilities for unrelated kinds of work; the self-employed can have handsome earnings; they tend to be highest in the Middle Atlantic and Northwestern states and the bigger and wealthier communities. (See Appendix A for 1967-68 benchmark figures.)

For People Who   Are perfectionists, enjoy working with people in a serving relationship; are things-oriented and like to see the results of their efforts frequently; have an urge to be creative; and prefer a measured work pace. Values associated with self-employment in dentistry are discussed on pages 109-114.

For More Information, see Appendix C or write The American Dental Association, Council on Dental Education, 222 East Superior Street, Chicago, Illinois 60611.

DIETICIAN

The Work   The proper feeding of people, normal or sick, as individuals or in groups. May involve menu preparation, purchasing food, equipment and supplies, the supervision of those who prepare food, writing and preparation of educational material, teaching, research, responsibility for sanitation and safety of feeding facilities, and stimulation of public concern for the bearing of proper nutrition on health.

Numbers and Prospects   About 31,000 employed, half in hospitals, the remainder dispersed in other areas: more than 90 per cent are women, though number of men is gradually increasing; most of the men are in generalized staff or administrative work.

Currently a shortage which may become aggravated, especially in nursing homes and hospitals, due to population growth, the large number who marry and leave field and growing affluence and concern for health; many part time opportunities expected.

Where Employed In hospitals and nursing homes, as therapeutic dietitians, dealing with the medically prescribed diets of patients; some others with the general feeding of patients and staff; or as a clinician, dealing with out-patients with weight, diabetes, pregnancy and similar problems; in restaurant, hotel, camp, company cafeteria, steamship, airline and railroad catering operations; in educational institutions; in home economics departments of utility and food equipment companies; in public health services; in the Military Service.

Preparation Four post-high school years, majoring in foods and nutrition or institutional management and, in either case, with other courses in everything from chemistry and mathematics to psychology, followed, if one wants membership in American Dietetic Association, by one year of approved internship or two to three years of supervised experience. To become a nutritionist, or to be involved in research or making surveys and analyses for public health services, or in teaching, additional postgraduate study is essential.

Advancement Depends, in most settings, on competence not only as technical expert but as manager and supervisor. Through research and advanced degrees leading to specialization. Particularly good profession for women who will be at home for a decade or so raising children, since it is relatively easy to keep in touch with "state of the art" during that time.

Salaries At levels, varying with seniority, experience, responsibility carried and field and place of employment, paid persons otherwise engaged with one-year Master's degrees in liberal arts; one can reach lower-middle management levels without taking on added responsibilities for unrelated kinds of work. (See Appendix A for 1967-68 benchmark figures.)

For People Who Like working with people in variety of contexts: supervisory doctors and administrators, supervised food workers, patients to be served, students to be fed and colleagues; have a yen to be creative; enjoy detail and precision and seeing the results of their efforts; often want to deal with tangibles and desire a high degree of job security.

For More Information, See Appendix C or write The American Dietetic Association, 620 North Michigan Avenue, Chicago, Illinois 60611.

EDUCATION WORKER (NON-TEACHING)

The Work There are many kinds of non-teaching work connected with the field of education, both within and without schools and colleges. Where they are to be found in a number of fields — general management and the various business disciplines, counseling, fund raising, library work and psychological research, for instance — they are described elsewhere in this book. Here attention will be focused on those non-teaching jobs peculiar to the academic setting. They will be described as functions rather than by job titles since the titles of those who perform them, where they are a full-time occupation, vary widely among institutions: since a single individual may be responsible for several, and since people whose principal duties and titles are in other areas may perform one or more of them.

Curriculum Is concerned with the number and nature of courses offered by the institution; which will be required of students and at what times and in what combinations to satisfy graduation requirements. With maintaining offerings which will be responsive to the changing outside world, the interests of students and the capabilities of available teachers. Usually most work closely with faculty, which has large say in the content of individual courses.

Admissions Is concerned with the quality, type and number of students admitted; in "selective" institutions may do extensive interviewing and screening of applicants.

Student Aid Where scholarships, loans and term-time employment are factors, screens applications, makes awards and keeps track of available resources.

Registrar work Attends to the facts and figures relevant to each student's academic and extracurricular progress through the institution; may handle classroom and examination schedules; prepares analyses and summaries for use of others concerned with student progress. There is increasingly use of computers for this work.

Alumni relations Concerned with keeping in touch with alumni and alumnae for the purpose of maintaining their interest in the institution and thus stimulating their direct or indirect support financially and in other ways.

Student standing Oversees action to be taken on students who, academically or otherwise, are entitled to special recognition or are liable to penalties on the basis of superior or substandard performance; usually handled by committittees.

Athletics Coaches individual sports or administers institution's sports program, including competition with other institutions, intramural sports and non-competitive athletic activity for recreation and to promote good health.

Foreign student supervision Concerned with all aspects of the welfare of students from other lands.

Residence supervision Involved in the comfort, behaviour and counseling of students who reside on the campus during the school year.

Extra curricular activities Concerned with all aspects of student activity outside the classroom, from fraternity parties to the student government to the school newspaper to the chess club.

Placement and Career Guidance Services See pages 71-72.

Numbers and Prospects Some 500,000 people are employed in non-teaching roles within the field of education, including many women; the proportion of these in the jobs peculiar to education is not available; prospects for all non-teaching workers, however, are excellent as population growth, in combination with increasing public concern that young persons assimilate all the learning they can, builds enrollments.

Where Employed Depending on the nature and size of the educational institution concerned, a majority if not all of these functions are performed in all educational institutions, except possibly in predominantly night, adult and extension school settings.

Preparation   A Bachelor's degree essential to all non-teaching functions listed above, the preferred major depending on the nature of the institution and the work to be done; teaching experience and certification often required in public schools; the bigger jobs, as specialists in larger institutions and/or as generalists in smaller ones, generally go to people with advanced degrees, the discipline again depending on the institution (Master's and Doctor's degrees in Education are a *sine qua non* for promotion in some settings and have little standing in others). Knowledge of computer uses increasingly important.

Advancement   No one who makes a specialty of one or another of the functions noted above can move above the middle-management level in the institution he serves, though by moving from a smaller to a larger institution he may increase his pay; however, assuming requisite postgraduate educational credentials and willingness to take on broader responsibilities, it is possible to move up into deanships (or the equivalent) and beyond from many of these specialties.

Salaries   At levels, varying with level of degree attained, seniority, experience, responsibility carried and place of employment, paid teachers and professors; normally do not have entire summer off; one can reach top-management levels but not without taking on responsibility for several different functions. (See Appendix A for 1967-68 benchmark figures.)

For People Who   Enjoy the relatively leisurely pace of academe — including the vacations, who like some freedom to come and go as they please, want to be involved with young people directly or indirectly, value job security, like to be involved in an activity that directly serves society, and are comfortable in a relatively unstructured working environment.

For More Information, write the president, superintendent, dean, principal or personnel director of the type of institution which interests you.

ENGINEER

The Work Concerned with converting the earth's raw materials and natural forces into products, processes and machines useful to man. An engineer picks up, in company with the "applied" scientist, where the "pure" scientist leaves off, to undertake research, using existing knowledge, which has a practical aim in view, and then proceeds to develop things that work, at reasonable costs in time and money. Normally concentrates in one or a few of 37 different areas (see list below).

Numbers and Prospects About 1,000,000 of whom only one percent are women. A breakdown on numbers in the ten principal branches of engineering follows: electrical and electronic, 215,000; mechanical, 195,000; civil, 175,000; industrial, 115,000; aeronautical, 55,000; chemical, 50,000; mining (extractive and physical), 14,000; agricultural, 10,000; ceramic, 7,000; and metallurgical, 5,000. Most of the remainder are in the following specialties or sub-specialties: accoustical-audio, air-conditioning and refrigeration, architectural, automotive, biomedical, bridge building, combustion, geological, geophysical, highway, hydraulic, instrumentation, management, materials, mechanics, methods and planning, nuclear, oceanographic, ordnance, petroleum, safety, sanitary, structural, systems, textile, traffic and welding.

Prospects are excellent for all types of engineers as emphasis on research and developmental activity increases dramatically, business and population grow and inter-industry competition puts added emphasis on efficiency and economy. A total of 830,000 additional engineers will be needed by 1976 as against a projected supply of only 500,000. However, prospects vary greatly as between types. The needs for more engineers anticipated in various areas are as follows: education, 66 per cent; aerospace and airframe industry, 61 per cent; construction and metals industries, 52 per cent each; chemical industry, 48 per cent; electrical and electronics industry, 40 per cent; consulting, 24 per cent; state governments, 21 per cent; petroleum industry, 17 per cent; machinery industry, 13 per cent; and the Federal government, 6 per cent. The transportation industry expects no need for a greater number, and utilities and local government to need fewer.

Where Employed In all six fields of work, with the great majority, however, in private profit-making concerns; civil engineers, most of whom are employed by government, are the only exception among the principal categories. Within these fields, one third are engaged in research, development and design, another third in administration, and perhaps 15 per cent in building construction and manufacturing, from skyscrapers to miniature bearings, and in planning and supervising production activities. Most of the balance about evenly divided among sales, teaching and independent consulting; a few write and invent; over 3 per cent are in the Military Services at any one time, many not practicing engineering as such.

Preparation Minimum of four years of engineering training to a Bachelor of Science in Engineering degree; some institutions offer a five-year curriculum, starting with three years of liberal arts; others offer alternating work and study programs, covering five or six years. All states require engineers who will be practicing where the public welfare is involved to be licensed or registered, and here four years of post-college experience and success in an examination are usually required. 25 per cent of BS-level engineers go on to higher degrees and this figure is expected to rise to 50 per cent by 1975. Constant reading and study during one's working life are necessary to avoid obsolescence in this fast-changing field. Knowledge of computers essential to practice. Graduates with credits in engineering are particularly welcome at graduate schools of business.

Advancement Along routes common to similarly trained fellow employees in whatever setting one finds oneself; or one can go into independent consulting. In many organizations today one can come close to the top while remaining a researcher and designer and eschewing administration. An increasing proportion of top-level management jobs are held by men with engineering or scientific background.

Salaries See Appendix A for 1967-68 benchmark figures. It should be added that the highest incomes in the field are earned by engineers who, if employed by others, take on managerial responsibilities, or by those who are self-employed.

For People Who Like work which demands precision and an analytical turn of mind; are intolerant of the inexact; prefer to work with others as professional colleagues; enjoy dealing with the concrete and seeing the results of their efforts often; like to plan and to have a feeling of being in control of the situation; and set some store on job security. Values associated with self-employment in engineering are discussed on pages 109-114.

For More Information, see Appendix C or write The Engineers Joint Council, 345 East 47th Street, New York, New York 10017.

ENVIRONMENTAL HEALTH SPECIALIST (SANITARIAN)

The Work Identifying and taking action to remove, or to develop protections against, environmental hazards to human health, including radiation, air and water pollution, contaminated food, waste, rodents, communicable disease and sub-standard housing; a sanitarian investigates, inspects, recommends, advises and takes corrective steps within his field of interest; may be involved in promotion of public concern about health hazards, court action, the drafting of legislation, teaching and surveys of conditions; may be specialist or generalist. Spends much time out of doors and often deals with unpleasant and at times dangerous conditions. Related occupations include toxicology, sanitary and environmental engineering and industrial hygiene.

Numbers and Prospects More than 15,000; very few women full-time workers; numbers are expected to rise dramatically as population increases and people crowd into cities, and as public concern with the healthfulness and safety of the environment grows.

Where Employed Great majority by public health agencies at all governmental levels; most of the rest in industry (canneries, dairies and utilities, for instance), and by hospitals, civil defense organizations and trade associations; a few teach or are self-employed consultants.

Preparation Increasingly at least four post-high school years specializing in sanitary science, public health or one of the relevant scientific disciplines. One may move from scientific work in another setting into environmental health (some physicians do this). Graduate degree in related field usually essential to reaching top posts;

about half the states require registration, based on either an earned degree or examination or both.

Advancement To administration, or to increasingly wide recognition as an expert in one or more facets of the problem, or into independent consulting.

Salaries At levels, varying with level of degree attained, seniority, experience, responsibility carried and field and place of employment, paid persons otherwise engaged with same type of schooling; one can reach uppermiddle management levels without taking on added responsibilities for unrelated kinds of work. (See Appendix A for 1967-68 benchmark figures.)

For People Who Want to feel they are of direct service to society; like to deal with tangibles and, so far as people are concerned, in helpful and persuasive roles, who value job security, can make decisions from imprecise data, and enjoy the challenge of confronting increasingly intractable problems. Values associated with self-employment in this field are discussed on pages 109-114.

For More Information, see Appendix C or write The American Public Health Association, 1790 Broadway, New York, New York 10019.

FOREIGN LANGUAGE WORKER

The Work Interpreting (speech), translating (writing material), or teaching one or more foreign languages. (Not included here are the many kinds of work and millions of jobs in government, business, education, the Military Services and elsewhere in which ability to read and communicate in other languages is either a necessity or useful. Such a worker may also do research, index or extract.

Numbers and Prospects About 1000 interpreters in all fields; otherwise no current estimates available; many women so employed. Prospects excellent as foreign travel increases, as business expands into foreign lands, as the "knowledge explosion" continues around the globe and as more and more international organizations take shape.

Where Employed As teachers of foreign languages at all educational levels in public or private schools, colleges and universities, in Military and other governmental training centers or in commercial "quicky" language schools; as interpreters for people without the necessary competence — in all fields of work — who must communicate with foreigners in their jobs; as translators and correspondents for such people, for publishers of foreign texts — for domestic consumption and for governmental and private organizations which need information contained in foreign language publications or have extracts available for reference, particularly "intelligence" and technical material; as interpreters in international organizations serving nationals of several countries; as scholars of language and of foreign lands. May practice as enterpreneur.

Preparation Intensive study of one or more foreign languages, preferably begun early, as well as, in some instances, solid grounding in the history, politics, economics, culture and other aspects of one or more foreign countries or areas, or in a particular subject (science, for instance).

Advancement No set patterns outside education and government where usual patterns obtain. Experts in the more esoteric languages are in short supply and in a position to be demanding. Setting up one's own language school or fee-charging translation service are possibilities.

Salaries Outside teaching and government, again no common patterns and again experts can call the tune up to a point.

For People Who Enjoy working precisely, are content with relative anonymity (unless teaching), prefer a leisurely pace (except in simultaneous interpretation), and value job security. Values associated with self-employment in this field are discussed on pages 109-114.

For More Information, write The Modern Language Association of America, 60 Fifth Avenue, New York, New York 10011.

FUND RAISER

The Work The planning of programs for raising funds from voluntary contributors for an institution, project or cause. A fund raiser, depending on the size of the organization does some or all of the following: organizes and trains volunteer solicitors, prepares letters, placards, speeches and other promotional materials for their use and quarterbacks promotional events, identifies prospective donors; seldom solicits personally; may work full time for a single employer or may serve a number of clients, either as an independent consultant or member of an organization which takes over all or part of the work involved in a given drive. May specialize in such areas as bequests, annuities, annual funds and school endowments.

Numbers and Prospects Because it is new as a profession (though fund raising for good causes is an American tradition as old as the Pilgrims) no figures are available. Many women are employed. Prospects excellent, as causes which must count on contributions, at least in part, proliferate, as recognition of the usefulness of professional help becomes more widespread and as resistance to added taxes, frequently the only other way of funding growing or new needs, increases.

Where Employed By such non-profit institutions as churches, schools, colleges and universities, hospitals, libraries and museums; by committees for cultural organizations such as symphony orchestras and community repertory theatres or by charities and community services such as community chests; and by the sponsors of a variety of worthy causes, from improving merit systems to the eradication of diseases to civil liberties to population control.

Preparation No set pattern, but a Bachelor's degree generally required and a Master's in Business Administration can be helpful. On-the-job training and attendance at short courses given by experienced practitioners are stressed since specific formal training is as yet unavailable.

Advancement From staff membership and specialization into supervision; from a small operation to a larger one; from management of fund raising in an institution to top administrative posts such as "Vice President, Relations"; into self-employment as consultant or proprietor of an independent fund raising organization.

Salaries At levels, varying with seniority, experience, responsibility carried and field and place of employment, paid persons with four-year liberal arts degrees otherwise engaged; one can reach middle-management levels without taking on added responsibilities for unrelated kinds of work. Consultants operating independently can have handsome earnings. (See Appendix A for 1967-68 benchmark figures.)

For People Who Want to get a sense of direct service to society from their work; enjoy persuading people and also dealing with them as professional colleagues; can tolerate the uncertainties involved in trying to marshall volunteers; like the challenge of a highly difficult assignment (no one hires a fund raiser if the contributions are easy to come by); want a degree of personal independence and some freedom to come and go as they please; can wait for results; and have considerable concern for job security.

Values associated with self-employment in this field are discussed on pages 109-114.

For More Information, consult the individual responsible for raising money through contributions employed by the institutions or causes which are of interest to you, and see "Designs for Fund Raising" by Harold J. Seymour; McGraw-Hill Book Company.

GENERAL MANAGER (EXECUTIVE, ADMINISTRATOR)

While the end products of their efforts and their earnings are not the same, in other respects there are more similarities than differences in the jobs of an executive vice-president of a bank, a superintendent of schools, a city manager, the proprietor of a small machine shop, a farm manager, a destroyer skipper and a hospital administrator. Further, the differences are narrowing as management increasingly becomes a profession in its own right rather than a job to be undertaken simply by the more competent or senior or aggressive people in the various fields of work. Savants in the matter foresee the day when most administrative posts in most fields will be manned by relatively interchangeable men and women whose principle training and competence is in the use of computers, psychology, organization and decision theory, operations and systems analysis, PERT (Program Evaluation and Review Technique), simulation and like disciplines. For these reasons management is here described as a distinct kind of work.

The following description departs from the usual pattern in that it does not discuss categorically place of employment, numbers and prospects and salaries. In these regards, be it noted that the country's 8-10,000,000 managers (only about one-tenth of them women) are ubiquitous; their number will grow with a growing population and workforce; and their salaries are at many levels, depending on the field and kind of work they are in and where they stand in their organization's hierarchies. These are obvious facts and need not be dwelt on.

The Work Direction, coordination and control of two or more different activities which, however, have a common goal, be it a product or a service. Decisions must be made promptly, be concerned with practicality as against theory, be clearly communicated and be endlessly followed up. A man in this position leads, motivates and trains those who report directly to him and is, further, concerned that such "manpower development" actions hold high priority with supervisors who report to him.

He pays constant attention to the financial aspects of the operation (without adequate funds continuously available it would cease to exist) ; almost always involved are the payroll, "working capital," the budget, accounting, efficiency, taxes, insurance and periodic reporting; he may also be responsible for sales, the granting of credit and the collection of overdue accounts, currently outstanding securities and the floating of new issues, borrowing or making loans, fund raising, acquisitions and mergers.

He must attempt to keep on good terms with all the "publics" which can influence the success of the operation: the list of these always includes the "consumers" of the goods produced or services rendered (buyers, interested segments of the general public, students, colleagues within the organization, union members, etc.) : the sources of income (donors, stockholders, taxpayers, legislatures, customers, alumni, company finance officer, etc.) : those to whom he is responsible (board of directors, legislature, immediate supervisor, etc.) ; employees and professional peers. Publics may also include government agencies, the community in which the organization is located, the financial community, special interest groups, powerful elements within the organization (faculty members in universities and doctors in hospitals, etc.), and others.

He must be an expert in one or more of the management disciplines. May enter self-employment as a "management consultant." May teach management courses part time.

Preparation Fewer and fewer managerial jobs of consequence will go to persons without at least a Bachelor's degree; in addition, in profit-making enterprises, non-profit organizations and government, relevant post-graduate training to at least the Master's level, undertaken in a full-time basis at a business or other graduate school, through correspondence courses, in company-run training programs or in evening or other spare time, is virtually essential today to reach the top. A Ph.D. frequently is required in science- and engineering-oriented operations; an increasing proportion of senior non-technical administrators have engineering or scientific schooling in their backgrounds. Mastery of one or more of the competences which will be one's management portfolio-to-be and sufficient understanding of the rest to make effective use of those who have them and to know good work from bad is essential.

In education, a Master's degree is more and more required for middle-management jobs and a Ph.D. for top jobs.

In the Military Services, the amount of post-college formal education undertaken, both in service schools and outside, correlates closely with promotion and retention.

In business self-employment, there are no clear patterns, but success obviously depends on knowledge and skill, however acquired.

Advancement In all fields accession to higher level management positions is largely but not entirely a matter of managerial competence and thorough training. In most settings one or more of the following factors have a bearing: willingness to conform to the standards of comportment which prevail; ostentatious hard work and willingness to sacrifice other interests and activities to the job; personal presentability; plenty of tact when expressing disagreement with superiors; knowing the right people; a concern and talent for timing; and if one is highly competitive, ambitious and anxious to take the initiative, a fine sense of how much of one's hand to show to whom. In government, education and the Military

Services, of course, rate of progress may also be conditioned to a high degree by law or custom.

For People Who Enjoy a more than usually rapid work pace; are pragmatic in their approach to problems; want to exercise control over others; like to analyze, plan and organize; thrive on the challenge of competition with peers; enjoy dealing with people in many different contexts; have a high tolerance for ambiguity (the product may be predictable but people seldom are) and, at the same time, have an eye for detail; who like to see what they have accomplished frequently; and, at the higher levels, do not feel strongly about job security. Values associated with self-employment in this work are discussed on pages 109-114.

For More Information, write The American Management Association, 135 West 50th Street, New York, New York 10015, The Civil Service Commission, Washington D. C., and The American Association of School Administrators, 1201 Sixteenth Street, N.W., Washington, D. C.

HOME ECONOMIST

The Work Is concerned with improving and helping others to improve all the tangibles and intangibles which can contribute to the comfort of a home. A home economist is knowledgeable about foods, cooking and nutrition, textiles and clothing, child development, family relations, household furnishings, supplies and equipment, home management and budgets, and consumer tastes. May be generalist or may specialize in one or more of these areas. May teach, write, advise, demonstrate, lecture, do research, consult, supervise or, as is frequently the case, do several of these things.

Numbers and Prospects About 90,000, of whom some 28,000 are dietitians and 5000 agricultural extension workers whose initial training was in home economics; very few men but numbers growing. Prospects excellent and related to the growing population and dramatically increasing public concern for the welfare of low-income families.

Where Employed Large majority as teachers, and large majority of these in secondary schools, the balance in adult education and college-level teaching. A substantial number by business concerns as experts on family tastes and needs, family budget advisers, demonstrators, designers, product testers and consultants to buyers. Some, either as specialists, dietitians or nutritionists, work in the food service operations of hospitals, hotels, business concerns and other mass feeding facilities; remainder employed by newspapers and other mass media, publishers, advertising agencies, social work agencies and government-sponsored extension services, and in overseas aid programs and research; a few are self-employed.

Preparation Bachelor's degree in home economics; additional year of interning usually essential to specializing in dietetics or institutional management; advanced degrees normally required for college-level teaching, practice as a nutritionist, and research.

Advancement In teaching and government settings, through the normal channels; elsewhere depends on competence, postgraduate training, personality and supervisory ability.

Salaries At levels, varying with level of degree plus internship level attained, seniority, experience, responsibility carried and field and place of employment, paid to persons otherwise engaged with liberal arts schooling; one can reach lower-middle management levels without taking on added responsibilities for unrelated kinds of work. (See Appendix A for 1967-68 benchmark figures.)

For People Who Like to persuade and to be helpful to others and also enjoy contacts with professional colleagues; want to deal with tangibles, are self-starters and like to get things done; have a streak of creativity in their make-up; and are concerned about job security.

For More Information, see Appendix C or write The American Home Economics Association, 1600 20th Street, N.W., Washington, D. C. 20009.

HUMANIST

Definitions of what a humanist is — and people frequently use the word reverentially — vary widely. For the purposes of this section a "humanity" will be defined as any field of interest which is non-natural scientific, non-social scientific and non-engineering (all of these are discussed elsewhere), and which requires graduate work if one is to pursue it as a career. More affirmatively, a humanist may be concerned with philosophy, language, literature (in all ages), the arts in terms of their history and practice and, in general, things cultural.

The Work   Teaching, scholarship and, on occasion through what a humanist writes or does, demonstrating that he can effectively practice what he preaches, be it plastic arts, music, writing or philosophical innovation.

Numbers and Prospects and Where Employed   Numbers have not been tabulated, but humanists are numerically consequential members of every college and university faculty in the country; a few work in museums and for government and non-profit organizations; some practice independently; prospects are good, as population increases, as more and more young people seek higher education and older ones find that they missed something, and as recognition that the cultural side of life, as well as the scientific and otherwise pragmatic sides, has importance to the viability of society.

Preparation   A Master's degree in the discipline of choice, at a minimum; usually a doctorate for successful lifelong practice — or consummate skill as a practitioner, if concerned with the plastic or performing arts, creative writing or, occasionally, philosophy.

Advancement   In academe, along the paths common to peers in other disciplines; elsewhere, no set patterns. It should be noted, however, that simple recognition by public and peers — through prizes, professional society officerships and otherwise — is of more consequence to humanists as a criterion of success than to those in most other kinds of work.

Salaries   At levels, varying with level of degree attained, experience, seniority, responsibility carried and field and place of employment, paid persons otherwise engaged with liberal arts schooling. (See Appendix A for 1967-68 benchmark figures.)

For People Who   Like work which demands preciseness and an analytical mind; enjoy working with ideas; can tolerate frequent lack of exact standards; and, so far as the academic setting goes, like to be able to think independently and to come and go as they please, value job security and prefer a measured work pace.

For More Information, see Appendix C and talk to the humanists you know.

INDUSTRIAL DESIGNER

The Work   Requires a knowledge of materials, machinery and production processes, combined with artistic talent and a feel for consumer taste to design products and their packages which are at once functional, economically feasible to produce and appealing to potential customers. An industrial designer may work on anything from spoons to limousines; may specialize in certain products or work on a wide variety; may create new products for the near or distant future or redesign old ones; works up models of alternative designs; may do layouts for facilities such as filling stations and trade fairs. A few teach. Security of employment is affected by volatility of consumer taste, rapid obsolescence of many products and fluctuations in national economy.

Numbers and Prospects   More than 10,000 working today, very few of whom are women though proportion is growing. Future tied to expected industrial expansion but always contingent upon the health of the economy at any given moment.

Where Employed   The majority by large manufacturers of consumer products in large industrial centers; some by consulting firms, architects and interior designers; a few freelance or set up their own consulting organizations or teach.

Preparation   At least three post-high school years of training, more usually four and sometimes five; a few master's degrees granted; curricula vary but all include some engineering, art and model-making, and most, in addition, some marketing or business courses. Some graduates go into industrial design with architecture, engineering and art degrees. No license required.

Advancement   Usually from routine work as assistant to a practicing designer to growing responsibility and independence and then to supervision or into private consulting. Teaching can lead to senior faculty standing.

Salaries   At levels, varying with level of degree attained, seniority, experience, responsibility carried and field and place of work, paid persons otherwise engaged with liberal arts schooling; one can reach middle management levels without taking on added responsibilities for unrelated kinds of work; independent consultants can earn in six figures. (See Appendix A for 1967-68 benchmark figures.)

For People Who Have strong desire to be creative and at the same time are practical and like to see the results of their work frequently; are naturally precise; enjoy competition with their peers and in the market place; prefer dealing with people as fellow businessmen; and set no great story by security. Values associated with self-employment as an industrial designer are discussed on pages 109-114.

For More Information, see Appendix C or write The American Society of Industrial Designers, 15 East 48th Street, New York, New York 10017.

INSURANCE WORKER

The Work The insurance industry — including life, property-liability (casualty), health and multiple line companies — employs people in a wide variety of different kinds of work, witness the horizontal dots following "Insurance" in the chart on page 82. (Contrary to the impression of many collegians, it is not almost wholly manned by salesmen, agents and brokers, though these constitute the majority of non-clerical workers.) Only three kinds of work, in fact, are peculiar to the industry — actuarial, claims analysis, examination and adjustment and home office underwriting, and only the last two will be discussed here. Actuarial work is described separately on page 123.

Claims analyst, examiner and adjuster Reviews claims for payment made by policy holders to be sure they fall within the specifications of the policy, works out any adjustments in the settlement which may be called for and follows up to be sure claims are promptly paid; works with technical, medical, engineering and other specialists where required during claims investigations. Similar work to be found in public carrier companies and in traffic departments of large industries.

Home Office Underwriter Evaluates the risks involved in each application for a policy, backing up the agent or underwriter in the field, and decides whether the company can accept the risk and issue the policy. Works, where appropriate, with a variety of specialists in making determinations. "Direct-writing" companies place much of the responsibility in this area and for claims analysis and other functions handled in the home office by other companies with their salaried representatives in the field.

Numbers and Prospects   Exact figures not available; are among the 200,000 non-clerical, non-sales employees of insurance companies. Few women have these jobs. Prospects good as public becomes more and more insurance-conscious, population increases, business expands and incomes rise.

Where Employed   In the home offices of the country's 5200 insurance companies; concentrated in Connecticut, Massachusetts, New York and New Jersey.

Preparation   A Bachelor's degree; capacity to acquire technical expertness in a variety of areas once on the job; top-level jobs may require relevant advanced degree.

Advancement   To supervision of home office specialists; to management of a broader range of insurance activities; to the field as an agent or independent insurance broker.

Salaries   At the levels, varying with level of degree attained, experience, seniority, responsibility carried and place of employment, paid persons in other work with four-year liberal arts or allied degrees; one can reach middle-management levels without taking on added responsibilties for unrelated kinds of work. (See Appendix A for 1967-68 benchmark figures.)

For People Who   Like to deal with things precisely and to see the results of their efforts often; prefer to deal with others as business colleagues and, in claims adjustment, in a persuasive role; who like a moderate work pace, and set some story by job security.

For More Information, see Appendix C and write to The Institute of Life Insurance, 277 Park Avenue, New York, New York 10017 and The American Mutual Insurance Alliance, 20 North Wacker Drive, Chicago, Illinois 60606.

INTERIOR DECORATOR-DESIGNER

The Work   The designing of interiors and their furnishings; consulting with customer in determining what will be done and at what price, and sometimes with architects and landscape architects on the design of buildings and their surroundings. A decorator-designer secures and organizes the arts, crafts, furniture, fabrics, rugs and other materials necessary to accomplish the design and supervises workers on the job; makes cost estimates and sketches; may sell materials used to customers at a commission; may consult and sell for a store, prepare advertising, write for periodicals or teach. Interior decorating and designing is sensitive to fluctuations in general economy; hours may be irregular.

Numbers and Prospects   More than 15,000, about half women. Substantial increase expected as growing population requires more homes and other buildings, and individuals become more aesthetically aware and can afford professional assistance. Prosperity or lack of it will affect employment at any given time.

Where Employed   By commercial, residential and institutional clients as an employee, or may be self-employed. As employee, role may be principally as a salesperson, or a consultant to management and buyers, or a designer, or an advertising worker; many openings with large furniture and department stores. May work in movies or TV as set designer; for hotel chains, theatres, architects, apartment and office building owners, manufacturers of interior furnishings, antique dealers, schools of interior design and decoration and magazines in the field. Employment concentrated in large cities and suburbs.

Preparation   Minimum of two to three post-high school years at institution specializing in subject followed by five to six years of on-the-job experience, or four years to a Bachelor of Fine Arts degree followed by four years of experience; one or the other program is required for membership in The American Institute of Interior Designers and The National Society of Interior Designers. Course work usually includes some history of art, painting, mechanical drawing, home economics and mathematics. No license required.

Advancement   From extended apprenticeship, often in such humble roles as salesperson, stockroom worker, receptionist or shopper, through assistantships to senior designer and decorator, or to supervision. Talent, personality, business sense and, surprisingly, increasing age count heavily.

Salaries For those employed by others and until one has "arrived," at lower levels, varying with level of degree attained, seniority, experience, responsibility carried and field and place of employment, than those paid persons otherwise employed with liberal arts schooling; once "arrived" professionals usually receive a good salary plus 5 to 10 per cent commission on the price of goods sold. Self-employed consultants, who can have large incomes, depend entirely on commissions running up to 33 per cent. (See Appendix A for 1967-68 benchmark figures.)

For People Who Have a strong creative bent and also like selling and business generally; want to see concrete results from their efforts frequently; do not object to the ambiguity of dealing with clients with whose taste they may not agree and the necessity this entails for persuasion, flexibility and compromise; who are not easily frustrated by seldom being able to make the final decisions; enjoy a fast work pace; can wait to make it to the top; and like working with others in a business setting. Values associated with self-employment in this field are discussed on pages 109-114.

For More Information, see Appendix C and write The American Institute of Interior Designers, 673 Fifth Avenue, New York, New York 10022.

INTERNATIONAL WORKER

The chart on page 82 lists international work among both the "fields" and "kinds" of work. The fit in both cases is extremely loose. Such is the tremendous diversity of international work (witness the number of dots, both horizontal and vertical, which appear on the chart that it actually defies categorization within a "kind-field" rubric. Nevertheless, many collegians have an interest in a career defined in their minds for the time being no more specifically than as "international work," and therefore this book could not claim reasonable comprehensiveness if it ignored the matter.

On the other hand, a thorough discussion of international work in all its aspects would take a book in itself. By way of compromise, what follows will be a rough sketch, somewhere between ignoring the matter and a book, designed to assure the reader that he or she has not overlooked any of the major possibilities.

The Work So far as what kinds and fields of work have international facets is concerned, the chart covers most of the ground. A consideration applicable to both kinds and fields may be worth adding. One can be a "professional" internationalist, that is, can make his living as an expert on one facet or another of the international picture (such people are found in the State Department, on college faculties and in foundations, among other places), or one can be an international "professional," that is, can make a living in a given kind of work— scientific, educational, financial, marketing or religious — by being a specialist in its international aspects. In both cases one may spend most or none of his time in foreign lands.

Where Employed and Numbers By Federal, international and foreign governments, and by profit-making companies, non-profit, educational and Military organization, both at home and abroad. There are no estimates available of number employed at home. Abroad, the majority — the actual numbers fluctuate considerably — work for the *Federal Government* (estimates run from 125,000 to 200,000 — out of 2,500,000 Federal employees — "permanently stationed" abroad at any one time). Within the Federal establishment, the majority of overseas workers are employed by the Department of Defense; other departments and agencies with substantial workforces abroad are State (about 7000, including about 3500 Foreign Service Officers), the Agency for International Development (about 4000), the United States Information Agency (upwards of 1000) and the Panama Canal Company (perhaps 1000). The following departments and agencies also have overseas employees: Agriculture, Labor, Treasury, Commerce, Health, Education and Welfare, the Atomic Energy Commission, the National Security Agency, the Central Intelligence Agency, the Peace Corps, the Export-Import Bank and the Library of Congress.

Those employed by *business and industry* in permanent assignments abroad probably number upwards of 50,000, though many times this number travel overseas occasionally or frequently on business. Banks, hotels, engineering firms, airlines and steamship companies, farm machinery, oil, auto, steel, fruit, mining and pharmaceutical companies are the principal employers. In general, private concerns attempt to man their foreign subsidiaries and affiliates with nationals; assignments for Americans overseas tend to be for extended periods in one place, unlike the Foreign Service's two-year rotational program. *Religious organizations* have representatives, including missionaries, numbering in the tens of thousands overseas. Also having staffs stationed abroad are such *community action organizations* as Accion, the International Voluntary Services, Inc., and the American Friends Service Committee, and such overseas agencies as CARE, the United Nations Educational, Scientific and Cultural Organization, the World Health Organization and Planned Parenthood-World Population. Other employers of Americans overseas include periodical and book publishers, foundations, international educational organizations and trade associations.

Preparation For the most part, jobs in the international field are held by those who have acquired a high competence in one or another of the kinds of work which are needed overseas (business disciplines, language, science, engineering, teaching, etc.) ; such competence backed up by one or two years of postgraduate training in one of the country's 90-odd schools of public and international affairs provides the best entreé into this highly competitive field; in some cases, such as the Foreign Service, rigorous examinations and other screening is involved; mere facility in one or more languages is not in itself a sufficient launching pad — most employers in and out of government are prepared to give otherwise qualified people "quickie" language training if they are weak in this area.

Advancement Obviously, amid all this diversity, there are no well-defined paths. In the Foreign Service it may be worth noting that 75 per cent of all ambassadors are "career" men. The state of the American and foreign economies, political developments at

home and abroad, American tax policy, the success of fund-raising
endeavors, the state of relations between America and other nations and like variables can, of course, bring dramatic advancement or stagnation or even sudden unemployment in many kinds
of international work.

Salaries Obviously, no generalization is possible. Foreign Service
Officers somewhat above levels, varying with level of degree attained, seniority, experience, and responsibility carried, paid persons otherwise engaged in the Federal civil service with liberal
arts schooling. Elsewhere the spectrum extends from board and
room only to upper-middle management levels. Since financing of
all salaries excepting those paid by business is supported either by
taxes or contributions, high salaries are rare; on the other hand,
living abroad may be inexpensive compared with state-side costs
and many employers provide liberal fringe benefits and generous
special allowances to those of their workers who live aboard. (See
Appendix A for 1967-68 benchmark figures.)

For People Who Want to be involved in the affairs of the globe;
beyond that, the diversity of the kinds of work possible permits
no generalizations.

For More Information, write the Editor, *Intercom,* The Foreign
Policy Association, 345 East 46th Street, New York, New York
10017, and ask for their most recent feature on careers in world
affairs.

LABOR RELATIONS WORKER

The Work Is concerned with one or more of the following aspects
of the 125,000-odd labor-management contracts which spell out
the wages, hours, benefits and other conditions of employment
which obtain in the country's "organized" workplaces (to be
found in all fields of work except the Military Services) : their
drafting, negotiation, administration and enforcement, the
settling of grievances which may arise; research, especially
economic and legal; legal representation of one of the parties
where an issue goes to court; acting as an arbitrator when management and labor are unable to settle their differences directly;
and teaching and writing about various aspects of the work,

which is often described as labor-management or industrial relations and frequently is a part of the job of a personnel manager. *Numbers and Prospects* Best estimate about 25,000, of whom relatively few are women and those few concentrated in the unions and largely employed in research and writing. Many of those involved, including lawyers, personnel directors, union leaders, and arbitrators, do other work part of the time. Prospects good, though growth in union membership — now about 18,000,000 in some 200 unions — has slowed in recent years.

Where Employed The great majority as members of the staffs of unions or of "organized" employers. A substantial number by government, largely at the Federal level though quite a few by the more industrialized states, as mediators, persons who attempt to get a voluntary agreement between the parties; as hearing examiners who make rulings under relevant law; as factfinders and as union election supervisors. About 1000 are arbitrators (a few of these in government employ but most are independents) — persons who are invited in by the parties to make a decision which both agree in advance to abide by; a few by colleges, universities and management associations, and by periodicals as writers specializing in labor relations.

Preparation This is a kind of work in which on-the-job experience plays a major role. Many people engaged in it, especially on the union side, still have less than Bachelor level educations: there is growing emphasis, however, on that level as a minimum in all organizations. Coursework in economics, psychology and other relevant disciplines preferred; higher degrees, in such fields as economics, business administration and law, often sought in filling posts in large companies and unions; with rare exceptions, an apprenticeship under an experienced practitioner essential to appointment to important jobs.

Advancement Through the steps common to other employments in business, unions and government. In business and unions top management positions are reasonable goals for those who start by specializing in labor relations. Into private practice as arbitrator or mediator, though the work is typically sporadic.

Salaries At levels, varying with level of degree attained, seniority, experience, responsibility carried and field and place of employment, paid persons otherwise engaged with same type of schooling; one can reach top-management levels without taking on added responsibilities for unrelated kinds of work; a few nationally known mediators and arbitrators earn handsome fees. (See Appendix A for 1967-68 benchmark figures.)

For People Who Like to deal with others in a persuasive or competitive role; (in unions particularly) want to feel that they are serving a cause; enjoy a pace which is occasionally frantic; have a high tolerance for acrimony and for uncertainty; like the challenge of "poker-playing"; and have a propensity for precision (one faulty word in a contract can mean a later strike). Values associated with self-employment in this work are discussed on pages 109-114.

For More Information see Appendix C or write, The American Management Association, 135 West 50th Street, New York, N.Y., or Headquarters, AFL-CIO, Washington, D.C.

LANDSCAPE ARCHITECT

The Work The planning and planting of outdoor areas for use and pleasure. Employs the skills of the creative artist, horticulturist, engineer, businessman and supervisor in designing, laying out and bringing to completion projects involving plant life, soil, rocks, artifacts, construction and open space. A landscape architect deals with employers or clients in the dual role of taste-maker and reflector of taste; may undertake many kinds of projects or may specialize; may teach. Long hours and outdoor work not unusual; frequently works part-time. Vulnerable to fluctuations in the economy.

Numbers and Prospects Over 5000 employed, of whom perhaps 15 per cent are women. Prospects good, due to the growth of the population, of urbanization of the country, of concern for recreation with the shortening of the work week, of interest in things aesthetic and of family incomes; somewhat dependent on state of economy since families may turn to less expensive landscape gardeners and nurserymen, or to their own devices, when their incomes drop.

Where Employed Majority in business for themselves or employed by other landscape architects; a third work for government, including city planning organizations, recreation agencies and park departments; a few work for architects, engineering firms, real estate developers, and nurseries, or teach. Concentrated in populous states and in areas where per capita income is high and the weather is moderate all year round.

Preparation Four to five post-high school years to a Bachelor's Degree in Landscape Architecture; curriculum includes both liberal arts and vocational courses; a few Masters' degrees granted; license to practice necessary in a few states and, where it is, two to four years of apprenticeship beyond college required.

Advancement Usually through two to three years as a junior draftsman to senior draftsman and thence to supervision or partnership in a firm or to independent practice.

Salaries For those employed by others, at levels, varying with level of degree attained, seniority, experience, responsibility carried and field and place of employment, paid persons with liberal arts schooling; one can reach middle-management levels without taking on added responsibilites for unrelated kinds of work; the self-employed landscape architect can have handsome earnings but may also experience wide fluctuations in income, depending principally on the general health of the economy. (See Appendix A for 1967-68 benchmark figures.)

For People Who Want creative work which includes a degree of practicality; like dealing with tangibles and seeing what they've accomplished frequently; do not put great emphasis on the security of their jobs; can live comfortably with the frequent uncertainty involved in trying to both follow and lead the aesthetic opinions of others; like to be free to come and go as they wish; and enjoy dealing with others in a business relationship. Values associated with self-employment as a landscape architect are on pages 109-114.

For More Information see Appendix C or write The American Association of Landscape Architects, Inc., 2000 K Street, N.W., Washington, D.C. 20006.

LAWYER

The Work Advising and representing individuals and organizations in those of their concerns which have legal aspects. May be concerned with one or more of the following matters: individual and family problems such as wills, deeds, trusts, and personal rights and obligations; corporation problems; securities; urban development (zoning, land use, property appropriation, interstate compacts, etc.); criminal and other prosecution (if in government employment); insurance; taxation; defense of accused law breakers; patent and copyright matters; labor law; real estate; international law (individual and business problems as well as governmental); maritime law; scholarship and research; teaching; writing; legislative and other drafting; lobbying; legal interpretation (judicial and administrative); law libraries; investigation; law enforcement and, most recently, such matters as space, poverty and the rights of psychiatric patients. A lawyer may appear frequently in court or not at all; may move around, on a full-time basis, among the six fields of work or may be active in several fields simultaneously.

Numbers and Prospects About 275,000, of whom only 3 per cent are women. Prospects for high ranking law school graduates and those from prestige institutions good but others may find the going slow and the competition stiff. Growing population, continuing business expansion and the increasing complexity of society and thus the number of new "rules of the game" which must be put on the books assure steady growth of need for lawyers, however.

Where Employed Ubiquitously; three-quarters in private practice, half of these practicing alone and the rest self-employed as partners (mostly in firms of ten or less) or employed by private law firms. The rest are employees of profit-making enterprises (business is turning more and more to "in-house" counsel); in government either as "attorneys general," serving total governmental complexes such as the Federal Government, states and cities, or as "solicitors" or "counsel" to one of the agencies which make up the complex (most of the 80 departments and agencies in the Federal establishment have their own lawyers). By non-profit organizations such as unions; in the Military Services

(Judge Advocate General Corps) ; in law schools; and by publications devoted to law; many with legal training are otherwise engaged, in management in all fields and in a variety of other pursuits, both related and unrelated to law.

Preparation A Bachelor's degree followed by graduation from an accredited law school is virtually a must today — latter takes either three years of full-time study or four or more years of part-time, night study (25 per cent get their degrees in this latter way). Undergraduate major is of less importance to law school entry than demonstrated intellectual competence. Success in a Bar Association examination in most states is essential to practice; states vary as to other requirements. Additional hurdles may be involved in becoming qualified to practice before various Federal courts and agencies. Law school is not today the best training for anything but the practice of law. The fast rising quality and quantity of good professional graduate schools of business and international affairs and in other disciplines make them a better bet than law school for those headed in those directions and uninterested in the practice of law.

Advancement All the way to top management possible in government and in profit-making and non-profit organizations; from employment by an organization into private practice; into the judiciary, or politics or diplomacy. The executives with law degrees one often finds at or near the top of business concerns and government agencies usually were successful lawyers before moving into general management.

Salaries If employed by others, at levels, varying with seniority, experience, responsibility carried and field and place of employment, paid holders of doctor's degrees in the sciences; one can reach top management levels without taking on added responsibilities for unrelated kinds of work; independent practitioners can earn in six figures. (See Appendix A for 1967-68 benchmark figures.)

For People Who Have a talent for precision and analysis — and this is the only common denominator; every other value discussed in this book can be satisified — or may be frustrated — by a career in law, depending on the nature of one's law practice. Values associated with self-employment in law are discussed on pages 109-114. *For More Information* see Appendix C or write The American Bar Association, 1155 East 60th Street, Chicago, Illinois 60637.

LIBRARIAN

The Work   Involves the maintaining of collections of books and other informative material for the use of a particular clientele or the general public. Includes evaluating, selecting, and purchasing books, periodicals, audio-visual aids, records, tape recordings, film in various forms, maps, pictures, and like materials; cataloguing and storing them for quick retrieval (microfilm and computers are increasingly being used) ; promoting their use through displays and other means; assisting library users in finding what they want. May include the making of bibliographies and abstracts, doing research, and preserving and repairing the collection's materials. Selection of additions requires capacity to both reflect and mold taste of clientele. Librarians may be generalists or may specialize or teach. Evening and weekend work may be frequent for full-time worker.

Number and Prospects   More than 81,000 full-time, 80 per cent of them women; in addition, 15 — 20,000 temporary or part-time. The proportion of men is increasing, especially in supervision and positions which require special technical knowledge. There is a shortage today and it is likely to continue, especially in schools, as the population's educational level increases and reading material pours from the presses in ever-increasing volume; many opportunities for partly trained and part-time workers will continue to be available.

Where Employed   Over a third in school and public libraries including branches and bookmobiles; remainder in virtually every field, including colleges and universities, professional schools, government agencies, industry, museums, professional and trade associations, hospitals, newspapers and law firms; some work overseas for the Military Services and the United States Information Agency.

Preparation   For full professional qualification, four college years (usually Liberal Arts — sometimes with pre-vocational course-

174

work) followed by year of graduate school in library science leading to Master's degree. Ability to read at least one foreign language may also be required. States require official certification of public librarians; most public schools require librarian to have teaching certificate. Four college years with library science major all that is needed to enter Federal service; directors of large libraries often have Ph.D. in Library Science or other discipline.

Advancement   From assistant's job to supervision or possibly into a speciality; from smaller to larger libraries.

Salaries   At levels, varying with level of degree attained, seniority, experience, responsibility carried and field and place of employment, paid persons otherwise engaged with same type of schooling; one can reach upper-middle management levels without taking on responsibilities for unrelated kinds of work. (See Appendix A for 1967-68 benchmark figures.)

For People Who   Like books and reading; enjoy detail, planning and organizing; want to deal with others in a serving relationship or as professional colleagues; prefer a usually unhurried pace; set considerable store on security; and have the urge to be of obvious service to society.

For More Information see Appendix C or write The American Library Association, 50 East Huron Street, Chicago, Illinois 60611.

MARKET ANALYST AND RELATED

The Work   The effort to determine public likes, dislikes, prejudices, motivations and buying capacities in connection with a product or service or idea; planning and research (by field interviewing or reading or both) and tabulation, analysis and reporting of findings to decision makers. A market analyst may use such techniques as consumer and dealer studies, media surveys, and copy and sales tests; often works closely with personnel in sales, advertising, public relations, buying, merchandising and production, or he may be responsible for one or more of these functions in addition to market analysis activities; often makes use of computers.

Numbers and Prospects   About 20,000 including a substantial but unknown proportion of women. Prospects excellent as business continues to expand, population increases and the techniques for taking the guesswork out of determining what will and won't sell become more and more sophisticated.

Where Employed   Principally by business concerns with products or services to sell; some by advertising agencies, such government agencies as the U.S. Department of Agriculture, public opinion polling organizations, educational institutions and private market research concerns which work for clients on a fee basis; the latter are concentrated in large cities.

Preparation   Bachelor's degree minimum requirement, with undergraduate concentration or business administration preferred. For upper level jobs relevant graduate work to the Ph.D. level sometimes required. Familiarity with computers increasingly important.

Advancement   From junior analyst, field interviewer and similar speciality jobs, up to broad top-level marketing or product management responsibilities and from there a good possibility of moving into top management, especially in the consumer goods industries; to self-employment as a fee-charging, independent expert. Moving from employer to employer on the way up is frequent.

Salaries   At levels, varying with level of degree attained, experience, seniority, responsibility carried and field and place of employment, paid persons otherwise engaged with same type of schooling; one can reach middle-management levels without taking on added responsibilities for unrelated kinds of work; top officers in independent consulting organizations at top management levels. (See Appendix A for 1967-68 benchmark figures.)

For People Who   Enjoy being systematic, precise and analytic in their work; prefer dealing with people as business colleagues; can tolerate the ambiguity of having to make decisions without all the relevant facts in hand; like planning and organizing; and don't put too high a premium on job security. Values associated with self-employment in market analysis are discussed on pages 109-114.

For More Information see Appendix C or write The American Marketing Association, 27 East Monroe Street, Chicago, Illinois.

MATHEMATICIAN-STATISTICIAN

The Work A *mathematician* is concerned either with "pure" mathematics, attempting to develop new principles and discover new relationships between mathematical forms with no immediate practical aim in view, or with "applied" mathematics, solving problems in higher mathematics encountered by scientists in all fields, engineers, businessmen and others. A *statistician* is concerned either with "mathematical' statistics, the equivalent of "pure" mathematics in the sense that this is an undirected search for new knowledge, or with "applied" statistics, the collection, analysis and interpretation of numerical data in a given area to help those concerned — scientists, engineers, businessmen, poll takers, psychometrists and other — understand the situation as it stands and to make knowledgeable decisions about next steps. Both disciplines make extensive use of the computer, and in both many teach. Some knowledge of both higher mathematics and statistics is essential to scientists, engineers, accountants, actuaries, computer scientists, operations researchers and systems analysts.

Numbers and Prospects *Mathematicians*—about 50,000, of whom 11 per cent are women. Prospects excellent as the usefulness of a mathematical approach to problems becomes more and more widely recognized, as more and more students, whatever their career plans, find they will need some mathematics, and as computers become more numerous and complex. *Statisticians* — about 20,000, of whom a third are women. Prospects excellent for the same reasons as for mathematicians.

Where Employed *Mathematicians* — the great majority, about equally divided, by colleges and universities and business and industry; the rest in the other fields of work, including a few self-employed consultants. *Statisticians* — majority by government at all levels, particularly the Federal; many of the rest by business in such areas as marketing, quality control and economic forecasting; others by universities and colleges and non-profit organizations or as self-employed consultants.

Preparation Bachelor's degree with major in mathematics or statistics essential. Supportive coursework relevant to one's particular area of interest — economics, engineering or marketing for

177

instance — useful. People with advanced degrees increasingly being sought in all fields, and Ph.D. essential for teaching at the university level.

Advancement Along the routes available to natural scientists (see page 203) in one's particular field; into private consulting.

Salaries At slightly lower levels, varying with level of degree attained, experience, seniority, responsibility carried and field and place of employment than those paid physical scientists; one can reach middle-management levels without taking on added responsibilities for unrelated kinds of work. (See Appendix A for 1967-68 benchmark figures.)

For People Who Like precise, analytical work; enjoy planning and problem-solving; prefer to deal with others as business or teaching associates and an unhurried work pace; who have substantial concern for job security. These are the only common denominators. The values associated with the pure and applied branches of mathematics and statistics are quite different. Values associated with self-employment in this type of work are discussed on pages 109-114.

For More Information see Appendix C or write The American Mathematical Society, 140 Hope Street, Providence, Rhode Island 02906 or The American Statistical Association, 810 18th Street, N.W., Washington, D.C. 20006.

MEDICAL TECHNOLOGIST AND RELATED

The Work Assisting physicians in detection and treatment of sickness and disease through laboratory observation, analysis and testing of body tissues, fluids etc. A technologist may specialize in one or more of such areas as microbiology, parasitology, biochemistry, hematology, histology, virology, cytology and nuclear medicine. Often works part time. (Other comparable members of the "health manpower team" are Medical Record Librarians and Medical X-ray Technicians).

Numbers and Prospects About 40,000, nine-tenths of them women. There are in addition more than 12,000 Medical Record Librarians and 70,000 Medical X-ray Technicians, also mostly women; the proportion of men is increasing. Prospects excellent as population continues to grow and public concern about health increases. Total health manpower team expected to grow from about 3,000,000 today to 4,000,000 in 1975.

Where Employed Great majority in hospitals and, of these, largest single group in Federal government institutions; others work in private laboratories, public health agencies, research institutions and pharmaceutical companies and as teachers.

Preparation Normal requirement three post-high school years with coursework concentrated in chemistry, biology and mathematics, followed by a year's training in school of medical technology; if school is accredited by the Board of Registry of Medical Technicians of the American Society of Clinical Pathologists, graduate then is designated as a registered "MT-ASCP."

Advancement To supervisory positions.

Salaries At levels, varying with seniority, experience, responsibility carried and field and place of employment, paid persons with four-year liberal arts degrees; one can reach lower middle-management levels without taking on added responsibilities for unrelated kinds of work. (See Appendix A for 1967-68 benchmark figures.)

For People Who Like detailed, precise work under close supervision; enjoy dealing with tangibles and seeing the results of their efforts frequently; prefer a measured work pace; like to deal with people as business colleagues; and are concerned about job security.

For More Information see Appendix C (Medical Record Librarians and Medical X-ray Technicians are also covered) or write any of the following: The American Society of Medical Technologists, Suite 25, Hermann Professional Building, Houston, Texas 77025; The American Association of Medical Record Librarians, 840 North Lake Shore Drive, Chicago, Illinois 60611; The American Society of Radiologic Technologists, 537 South Main Street, Fond du Lac, Wisconsin 54935.

MINISTER—PRIEST—RABBI

The Work Whether Protestant minister, Catholic priest, Jewish rabbi, or leader of another religion, his work is concerned with the

179

spiritual, moral, and, in some contexts, educational and physical needs of people of his faith (excepting those priests who devote their lives to contemplation and prayer).

Numbers and Prospects Some 250,000 serve as ministers in the churches of 225 Protestant denominations; thousands of other ordained Protestant clerics engage in non-parish work; 5 per cent of Protestant ministers are women; 35,000 other women are religious education and church youth workers, missionaries, Christian Science practitioners, nuns and teachers of religion. There are 60,000 Catholic priests and more than 5000 rabbis. There is an increasingly acute shortage of clergymen in all three faiths. The newly ordained each year are too few to replace losses due to death, retirement and departures from the ministry for other callings.

Where Employed Great majority preside over or work in churches and parishes, which involves round-the-clock activity including preaching, performing religious rites, visiting troubled or sick parishioners, leading charity endeavors, participating in the organizations of the church's laymen, and taking part in the community. Others teach, devote themselves to scholarship, work in hospitals or homes for the elderly or for children, write, administer, work as missionaries, do professional vocational and other counseling, act as chaplains to military organizations, campuses and hospitals, edit religious publications, do social work, lead youth organizations, specialize in church music, and (increasingly) take leadership roles in such causes as the drives for civil rights and poverty elimination.

Preparation Most Protestant faiths require for ordination several years of post-college training; candidates for the Catholic priesthood face eight to twelve years of post-high school training, usually including four years of college; three to six years of post-college training is required for ordination as a rabbi.

Advancement From parish assistant to pastor in charge, to leadership in increasingly larger parishes; or up through the internal church hierarchy; or from teaching into educational administration.

Salaries In educational and military settings, at levels, varying with academic degree (in education), seniority, experience, responsibility carried and place of employment (in education), paid persons with liberal arts schooling. In other settings, for Protestant ministers and rabbis salaries are very modest; they may be supplemented by gifts and fees for performance of rites. Priests receive no salaries as such. Housing and other necessities often provided by church served. (See Appendix A for 1967-68 benchmark figures.)

For People Who Want to devote their lives to the service of God and their fellow men; like some feeling of power, independence and freedom to determine how they use their time; want job security; enjoy planning and organizing; who are patient, sympathetic and intelligent listeners, can deal warmly with many different kinds of people, and cheerfully live a life beyond reproach in fact and in appearance.

For More Information see Appendix C or consult a clergyman of your faith.

NURSE (REGISTERED)

The Work Helping in the restoration and preservation of human health as a principal assistant to the medical profession in its dealings with individuals. A nurse may tend the sick and injured in an institution or privately or may participate in preventive medicine and public education programs, undertake administrative and secretarial duties, specialize in such fields as anesthesia, children's diseases or emotional sickness, teach student nurses or do research. May work with patients one at a time or have responsibilities covering many; may work full time (three-quarters do so) or part time; may have single workplace, or may travel to homes of patients. Frequently is on her feet during much of workday.

Numbers and Prospects About 625,000, of whom only 1 per cent are men. Prospects excellent as population continues to increase, public concern about health and preventive medicine continues to rise, pre-paid health insurance plans proliferate and turnover remains high; supply of nurses, however, improving.

Where Employed Two-thirds as hospital staff members (general duty), about 10 per cent as private duty nurses in hospitals or homes. A substantial number are "office" nurses and public health nurses, the latter typically "on the road" or in clinics as employees of governmental and private non-profit organizations. Others are nurse "educators," "occupational" nurses employed by large business and governmental organizations, Military Service officers, researchers and writers.

Preparation Three principal methods: earning a "diploma" after three years of training in a hospital school of nursing (75 per cent of nurses are so trained today); earning a Bachelor of Science in Nursing degree after four or five years work at a nursing school; and earning an Associate in Arts in Nursing degree, which requires two years of training in a junior or community college. All graduates must, further, pass a state examination and, in some cases, meet other standards to become "registered" nurses. Added formal training usually needed to teach, do research, undertake certain public health duties, specialize and hold high administrative posts. Some effort is being made to persuade married women with non-nursing college backgrounds to take nursing training.

Advancement From "general duty" into private practice, or increasingly responsible administrative posts, or specialization, or research, or industrial practice or management of a doctor's office.

Salaries Industrial, office and Federally-employed nurses, at levels, varying with experience, seniority, responsibility carried and field and place of employment, somewhat higher than those paid persons with four-year liberal arts degrees. Public health nurses tend to earn a little more, general duty nurses in private hospitals and private duty nurses (many working part time), less; one can reach upper-middle management levels without taking on added responsibilities for unrelated kinds of work. (See Appendix A for 1967-68 benchmark figures.)

For People Who Want to deal with people in a helping relationship and to be in work which is of obvious service to society; enjoy being meticulous and seeing the results of their efforts frequently; like to have the feeling of being in control to a degree; and set considerable store on job security.

For More Information see Appendix C or write The National

League for Nursing, Committee on Careers, 10 Columbus Circle, New York, New York 10019.

OPERATIONS RESEARCH WORKER

The Work The study of complex operations, present and prospective, with a view to giving the ultimate decision makers the best possible analytic basis from which to make up their minds; concerned with men, machines, material, equipment and costs in various combinations, and with their distribution, control, direction and effectiveness. Uses such tools as mathematical models, simulation, game theory and linear programing in determining relationships, alternatives, averages and probabilities; often is a member of a team which includes experts in several disciplines; frequently uses computers.

Numbers and Prospects Over 7000, almost none of them women. Growth expected to be dramatic as business learns to accept and use operations research to improve efficiency; as organizations in all fields increase in size and complexity; as computer capabilities continue to expand and as new techniques are developed.

Where Employed Principally by the Military Services (in and out of uniform) and government, but increasingly by larger profit-making enterprises; some in non-profit and profit-making "think tanks" which serve the Military, government, business, educational institutions, urban redevelopment organizations and others for a fee.

Preparation Bachelor's degree in the physical sciences, supported by coursework in mathematics with emphasis on probability and statistics, or in engineering, economics or related disciplines. Few institutions offer degree in OR as such at present. Many organizations require postgraduate degrees, some even postdoctoral work. Ph.D.'s in some disciplines not mentioned above find work on OR teams.

Advancement Along routes common to those with comparable training doing other kinds of work.

Salaries At levels, varying with level of degree attained, experience, seniority, responsibility carried and field and place of employment, paid persons otherwise engaged with the same type of schooling; one can reach upper-management levels without taking on added responsibilities for unrelated kinds of work. (See Appendix A for 1967-68 benchmark figures.)

For People Who Like to deal, both creatively and pragmatically, with facts and ideas; enjoy analysis and precision but at the same time can reach conclusions and make recommendations from data which may be inconclusive; who want the challenge of tackling problems where the ground rules are few and where, on occasion, no one even knows what the question is, and who set some store by job security.

For More Information write The Operations Research Institute, 420 Lexington Avenue, New York, New York.

OPTOMETRIST

The Work The examination, treatment and protection of the eyes to the extent that this can be done without surgery or drugs (when the latter are needed the opthalmologist or occulist, who are fully trained physicians, take over). An optometrist may supply and fit glasses (which is all the optician does) as well as prescribe them. May teach.

Numbers and Prospects More than 17,000, of whom only 5 per cent are women. Prospects good due to the increasing population, the rising number of elderly people, the increasing incidence of eyestrain and the greater general concern for health. Excellent opportunities in smaller communities and in the southern states.

Where Employed Eighty per cent in private practice; the rest work for other optometrists, in hospitals and health clinics, for the Military Services, in government agencies and in industry, particularly for optical instrument manufacturers. Concentrated in large cities and industrial areas. A few teach.

Preparation A minimum of five years (the figure is climbing) of post-high school training, including two years of pre-vocational coursework and the rest concentrated in optometry. A license is required in all states issuance of which is based on graduation from recognized school and a state examination. Bachelor's degree is called Doctor of Optometry or Bachelor of Science in Optometry.

Advancement By joining an established optometrist as associate, or buying a practice, or opening an office; a good location is important; also to senior staff positions or supervision if employed by others.

Salaries When employed by others, at levels, varying with seniority, experience, responsibility carried and field and place of employment, paid to persons with Liberal Arts Bachelor's degrees; one can reach middle-management levels without taking on responsibilities for unrelated kinds of work; the self-employed can make very comfortable livings, though establishing a practice may take a long time. (See Appendix A for 1967-68 benchmark figures.)

For People Who Like working precisely; enjoy dealing with people in a serving relationship; want to work with tangibles, see the results of their work frequently, and prefer a moderate work pace. Values associated with self-employment as an optometrist are discussed on pages 109-114.

For More Information see Appendix C or write American Optometric Association, 7000 Chippewa Street, St. Louis, Missouri 63119.

PERSONNEL WORKER

The Work Is concerned with matters bearing directly and indirectly on the effectiveness of the manpower in any organization. A personnel worker may be involved in one or more of the following activities: recruiting, testing, hiring, orientation, firing, exit interviewing, job classification, wage and salary admnistration, promotion screening, counseling, training and other developmental work, record keeping, administration of credit unions and of health, welfare, safety, incentive, suggestion and retirement programs, with labor relations, employee recreational, social and recognitional activity, management-employee relations, morale building, house organs, hearing grievances, improving physical working conditions and research. He, or she, may teach in one or more of these areas. The work is also described as employee, industrial or labor relations.

Numbers and Prospects About 100,000, of whom three-quarters are men. The proportion of women is increasing and is concentrated in organizations where women employees are most numerous, i.e., telephone companies, banks, department stores, insurance company home offices and some government agencies. Prospects excellent as work force continues to grow, management increasingly recognizes that manpower is its key resource and personnel techniques become increasingly sophisticated.

Where Employed   More than 50 per cent by private profit-making enterprises; a large proportion of the rest by government at all levels; some in the Military Services, education (both as administrators and teachers) and non-profit organizations. Others are self-employed as employment agency proprietors or "executive recruiters" (whose number has grown tremendously in past decade).

Preparation   Bachelor's degree not essential but becoming increasingly important to success. A large number of institutions now offer specific coursework. Psychology, sociology, business administration and English also considered "pre-vocational," but almost any curriculum acceptable. Postgraduate degree important only for specialist, in testing or employee communications or labor relations, for instance, in larger organizations. Many gravitate into personnel work from other jobs.

Advancement   To the vice-presidential level a possibility in most organizations; or into self-employment.

Salaries   At levels, varying with level of degree attained, seniority, experience, responsibility carried and field and place of employment, paid persons otherwise engaged with liberal arts schooling; one can reach top-management levels without taking on added responsibilities for unrelated kinds of work; independent "executive recruiters" can earn handsomely. (See Appendix A for 1967-68 benchmark figures.)

For People Who   Want to deal with others in a helping relationship and as professional colleagues; enjoy a feeling of being in control of others to a point; have the high tolerance for ambiguity needed by anyone who is heavily involved with human nature; like to plan and organize and to see the results of their efforts frequently; prefer a fast pace and do not object to frequent long hours; and value job security. Values associated with self-employment in personnel work are discussed on pages 109-114.

For More Information see Appendix C or write The American Society for Personnel Administration, 52 East Bridge Street, Berea, Ohio 44017.

PHARMACIST

The Work Is primarily that of the "corner druggist" familiar to all, but a pharmacist may also do research including pharmacology (the study of the effect of drugs on the body) and pharmacognosy (the study of drugs derived from plant and animal sources), or teach or sell. May work long hours and at nights and weekends. Much standing.

Numbers and Prospects Over 125,000 licensed, of whom about 8 per cent are women; 33 per cent of those in hospitals, however, are women. Prospects good (though drugs increasingly come pre-mixed) because of population growth, the increasing use of drugs in medicine and treatment, and expanding health care plans.

Where Employed Ninety per cent in drug stores, one half of them either owners of or partners in the enterprise; the rest in hospitals, such government agencies as the Public Health Service, the pharmaceutical industry as researchers (400 new drugs each year) or "detail men," (who sell to and consult with drug buyers), and in nursing, medical and pharmacy schools.

Preparation Five to six post-high school years, including two of pre-vocational studies and the remainder vocational training. A license is necessary in all states, based on graduation from approved school, examination and often a year of internship. Masters and Doctorates increasingly necessary for research and teaching.

Advancement Usually from post as assistant in drugstore to partnership or ownership; those employed by others may rise through the routes typical of comparable fields of employment.

Salaries For those employed by others, at levels, varying with level of degree attained, seniority, experience, responsibility carried and field and place of employment, paid persons otherwise engaged with a Bachelor's degree in accounting; one can reach middle-management levels without taking on added responsibilities for unrelated kinds of work; the self-employed can earn handsomely. (See Appendix A for 1967-68 benchmark figures.)

For People Who Like orderliness and precision and dealing with tangibles; want to see the results of their work frequently; and prefer associating with others as co-workers or in a serving relationship. Values associated with self-employment in pharmacy are discussed on pages 109-114.

For More Information see Appendix C or write The American Pharmaceutical Association, 2215 Constitution Avenue, N.W., Washington, D.C. 20037.

PHYSICIAN AND OSTEOPATH

The Work *Physicians* are concerned with the treatment and prevention of human diseases, disorders and injuries; they make diagnoses and take appropriate action through surgery, therapy, or the prescription of medication. A physician may engage in family practice (today this usually means internal medicine — as contrasted with general practice — and identification of non-internal problems to be referred to other specialists) or in one or more of some three dozen specialties, among them obstetrics, gynecology, psychiatry, pediatrics, gerentology, radiology, anesthesiology, opthamology, pathology, proctology, orthopedics, dermatology and surgery, some of these containing specialties within them. He may simultaneously or exclusively work in the fields of community and environmental health, industrial medicine, administration or rehabilitation, or teach, do research or write. *Osteopaths* concentrate on manipulation of the body to cure disorders of the bones, muscles, nerves and blood vessels, though in three-quarters of the states they are also permitted to practice all aspects of medicine and surgery when appropriately qualified.

Numbers and Prospects Close to 300,000 physicians and about 12,000 osteopaths, of whom 7 per cent in both cases are women. Prospects in both cases tremendous (in the case of physicians there is an estimated shortage of 50,000 today and a need for 140,000 more by 1975). The growing population, fast increasing public concern about health, the growing number of Federal and other pre-paid health care plans and the shortage, present and prospective, of training facilities (less than 8000 physicians are being graduated annually) account for the situation.

Where Employed About 60 per cent of *physicians* are in private practice, alone or with colleagues; over 15 per cent are staff members, residents and interns in hospitals, public, private and military; the rest are employed by medical schools, government at all levels and business and industrial concerns, and by such private, non-profit organizations as Planned Parenthood-World Population. Concentrated in populous areas, thus many smaller communities are undermanned. The proportion of those in specialties expected to rise from a third to two-thirds in next decade; the present small proportion in research is increasing even faster. Ninety-five per cent of all *osteopaths* are in private practice, half of them in Michigan, Pennsylvania, Missouri, Ohio and Texas.

Preparation For both physicians and osteopaths, occasionally three but almost always four college years, including, without exception, coursework in biology, physics, and chemistry; followed by four years in medical or oseopathic school, the last two including much on-the-job training in a hospital. A degree is granted upon passing a state examination and, with few exceptions, at least a year of internship in a hospital is required. To enter a specialty, one must have from one to four additional years of hospital residency in one's chosen field and two years of practice to achieve recognition by the national board in that specialty. Medical school admission requirements vary in a number of ways, but all schools require the taking of the Medical College Admissions Test. There is room in medical schools today for only half (about 9000 each year) of the applicants; a similar situation obtains in schools of osteopathy.

Advancement By the routes peculiar to the kind of practice one undertakes.

Salaries For those employed by others, at levels, varying with experience, seniority, responsibility carried and field and place of employment, paid scientists and engineers with doctorates; one can reach upper-middle management levels without taking on added responsibilities for unrelated kinds of work. The private practitioner faces at least several years of bare subsistence living, in all probability, before moving toward levels that can be handsome and are basically controlled by his location, competence and reputation. (See Appendix A for 1967-68 benchmark figure).

For People Who Such is the diversity of the kinds of work that a physician may undertake that the practice of medicine in general can be said to surely satisfy only two values, a desire to be of obvious service to society and for job security, the latter a factor of the acute shortage of qualified practitioners. Values associated with self-employment in medicine are discussed on pages 109-114.

For More Information see Appendix C or write The American Medical Association, 535 North Dearborn Street, Chicago, Illinois 60601, or The American Osteopathic Association, 212 East Ohio Street, Chicago, Illinois 60611.

PILOT (CIVILIAN)

The Work Flies an airplane, usually from one place to another, and may, in addition, have some responsibility for comfort of passengers, mechanical soundness or testing of the equipment, reporting, photography and surveillance of land beneath him; never flies eight hours a day and may not be at controls more than 50 hours a month; ground duties may consume considerable time; employments depends not only on skill but continuously superior physical and emotional health; in some employments there are restrictions on a pilot's physical dimensions.

Numbers and Prospects Over 80,000 fly planes for a living; almost none of them women. The number will increase only slowly, and largely outside the scheduled airlines, where larger planes will balance off the increased passenger traffic, though there will be substantial replacement needs. Greatest new opportunities in air taxi and business flying.

Where Employed More than a third by business concerns (who own some 20,000 private craft), about a third by scheduled airlines, the rest in crop dusting, non-scheduled flying, air taxi services, testing, patrolling, inspecting (pipelines employe 2000), examining other pilots, photography and teaching.

Preparation Minimum requirement is high school education, but increasing emphasis on preliminary non-vocational college training; largely a matter, in any event, of flight, engineering, navigation, instrument and similar formal schooling, wherever obtained, plus experience, leading to qualification for taking and passing increasingly rigorous examinations. Physical condition always an issue.

Advancement On scheduled airlines from co-pilot (preferred age mid to late twenties) to captain, which usually takes five to ten years. Elsewhere, depends on competence and good luck; most commercial pilots fly until retirement at about 60, but some move into administrative positions with airlines or aircraft manufacturers, or turn to self-employment.

Salaries Start for qualified commercial pilot at lower-middle management level; senior airline captains at top middle-management levels (and they may retire at full pay at 60 if they have long enough service); others can reach earnings comparable to the upper end of the Federal Civil Service scale; competence and luck determine earnings of entrepreneurs. (See Appendix A for 1967-68 benchmark figures.)

For People Who Are naturally precise; enjoy dealing with tangibles and getting prompt results; like to be in control and their own masters; want the challenge of omnipresent danger and uncertainty; and are largely unconcerned with security. Values associated with self-employment in this line are discussed on pages 109-114.

For More Information see Appendix C or write The International Airlines Pilots Association, 55th Street and Cicero Avenue, Chicago, Illinois 60600.

PODIATRIST (CHIROPODIST)

The Work The diagnosing and treatment, by surgery, drugs, physical therapy and the prescription of special shoes and other corrective devices, of diseases and deformities of the feet. Major foot problems, especially those connected with other parts of the body, are referred to physicians. A practitioner may specialize in podopediatrics (the foot problems of children), or orthopedics (bone, muscle and joint disorders). May teach. Regular hours with few house calls.

Numbers and Prospects   Almost 9000, of whom some 5 per cent are women. Substantial increases expected as population grows, especially proportion of the elderly among whom the incidence of foot disorders is highest, and as concern for health and preventive treatment generally increases. Local popularity of the profession is a factor.

Where Employed   Great majority in private practice; the rest in hospitals, the Military Services, private and government health agencies. A few are employed by shoe manufacturers. Some teach or do research. Concentrated in large cities and populous states.

Preparation   Six post-high school years, including two of general pre-vocational college study, two of formal podiatric study and two of clinical work to graduate (Doctor of Podiatrics or of Podiatric Medicine). A license is required in all states, granted to those who pass an examination and, in some states, a year of internship.

Advancement   Directly into self-employment through purchase of a practice, by hanging out one's own shingle or by entering into partnership with an established practitioner or, indirectly, through initial employment by such a practitioner. If employed by others, to senior staff or administrative positions.

Salaries   For those employed by others, at levels, varying with seniority, experience, responsibility carried and field and place of employment, paid persons otherwise engaged with four-year liberal arts degrees; eventual upper-middle management level earnings possible for the self-employed. Acquiring a reputation and clientele against the heavy competition typical of populous areas may take considerable time. (See Appendix for 1967-68 benchmark figures.)

For People Who   Like working with tangibles and seeing the results of their efforts often; have a propensity for precision; want to deal with people in a serving relationship; and prefer an unhurried work pace. Values associated with self-employment in this work are discussed on pages 109-114.

For More Information see Appendix C or write The American Podiatrics Assn., 3301 16th Street, N.W., Washington, D.C. 20010.

PRODUCTION MANAGER

The Work The combining of men, machines and materials in manufacturing concerns to convert blueprints into goods ready for sale. Includes the purchasing of raw materials, parts, tools and machinery, hiring of workers, training and supervision of plant workforce usually through foremen, and continuing attention to plant safety, layout, design and work scheduling. A production manager institutes time and motion studies as needed; sets up quality and cost control procedures; participates in decisions on pay scales, hours and working conditions and in labor negotiations if plant is organized. He is responsible for packaging the end product and often for arranging for its shipment, for record-keeping and for organizing suggestion and other incentive systems. Highly automated machinery is increasingly used in this work. End product may be in one or more of the following manufacturing fields: food, tobacco, textiles, apparel, lumber and wood, furniture and fixtures, pulp and paper, printing and publishing, chemicals, rubber, leather, petroleum and coal products, stone, clay and glass, primary metals, fabricated metals, machinery, transportation equipment and instruments. Sometimes called "plant," "works" or "manufacturing" manager.

Numbers and Prospects About 300,000, of whom very few are women. Prospects are tied directly to growth of business and industry with trends in some industries towards larger and larger plants balanced off by moves in others to decentralize manufacturing operations.

Where Employed In each of the country's more than 300,000 self-sufficient manufacturing plants.

Preparation Generally a Bachelor's degree, usually in industrial or other engineering disciplines, business management or a field related to the product (chemistry in the industrial chemical business, for instance). There is still some possibility of working up through the ranks without such a degree; extended on-the-job experience and training normally necessary; jobs are occasionally filled by transfers from other departments such as sales, research and development or finance.

Advancement   To management of larger plants in same company or elsewhere or of a number of plants; can lead, also, to top overall management posts.

Salaries   At middle to upper-middle management levels, varying with experience, seniority, responsibility carried and field and place of employment; academic degree level attained and discipline studied not a matter of great consequence. (See Appendix A for 1967-68 figures on engineers, business administration majors and others with relevant schooling.)

For People Who   Like to deal with tangibles and to see the results of their work frequently; enjoy control over others and a substantial degree of autonomy; like to organize and plan; have a liking for detail and precision; and thrive on a lively work pace.

For More Information write The National Association of Manufacturers, 277 Park Avenue, New York.

PUBLIC RELATIONS WORKER

The Work   The presenting of a company or industry or sometimes a person to the public in the most favorable possible light. Concerned more with employer's reputation than the excellence of a product or service supplied. Among other things a public relations man writes newspaper stories, speeches and radio and TV materials, edits house organs and annual reports, lays out brochures, posters and displays, cultivates the good will of all varities of media, arranges anniversary celebrations, new facility openings and other promotional events, sets up convention exhibits, makes speeches, attends meetings alone or as a member of his employer's entourage, entertains people of consequence to his employer, bones up on the facts about various sections of the public and their opinions and interprets these to his employer, develops and recommends (usually directly to top management) long- and short-range "best-foot-forward" programs, fights adverse opinion fires and moves quickly to capitalize on favorable developments. He may travel extensively. His hours are long, irregular and often filled with emergencies. He is generally anonymous so far as the public is concerned; must take his lead from his employer and sometimes must try to put two faces on same set of circumstances. May be liable to sudden dismissal if he miscues.

Numbers and Prospects About 50,000 full time, a quarter of them women who are concentrated in department stores, hospitals, hotels and restaurants. Prospects excellent and tied to population growth, business, government and education expansion, and growing awareness of importance of good public relations.

Where Employed Full- or part-time by all organizations in all fields of work — education, government, profit-making enterprise, non-profit organizations, and the Military Services; may be employee of or be self-employed as consultant (there are over 2000 public relations firms in America, more than half of them in Los Angeles, New York, Chicago and Washington, D.C.).

Preparation A liberal arts degree is usually required, with a major in public administration, journalism, English or the social sciences preferred. Scientific, language or other special training needed for some jobs. Entry into work frequently from employment as a journalist or other "communications" worker. Some Masters' degrees in public relations are granted.

Advancement Usually from specializing in one facet of work to increasingly broad responsibility and eventually, if employed by others, to responsibility for employer's entire program (titles include Vice President-Relations, Director of Information, Director of Communications and others) ; or into self-employment, launching out alone or in partnership or working one's way up in a consulting firm.

Salaries For those employed by others, at levels, varying with level of degree attained, seniority, experience, responsibility carried and field and place of employment, paid persons with liberal arts schooling; one can reach middle-management level without taking on added responsibilities for unrelated kinds of work. Independent consultants can earn in six figures. (See Appendix A for 1967-68 benchmark figures.)

For People Who Have a highly varied value structure; enjoy dealing with people as business associates, social acquaintances, objects of psychological study, and bosses to be studiously served;

who like to see the tangible fruits of their work but can live with ambiguity and uncertainty, since pinpointing results of one's work is often difficult or impossible; who are creative and take pleasure in originating and selling ideas; are self-starters but at the same time can take sometimes unwelcome direction in stride; want a fast, pressureful pace and some freedom to come and go as they wish; and do not lay great store by security. Values associated with self-employment in public relations are discussed on pages 109-114.

For More Information see Appendix C or write The Public Relations Society of America, Inc., 845 Third Avenue, New York, New York 10022.

PURCHASING AGENT

The Work   The purchasing of raw materials, machinery, office supplies, services, and other things necessary to the effective functioning of an organization. Unlike a "buyer," a purchasing agent does not usually purchase finished goods for resale. He is concerned with such things as specifications, quality, prices, inventories, shipping, delivery schedules and packaging.

Number and Prospects   About 150,000, of whom 10 per cent are women. The number is likely to grow at the rate the economy in general does.

Where Employed   By all substantial organizations in all fields. When an organization's annual purchasing volume reaches $100,000, it usually needs one full-time agent; industrial giants employ hundreds of purchasing specialists. Half of all purchasing agents are employed by manufacturing concerns.

Preparation   College training not an absolute essential but there is a growing trend towards requiring a Business or Liberal Arts degree with coursework in economics, statistics, accounting and related subjects and an increasing demand for scientists and engineers as materials and processes become more complex.

Advancement   Either into supervision (Bachelor's degree increasingly important) ; or into non-supervisory specialization; or by moving to larger organization. Does not frequently lead, as can finance and marketing, for instance, directly to top management, though some top management executives have worked for a time as purchasing agents on the way up.

Salaries At levels, varying with level of degree attained, seniority, experience, responsibility carried and field and place of employment, paid persons otherwise engaged with same type of schooling; one can reach middle-management levels without taking on added responsibilities for other kinds of work. (See Appendix A for 1967-68 benchmark figures.)

For People Who Have an analytical turn of mind and a liking for precision, have something of the horse-trader in them, like constant contact with others on a business level (in this case with salesmen, suppliers and the company personnel for whom they buy); who find the role of good servant to others agreeable, can tolerate the "Caesar's wife" posture of probity essential in a job where there is a constant pressure and temptation to play favorites; who want job security, and enjoy dealing with tangibles and seeing the results of their efforts often.

For More Information see Appendix C or write The National Association of Purchasing Agents, 11 Park Place, New York, New York 10007.

RADIO-TELEVISION WORKER

The Work (Only the few kinds of work more or less peculiar to radio-TV will be discussed here. Other radio-TV occupations common to several fields of work — engineering, scientific, artistic, "business," managerial, sales, writing, etc. are covered elsewhere in this book — see chart page 82.) Involves the preparation and production of and sometimes participation in a variety of programs designed to be broadcast. A person may produce an entire program or series of related programs, bringing together all the specialists and the work of specialists needed (as in movie and live theatre production), or may control the daily sequence of programs and advertisements or may be an announcer or do several or all of these things — and others — largely depending on size of station. He may work with tape or film for later rebroadcast or on live productions. The hours of work are frequently abnormal.

Numbers and Prospects About 100,000 full time, including those in jobs peculiar to radio-TV and otherwise; a quarter of the total are women. In addition, some 20,000 people work in the industry part time. There are 14,000 announcers, 85 per cent in radio; the four major radio networks account for perhaps 1000 persons, the three major TV networks for 10,000. Prospects only fair, except in Educational TV and related areas, which have recently received mounting support from government and foundations. While the number of new commercial stations may grow and technology (use of satellites, for instance) will open up new possibilities, increasing use of automation and of taped and filmed programs and of material emanating from network headquarters will prevent corresponding rise in employment. Competition is stiff because this is a "glamour" field of work.

Where Employed   A majority by the more than 6000 radio stations across the country and the rest by the nation's 600 TV stations. Nearly all of them are commercial ventures, often affiliated with newspapers, but some are non-profit, Educational TV and the closed circuit operations of some educational institutions and businesses, for instance. More than half by stations which have 10 employees or fewer; a quarter in New York and California.

Preparation   Bachelor's degree not essential though increasingly in demand; relevant coursework, talent and experience of great importance; the number of colleges and universities offering majors in the field is increasing; the bigger stations and networks draw new employees largely from smaller stations and from related fields such as advertising, the theatre and journalism.

Advancement   From specialization to responsibility for a variety of functions and eventually, possibly, to top management; occasionally to proprietorship of small station.

Salaries   In TV, at level, varying with level of degree attained, seniority, experience, responsibility carried and field and place of employment, paid persons otherwise engaged with same type of schooling; in radio, at a considerably lower level; in both, promotional paths are seldom preset and progress depends heavily on ability, energy and good luck. (See Appendix A for 1967-68 benchmark figures.)

For People Who   Have a strong creative bent; like to work with precision (split-second timing is of the essence in radio-TV) ; enjoy planning and organizing and seeing the fruits of their efforts often; prefer a fast pace; and have little concern for security (the turnover in radio-TV is notably rapid). Values associated with self-employment as such (if one elects this route) are discussed on pages 109-114.

For More Information see Appendix C or write The National Association of Broadcasters, 1771 N Street, N.W., Washington, D.C.

RECREATION WORKER

The Work   Helping others of all ages and conditions to make enjoyable and constructive use of their leisure time. A recreation worker organizes and leads individual and group activities; administers physical, cultural and social programs; may work with therapists of various kinds; may be generalist or may specialize in one kind of recreation or of clientele. Raising money may be a duty. May teach. The hours, especially at start, may be long and irregular.

Numbers and Prospects   Over 45,000 full-time workers and another 100,000 employed part time; one third are women. Prospects excellent due to mounting concern about urban youth, lengthening vacations and briefer work weeks, increasing per capita income, earlier retirement, more travel and growing national attention to physical fitness.

Where Employed   Majority by local government and voluntary agencies, with those served usually the young or the elderly; also by religious organizations, the Federal government (in national parks, for instance), the Military Services, prisons, schools, hospitals and industry; a few teach.

Preparation   Four-year Bachelor's Degree in Recreation, Physical Education or Health (and sometimes Social Work) preferred, but only half of those employed are so qualified; the others have variety of Bachelors' degrees. On-the-job experience weighs heavily; Masters' and Ph.D. degrees often required for teaching and senior administrative posts; large cities may require a year of post-college internship.

Advancement   From staff member into administration and supervision, with experience and higher degrees an important consideration.

Salaries   At level, varying with level of degree attained, seniority, experience, responsibility carried and field and place of employment, paid persons otherwise engaged with liberal arts schooling; one can reach lower-middle management levels without taking on added responsibilities for unrelated kinds of work. (See Appendix A for 1967-68 benchmark figures.)

For People Who   Like working with people in a variety of relationships, as leader, teacher, helper and supervisor and in the difficult role of recruiter, organizer and stimulator of volunteers. Who enjoy control (individual responsibility comes early in the recreation field), planning and organizing; can tolerate a good deal of ambiguity in their environments; like a fast work pace, seeing the results of their work and an opportunity to be creative; want to feel that they are serving society directly; value job security; and find that enthusiasm comes naturally.

For More Information   see Appendix C or write the National Recreation Association, 8 West Eighth Street, New York, New York 10011.

SALES WORKER

A sales worker, as here defined, is one who is actively engaged in efforts to persuade someone else to part with his money, sooner or later, for a product or service he otherwise would not have bought at all or would have bought from someone else, not the "salesperson," to whom others come of their own initiative to buy — in retail store selling alone there are 3,000,000 of the latter. Nor will we be discussing efforts to sell oneself or one's ideas. The only people not so engaged, much or all of the time, privately or professionally, are hermits.

Because the only thing of major consequence that differentiates the work of one sales worker from that of another is the product or service he sells, this is the only section in which selling will be discussed. The alternative, an attempt to cover sales work in describing each kind and field of work in which it takes place, would be noxiously repetitive. Further, something in the nature of an essay seems more appropriate to the subject matter than the usual categorical analysis. As a matter of consistency, however, be it noted that sales workers are to be found in all private profit-making enterprises as employees or proprietors and that they are therefore ubiquitous; that they number more than 2,000,000 full-time workers, of whom a quarter are women, and that the prospects are excellent; that preparation involves learning what is necessary in order to discuss the product or service intelligently with prospective customers and how to be personally attractive to those customers (examinations are also sometimes given); that salesmen advance by selling more and more or by going into management jobs (with a caution to be touched on later); and that salaries range from peanuts to six figures, principally based on preparation and ability, the health of the economy and the desirability and quality of what is sold. As to the *For People Who* category, much of what follows falls into it.

Salesmen are thought of by many collegians as con-men or peddlers or arm-twisters whose business it is to create and fan unneeded wants, who are perpetually on the road, living out of a suitcase, who constantly have doors slammed in their faces, whose hours are odd and filled with the pressures of competition, who can succeed only if adept at eyeball-to-eyeball persuasion, who alternately feast and starve, and who deal largely in insurance, brushes, automobiles, magazines and soap. For this reason employers looking for sales recruits often talk in euphemisms, witness this partial list: manufacturers' representatives, insurance agents and underwriters, real estate brokers, computer technical representatives, advisers and consultants, circulation managers, merchandising managers, marketing managers, product managers, securities and advertising account executives, fund raisers, publishers' representatives, literary agents and drug company detail men. Selling is a principal if not the only business of all of these people.

The perhaps prevailing collegiate concept, *in toto*, rarely squares with the facts today. But the Willie Loman image is not inaccurate to the extent that it suggests that to succeed in sales one must be willing to spend much of his time trying to persuade others in a face-to-face situation to buy what he has to sell (he may or may not face competition from other salesmen or from the potential customer's lack of felt need, or inertia, and reluctance to part with his money) ; and that he can accept the way of life which dependence on the predilections and convenience of others necessarily involves.

A dozen considerations can prompt a person to go into sales. It may be that he enjoys persuading people, or the challenge of the competition invariably to be found, or the fast work pace, or the independence and freedom to come and go as he pleases frequently associated with saleswork, or simply constant contact with people. Or he may have learned that he was good at selling and sees it as his shortest road to riches. Or he may be moved by conviction that his service or product meets an important but unrecognized human need. Again, knowing that aggressive selling is one of the factors which has brought the country to its present level of material well-being (it has been estimated that two-thirds of all farm and factory workers would be jobless if Americans lived at the subsistence level), he may want to be a participant in its on-going contribution. Or he may like it because he can often see the results of his efforts or because of the power the salesman inevitably wields in business, where nothing happens unless something is sold. And one school of thought maintains that most salesmen were rejected as children and are spending their lives trying to compensate.

Whatever the motivation, all successful salesmen have several things in common — and I will be repeating myself in several instances by way of emphasis. They have sufficient self-confidence to take in stride the word "no" which they are bound to hear at least occasionally. They are self-starters. They are more concerned with what the customer wants than what they think he ought to want. They know their product or service and believe in it, and are students of their markets and competition. They work hard. And job security is not a matter of overriding consequence to them.

A word about sales management. The qualities which make a person a good salesman do not necessarily mean effectiveness as a sales manager. Recognizing this, many salesworkers turn down offers to move into management and many others, not recognizing it, are disappointed when they receive no such offers. On the other hand, few people can hope to be promoted into sales management — or top management — who are not adept at selling.

Whether or not what has gone before has produced for the reader a red or green light so far as his or her interest in pursuing sales as a kind of work is concerned, a number of other considerations may be worth exploring. One is one's record to date. How much has one attempted and enjoyed selling himself, his ideas and things to others and how has he fared in these efforts? Another is testing. There are a number of tests which measure one's aptitude. And finally, if the interest is tentatively there but capacity is in question, it should be noted that most employers today conduct extensive training programs for salesmen, initially and along the way, recognizing that salesmanship can be learned — may even be approaching the status of a profession — and that even "born" salesmen will go less far, if anywhere, without entry-level and continued learning.

For More Information see Appendix C or write The Council on Opportunities in Selling, Inc., 630 Third Avenue, New York, N.Y.

SCIENTIST-NATURAL

If the reader's interest is in bionics, paleoecology, etiology, phytochemistry or limnology, he will have to go to his professors or textbooks or the Encyclopedia or the dictionary or the references cited in the Appendix for elucidation. There are hundreds — perhaps thousands — of natural scientific disciplines old and new, and they are proliferating with each passing year as the basic areas — the physical, biological and earth sciences — are further subdivided and as "crosses" between them (and engineering and even with the social sciences) spring up. Here only a rough and rudimentary sketch of natural science (which is concerned with the history, structure and composition of earth's land, interior, oceans and atmosphere, the basic laws of the physical world, the properties of matter and energy and the living things which inhabit the globe) as a kind of work will be possible, with emphasis on the things that these many facets have in common.

The Work Natural scientists, be they physical (physicists, chemists, biochemists, astronomers or other), biological, or earth (geologists, geophysicists, oceanographers, meteorologists or other) are all engaged in one or a combination of activities, including research, development, teaching, consulting, administering, writing, or otherwise applying their special knowledge to the job at hand. If in research, they may be involved in its "pure" aspect or its "applied" aspect or both. The pure scientist is concerned with the discovery of new facts and a better understanding of nature without any expectation or intent that his findings will have practical application. The applied scientist is interested in doing something practical with known facts. He aims at meeting an old or a new need. He does not know whether or not he will succeed, either in coming up with a possible answer or, if he does, whether it will prove to be feasible. Developmental scientists, but more usually engineers, are those who concern themselves with this final step, that is, taking a potentially feasible idea and achieving economical, effective and safe results from its practical use.

Where Employed, Numbers and Prospects In general, "pure" science is pursued almost exclusively in university and governmental settings, though a few companies and non-profit organizations permit their scientific employees to spend some of their time in non-pragmatic investigations if they wish to. Applied scientists are found in all settings — government, education, profit-making and non-profit organizations, the Military Services and self-employment. No figures are available on how many scientists are engaged in each of these kinds of research or in other applications of their knowledge. They are, however, available on the numbers in each of the major disciplines, and, in general, on who employs them. The following list gives this information approximately:

Astronomers — 1,100 (almost no women). Half in colleges and universities, half in a variety of settings.

Biochemists — 10,000 (15 per cent women). Great majority, split about evenly, in industry and colleges and universities.

Biologists — 145,000 (70,000 in biology as such, 45,000 in agricultural science, 30,000 in medical field — 11 per cent women in various fields). Half in colleges and universities, most of balance evenly divided between government and industry.

Chemists — 120,000 (5 per cent women). Three-quarters in industry.

Geologists — 16,000 (few women). Most in industry.

Geophysicists — 6,000 (few women). Most in industry.

Meteorologists — 7,000 (few women). About half in uniform with Air Force, most of the rest in U.S. Weather Bureau.

Oceanographers — 3,000 (few women). Three-quarters in government and colleges and universities.

Physicists — 40,000 (3 per cent women). The great majority, split about evenly, in industry and in colleges and universities.

In regard to prospects, the demand is expected to be greatest for physical scientists and least for earth scientists, excepting oceanographers, with biologists falling somewhere in between. But it should be stressed that all types, and particularly those with doctorates, will be in short, in some cases, critically short supply into the foreseeable future.

Preparation   The natural scientist with no more than a Bachelor's degree will usually find that he cannot get into "pure" or "applied" research, except as a technical assistant to persons with advanced degrees. In general, he must put his knowledge to immediate use in such occupations as sub-college level teaching, conservation work or development activity in industry. The same is true to a lesser degree of the holder of a Master's degree. Only the holder of the doctorate has all options open to him.

It may be worthwhile to note that, while, as a man pursues higher and higher degrees he will become more and more specialized, he will find — such is the basic unity of nature — that he will continue to be able to work with scientists in other disciplines and, further, that all must have mastered to a point a variety of common tools such as mathematics in order to progress. It is also worth pointing out that because scientific knowledge is accumulating at a progressively rapid rate, no natural scientist can long perform adequately, whatever his degree level and particular activity, unless he reads and studies constantly in his own field, in those allied to it and in science generally.

Advancement   Along the avenues common to non-scientists, be it in teaching, government service, the Military, self-employment, industry or non-profit organizations. Scientists, however, more than most other kinds of workers, look on simple recognition for accomplishment: prizes, professional society officerships, etc., from their colleagues and the public as a principal criterion of success. *Salaries* See Appendix A for 1967-68 benchmark figures. Two footnotes may be useful. First, among natural scientists, those in physical science usually have a small edge over those in the other branches. Second, top earners in all branches are usually those who have been willing to take on managerial responsibilities and have proved themselves competent managers.

For People Who Like work which demands precision and an analytical turn of mind and who have little tolerance for ambiguity. Because of the diversity of the roles that a scientist can play, no other values can be said to be generally relevant. Values associated with self-employment in this work are discussed on pages 109-114.

For More Information see Appendix C.

SCIENTIST-SOCIAL

Although social scientists — and we will here include economists, historians, sociologists, psychologists, anthropologists, geographers and political scientists — differ in terms of what their interests are, where they are principally employed and the anticipated future demand for them, most have a number of things in common. We will start with the similarities and conclude, considering each discipline separately, with the differences.

The Bachelor's Degree The social sciences are generally considered to be among the "liberal arts." One who has majored in one of them, therefore, is in the same position relative to his career at the point of graduation as are other Bachelor of Arts graduates. (See daggers in chart on pages 82-83.) He can teach social studies or in his specialty (to the extent it is offered and he has whatever teacher training is required) up through the secondary school level. He is equipped to undertake a wide variety of entry-level jobs in government, business and non-profit organizations. He can undertake officer training in the Military Services. And he can go on to graduate school in his field or to those professional schools which do not, as for instance does medical school, require specific undergraduate coursework. He has, in general, foreclosed only scientific and engineering careers and careers requiring arts and sciences graduate work outside his field. He is not yet, however, with two possible exceptions, a professional social scientist.

Higher Degrees Excepting economics and geography, to "practice" as a social scientist one must have a Master's degree in his field, at the very least, and more usually a doctorate. In addition, in some cases, notably in clinical and counseling psychology, he must pass an examination set by the state to obtain a license and an internship may also be required for practice. It might be added here that while future demand is expected to vary as between the social science disciplines, as will appear later, in all areas it is likely to be lively for those holding the doctorate. And two footnotes: most practicing social scientists today, possibly excepting historians and geographers, must be conversant with computers; and constant reading and study throughout one's worklife are vital in these constantly changing disciplines.

The Work Social scientists principally teach and do research. They may also consult, write, administer, maintain private practices or apply their knowledge daily as workers in such fields as urban development, industrial relations, marketing and international affairs.

Where Employed Social scientists in one or more of the seven disciplines are employed by government, business, non-profit organizations, the Military Services and education, and in most of the disciplines some are self-employed, principally as consultants or writers. The fast-growing field of urban and regional development is using increasing numbers in all disciplines.

Advancement Along the paths, within one's particular field of work, common to people in comparable callings. It should be noted, however, that social scientists, like other scientists and more than most other kinds of workers, consider simple recognition for accomplishment, in terms of prizes, professional society officerships and so on, from colleagues and the public as a principal criterion of success.

Salaries At levels, varying with level of degree attained, seniority, experience, responsibility carried and field and place of employment, paid persons with liberal arts schooling; psychologists who practice as clinicians and counselors independently and independent writers and consultants in other social science areas can earn substantial incomes. (See Appendix A for 1967-68 benchmark figures.)

For People Who Enjoy working painstakingly and analytically and prefer a substantial degree of independence of thought and action. Otherwise the roles social scientists can play are so varied that no value can be said to be relevant across the board.

By Discipline:

Anthropologists Are concerned with primitive and civilized man — his origins, physical characteristics, customs, languages, traditions, material possessions and social and religious beliefs and practices; number about 2700, of whom 20 per cent are women. The great majority work in colleges and universities; some are employed by government, especially in museums. Prospects excellent for those with doctorate, particularly in college teaching field where student interest is growing rapidly.

Economists Are concerned with distribution and use of world's not unlimited supplies of land, raw materials, manpower and productive capacity; number over 20,000, of whom 14 per cent are women; the large majority about equally divided between colleges and universities and industry; most of rest in government. Prospects good including Bachelors with economics majors who wish to go straight to work.

Geographers Study physical characteristics of the earth and relate them to patterns of human habitation and employment. Number over 3,500 of whom 10 per cent are women; concentrated in colleges and universities, but with substantial numbers in various government settings. Prospects favorable, especially for those with advanced degrees.

Historians Study the past and often interpret the present and future from their findings; may specialize in a country or region, or in a particular period of time, or in the historical developments in such fields as economics or science. Number about 9000, a small fraction of whom are women; great majority employed by colleges and universities; most of rest by the Federal government. Prospects are moderate for advanced degree holders and largely in academe.

Political Scientists Study the structure and theory of governments, past and present. Number about 9000 of whom 9 per cent are women; majority work in academe; most of rest in government. Prospects excellent for advanced degree holders, in both academe and government.

Psychologists Study the intellectual, emotional, aptitudinal and personality aspects of human beings and frequently work full or part time counseling or treating private or institutional clients; number about 27,000 of whom small fraction are women; a third employed by colleges and universities; remainder concentrated in government and school settings, in industry and in non-profit organizations. Prospects excellent for advanced degree holders including the Master's.

Sociologists Study the interaction between groups of people, past and present; great majority work in colleges and universities. Number about 5000, of whom about 10 per cent are women; some in government, non-profit organizations, and industry, frequently teamed with other social scientists. Prospects excellent for advanced degree holders, including the Master's.

For More Information see Appendix C.

SECRETARY

The word "secretary" has more rubber content than any other in the lexicon of occupational titles and at the same time is nailed down along its stretch with more stereotypical images in people's minds. At the one end is the image of the last and fast becoming vestigial precursor to the computer, a coffee-break-oriented, amoral robot in a skirt who transforms executive decisions into tidy letters and infallible files from just after nine to just before five. At the other is the power-behind-the-throne, an anonymous amanuensis who directs the entire operation through a combination of brilliance, aggressiveness, guile and the capacity to duplicate the boss's signature, while he practices golf shots in the inner office — if he isn't, in fact, all the while down at Palm Beach.

Most college-trained women are victims of the vestigial robot image. Some even go so far as to refuse to learn typing and shorthand — which the power-behind-the-throne had to have to get started — because they are afraid of getting stuck as robots. Most men and women in positions of importance, on the other hand, will pay a king's ransom to get an authentic power-behind-the-throne, even if they aren't golfers.

The point is that a thinking secretary, one to whom an executive can confidently delegate a fascinating variety of editorial, planning, research and administrative work and who, at the same time, can handle and stomach stenographic chores, is a pearl beyond price — or at least she can come close to naming her own.

And many's the professional woman, in publishing, advertising, banking, personnel work, general administration, museum work and many other fields who started out as a thinking secretary and would never have arrived if she had been "above" such a start.

SECURITIES WORKER

The Work Is concerned with stocks, bonds, mutual shares, notes and other types of securities; Worker may buy and sell as directed by many different clients or on behalf of a single employer. He may analyze the "market" as a whole, or only particular companies or industries, or security "portfolios," again, for many different clients or for a single employer. He may advise individuals or organizations on their investments, participate in the underwriting ("floating") of new issues of securities, or engage in several of these activities.

Numbers and Prospects No figures, except for securities salesmen are available. There are about 100,000 of these (few of them women), 60 per cent of whom are employed by investment firms and are largely concentrated in a few of the largest ones. An additional 30,000 people sell securities part time, often mutual fund shares. Prospects for all security workers excellent as national income grows, individuals become more and more interested in investing (25,000,000 shareholders anticipated by 1970), mutual funds and the investment clubs increase and business expands. *Where Employed* By government at all levels (the "floating" of municipal bonds, for instance) ; by investment banks (underwriting of a new stock issue for a company planning expansion, for instance) ; by bank trust departments (handling the portfolios of clients) ; by savings banks (investing the savings) ; by mutual funds (investing assets and selling shares) ; by brokerage firms and dealers (buying and selling for customers) ; by insurance companies (investing assets) ; by business organizations (attending to their stocks and bonds) ; by universities (investing their endowment funds) ; on the various security exchanges (as a "trader," for instance) ; and by investment firms (as registered representatives, account executives or customer's men, selling the firm's and their own services to new customers). Most of these organizations employ analysts and advisers or contract for such assistance from outside consultants even if this is not their principal business. New York City is the financial and investment capital of the world.

Preparation A four-year college degree virtually essential and some investment organizations want Masters in Business Administration; liberal arts or business curricula preferred but major of no great consequence, providing one has a good head for figures; much of training takes place on the job. Investment houses often prefer to hire people who have had several years experience in other business jobs; personality and appearance are important in sales and counseling work.

Advancement Through normal channels in larger organizations with top posts clear possibilities; able and persuasive salesmen can rise very rapidly in investment firms and this can lead to a partnership or setting up as an independent.

Salaries In large firms, at levels, varying with level of degree attained, seniority, experience, responsibility carried and place of employment, paid persons otherwise engaged with liberal arts schooling; in smaller firms, initial salaries at lower levels; those who engage in selling on commission can become among the highest earners in the country; knowledge acquired on the job can make one's personal investments exceptionally successful. (See Appendix A for 1967-68 benchmark figures.)

For People Who Combine a capacity for precision with a high tolerance for uncertainty, enjoy working with people as customers and professional colleagues, and want to be able to see the results of their work frequently; who like a fast pace, the challenge of sharp competition with their peers, and considerable freedom to come and go — in jobs where selling is involved — and who are unconcerned with job security. Values associated with self-employment in this work are discussed on pages 109-114.

For More Information see Appendix C or write The New York Stock Exchange, 11 Wall Street, New York, New York 10005.

SOCIAL WORKER

The Work The prevention or alleviation of personal, family and community distress caused by such factors as poverty, unemployment, illness, inadequate housing, broken homes, limited recreation space, family maladjustments and individual occupational, physical, mental and emotional handicaps. The majority of social workers are caseworkers, dealing with persons and families individually and frequently in their homes; others do social group work, activity designed to prevent social ills and concentrated principally on young people in underprivileged neighborhoods, or community organization work, in the planning and developing of programs and in the recruiting and training of lay leaders and workers. Some also teach and administer at various levels; many work part time. Special fields include family service, child welfare, adoption, medical-social work, psychiatric counseling, probation and parole work, gerentological work and rehabilitation.

Numbers and Prospects About 155,000, 60 per cent of whom are women; the proportion of men is increasing. Prospects excellent as the nation's inner city and urban decay problems become more acerbated, as public concern about these problems grows and as funds become increasingly available.

Where Employed Sixty per cent by Federal, State and local governments; most of the rest by private, non-profit organizations; some by colleges and universities; a few by a new phenomenon, private, profit-making consulting enterprises which specialize in social welfare problems.

Preparation Master's degree, following broad liberal arts college training, necessary to full-fledged professionalism and advancement; teachers and top administrators frequently hold doctorates. An acute shortage of social workers, however, makes it possible to find a job with a Bachelor's degree in social work, sociology, anthropology, psychology or a related area but without further training opportunities for promotion are likely to be limited.

Advancement From staff membership into supervision of growing breadth; governmental welfare department heads usually are former social workers.

Salaries At levels, varying with level of degree attained, seniority, experience, responsibility carried and field and place of employment, paid persons otherwise engaged with liberal arts schooling; one can reach middle-management levels without taking on added responsibilities for unrelated kinds of work. (See Appendix A for 1967-68 benchmark figures.)

For People Who Enjoy being helpful to others and having a sense of being of direct service to society; like to see the results of their efforts frequently but at the same time can wait patiently when necessary; are happiest with a fairly high degree of autonomy; prefer a rapid work pace and the challenge of continually being confronted with problems which defy easy resolution; who like to plan and direct, and who desire job security.

For More Information see Appendix C or write The National Commission for Social Work Careers, 345 East 46th Street, New York, New York 10017.

SYSTEMS ANALYST

The Work The attempt to discover the best solutions, in terms of cost and effectiveness, to scientific, engineering, procedural, logistical, processing, information-gathering and like problems. A systems analyse studies alternatives, capabilities, reliabilities, costs, benefits, sequences, schedules and their interrelations to determine how employer can get most for his money; uses computers extensively and such techniques as simulation, inventory and demand theory and linear programing; designs problems for computer solution which are then translated into machine's language by programers. The dividing lines between systems analysts, sometimes called "software" specialists, computer scientists, called "hardware" specialists, and operations researchers (the latter two kinds of work are described elsewhere in this book) are not always distinct.

Numbers and Prospects About 60,000, including very few women. Prospects as good as, if not better than, those for any other profession, as decision makers in all fields of work learn what systems analysis can do for them and as computers become more numerous and sophisticated and capable of solving a broader range of problems.

Where Employed Mainly in the insurance, manufacturing, banking and wholesale and retail businesses; some in the Federal government, in urban redevelopment settings and in the Military Services; a few in universities and as independent fee-charging consultants.

Preparation In this, a very new field, no set patterns have developed. Companies are offering low five-figure salaries for people with high school diplomas and four or five years experience. Increasingly, degree at least to Bachelor's level in a physical science, engineering, accounting, statistics, mathematics or business is preferred and, in some cases, an advanced degree for senior positions. Computer programing training and experience almost always essential; continuing study and training on the job necessary as new techniques and computers are developed.

Advancement From programer or analyst trainee to junior analyst to senior analyst and on into supervision of team of analysts or management of broader range of functions; or into private consulting.

Salaries At levels, varying with level of degree attained, seniority, experience, responsibility carried and field and place of employment, paid persons with schooling in the sciences; one can reach middle-management levels without taking on added responsibilities for unrelated kinds of work. (See Appendix A for 1967-68 benchmark figures.)

For People Who Enjoy being precise and have an analytical turn of mind; like an opportunity to be creative, to deal with ideas and to see the results of their efforts frequently; prefer a measured work pace and businesslike contacts with others; and set considerable store by job security. Values associated with self-employment in this work are discussed on pages 109-114.

For More Information see Appendix C or write The American Federation of Information Processing Sciences, 211 East 43rd Street, New York, New York 10017.

TEACHER-PROFESSOR

Since all to whom this book is addressed have first-hand knowledge of the outwardness of teaching as a kind of work, from kindergarten into the college and university level, there will be no discussion of this aspect of the profession. Nor will there be comment on "Numbers and Prospects" since this was touched on in the discussion of education as a field of work on page 92; or on "Where Employed" since this is obvious, or will be from the following description of "The Work." Here, then, the stress will be on the non-apparent and elsewhere undiscussed aspects of teaching.

The Work The great majority of teachers are engaged in work familiar to all. An increasing proportion, however, are occupied with one or more of such less apparent activities, full or part time, as: teaching in schools for adults, open to the public or set up by business organizations for their employees, or in institutions such as prisons or the Veterans Administration; teaching on Educational TV; team teaching; working with the emotionally, intellectually and physically deprived; teaching at vocational institutions; conducting "extension" courses away from campus; working in the burgeoning "learning industry," composed of business concerns, largely in publishing and communications, which are developing sophisticated teaching aids and doing research in support of education; specializing in the development of tests and doing testing; doing research in the content, aims and processes of education; working on the development of audio-visual aids to teaching; engaging in "cooperative education," that is, teaching teachers at a nearby college or university as well as teaching pre-college young people; and conducting experiments in connection with such new developments as programed learning, speed reading, ungraded curricula and the possibility that teacher expectations have as much to do with learning as pupil competence.

Preparation   Up through the secondary level, a Bachelor's degree is a minimum requirement; to teach in public schools, coursework must include the subjects and practice teaching required by a particular state (and states vary) for certification. Private schools up to this level may not require "pre-vocational" courses. At the college and university level, Master's degree in subject to be taught is the minimum requirement with, in some cases, additional courses in teaching techniques. Assistant professorships in most, and full professorships in virtually all, institutions of higher education go only to Ph.D.'s. Substantial contributions in research are essential to promotion in many such institutions.

Advancement   Usually through fairly rigid, pre-set routes, based on seniority, additional courses taken or degrees attained, willingness to undertake non-teaching duties and, in some instances, research and scholarship attainments. Capacity to teach well is still too difficult to measure to be a major factor in most settings. An exception to the steady, pre-ordained path is at the instructor-assistant-professor level in colleges and universities, where competition can be stiff and one either goes up or out after several years.

Salaries   Appendix A includes typical figures for all levels, as of 1967-68. In weighing these figures, a number of things should be kept in mind. First, the "fringe benefits" enjoyed by teachers compare favorably with those in all other fields of work. Second, the discrepancy usual between teaching and business salaries is recognized and accepted in most communities. Teachers are not expected to "compete" where money is concerned. And where, as in a "college town," they predominate, they determine the levels of adequacy in connection with entertaining, education of children, dress, travel and so on. Third, most teachers have the summer off and many use it to supplement their regular earnings. Also, at the college and university levels particularly, many bring in added dollars, both in and out of term, by consulting, lecturing and writing textbooks.

For People Who   (Aside from the values noted in the chapter on

Education) like to deal with people, especially younger people, in the role of a helper, persuader, controller and counselor. There are no other common denominators so far as values are concerned. Teaching and related jobs, depending on exactly what one is doing, can satisfy or may frustrate any of the values discussed in this book.

For More Information see Appendix C or write The Office of Education, Department of Health, Education and Welfare, Washington, D.C. 20202, or The National Education Association, 1201 16th Street, N.W., Washington, D.C. 20036, or The American Council on Education, 1785 Massachusetts Avenue, N.W., Washington, D.C. 20036.

THERAPIST AND RELATED

The kinds of work covered here are physical (and corrective) therapy, occupational (and manual arts, education, recreational) therapy, speech pathology and audiology. These disciplines, all supportive to the physician, differ in the problems to which they address themselves but otherwise have much in common and are therefore treated as a group.

Physical Therapists Are concerned with muscle, nerve, joint and bone deformities, injuries and disabilities, using exercises, mechanical apparatus, massage heat, light and water treatment.

Occupational Therapists Are concerned with the whole range of physical, mental and emotional sicknesses, disabilities and injuries for which individually prescribed recreational, creative, handicraft and educational activities may be helpful in bringing about self-sufficiency, recovery and eventual ability to earn a living.

Speech Pathologists Are concerned with the diagnosis and treatment of speech defects, whatever the cause. They use exercises, counseling and mechanical and electrical equipment to effect cures.

Audiologists Are concerned with the diagnosis and treatment of hearing defects and use techniques similar to those used by speech pathologists.

Numbers and Prospects About 12,500 physical therapists, 6500 occupational therapists and 15,000 speech pathologists and audiologists. At least 75 per cent of practitioners in each discipline are women but the proportion of men is increasing. Prospects in all are excellent as population continues in increase, people live longer, government funding grows and the potential of these kinds of treatment becomes more widely recognized.

Where Employed By government, private non-profit, the Military Services, profit-making (nursing homes, for instance) and educational organizations, in hospitals, clinics, rehabilitation centers, classrooms, homes for children and the elderly and sanitaria; some visit patients at their homes; a few practice privately as consultants.

Preparation For physical and occupational therapists, four years of post-high school pre-vocational study, followed by one or two years of internship, or several years of study and an internship following a Bachelor's degree in another field. License or registration, with or without examination, required in most states. For speech pathologists and audiologists, four post-high school years of training a minimum, with growing trend towards a Master's degree as the standard requirement for entry. The Federal government hires only those who have completed work for a doctorate.

Advancement From staff membership to supervision or into private practice.

Salaries At levels, varying with level of degree attained, seniority, experience, responsibility carried and field and place of employment, paid persons with liberal arts schooling; one can reach lower middle-management levels without taking on added responsibilities for unrelated kinds of work. (See Appendix A for 1967-68 benchmark figures.)

For People Who Like to work with others in a helping relationship and to feel that they are directly serving society; prefer to deal with the concrete; have a high order of patience; enjoy the challenge of tackling sometimes apparently insoluble problems and of a continuing demand for creativity; and have substantial concern about job security.

For More Information see Appendix C or write The American Physical Therapy Association, 250 West 57th Street, New York,

New York 10019, or The American Occupational Therapy Association, 1790 Broadway, New York, New York 10019, or The American Speech and Hearing Association, 1001 Connecticut Avenue, N.W., Washington, D.C. 20036.

TRAFFIC WORKER (INDUSTRIAL)

The Work A traffic worker is responsible for seeing that purchased raw materials, parts, machinery and other inanimate production necessities arrive at and finished goods depart for market from his employer's premises at the proper time and at the lowest possible transportation cost (work flow within installations is the responsibility of such people as industrial engineers, production managers, systems and procedures experts and office managers). He must know costs, schedules and the appropriateness of such transportation alternatives as railroads, trucks, pipelines, airplanes, freighters and barges and be familiar with the laws and regulations applicable to them. He is concerned with loss, damage and delays, inventories and insurance; may supervise receiving and shipping personnel or operate company-owned carrier equipment; may represent his company in cases before Federal agencies which control and regulate interstate and international commerce. (Traffic management in Radio-TV refers to scheduling of programs, and in the air transportation industry, to controlling incoming and departing flights.)

Numbers and Prospects About 15,000; almost no women. Prospects excellent as producers go further and further afield to buy and sell, making transportation costs an increasingly important consideration; as methods of transportation grow in complexity; as business continues to expand, and as transportation regulations become more complicated.

Where Employed Great majority in the manufacturing industries; some by government agencies in connection with what they buy and produce or with their regulatory responsibilities; some by large wholesale and retail organizations; and some by the Military Services (a part of the logistics function) ; a few are independent consultants.

Preparation For important jobs, Bachelor's degree in transportation, business management, economics, statistics or commercial law is of increasing significance. To become a certified member of the American Society of Transportation and Traffic, Inc., an examination must be passed.

Advancement From such staff jobs as rate analyst or shipping and receiving expert into managerial posts; into larger firms; and into independent consulting. This is not a type of work which often leads to top general management.

Salaries At levels, varying with seniority, experience, responsibility carried and field and place of employment, paid persons otherwise engaged with the same type of schooling; one can reach middle-management levels without taking on added responsibilities for unrelated kinds of work. (See Appendix A for 1967-68 benchmark figures.)

For People Who Want to work with things, to see the results of their work frequently and to plan, direct and control; who prefer dealing with others as business colleagues, like to be precise, and value job security. Values associated with self-employment in this work are discussed on pages 109-114.

For More Information see Appendix C or write The American Society of Transportation and Traffic, Inc., 22 West Madison Street, Chicago, Illinois 60602.

VETERINARIAN

The Work A veterinarian is concerned with the physical well-being of animals and with the wholesomeness of animal flesh used as food. Treats sick and injured animals, takes action to prevent disease, inspects such foods as meat and milk. He may engage in research or teach, or specialize in the care and breeding of animals. His hours may be long and irregular; the work often requires physical strength and courage, sometimes takes place in difficult surroundings and may involve danger to a practitioner's health.

Numbers and Prospects Close to 25,000, only 5 per cent of whom are women (women are not even accepted by many schools of veterinary medicine). Prospects excellent due to growth of population which means more food consumption and more pets, to increasing emphasis on scientific breeding of animals, and to greater and greater concern for food purity.

Where Employed Two-thirds in private practice, both in and around cities where small animals are kept (the larger the city, the smaller the animals), and in rural areas where large animals may be the principal concern (continual travel to treat them may be involved) ; about a tenth by the U.S. Public Health Service and the Department of Agriculture; the rest by large ranches, dairies, stables and kennels, by state and local government, as Army officers, in zoos, in research, as teachers and, most recently, in connection with the space program where animals always take the first rides.

Preparation Two to four years of college including pre-vocational coursework, followed by four to five years in school of veterinary medicine (only half of those who apply are admitted today). License necessary for private practice and depends on graduation from approved school and passing an examination. It is possible to work for government and to teach without a license. Advanced degrees often needed for public health, teaching and research work and for top level administrative posts.

Advancement For the self-employed, through buying or setting up a practice, becoming the partner of an established practitioner or working up from a position as an assistant. If employed by others, through the usual channels in the field of work entered.

Salaries If employed by others, at somewhat lower levels, varying with seniority, experience, responsibility carried and field and place of employment, than those paid physicians ; the self-employed can earn at upper-middle-management levels and even higher. (See Appendix A for 1967-68 benchmark figures.)

For People Who Not only like animals but enjoy dealing with their owners in a sympathetic, serving relationship; have a high tolerance for ambiguity (an animal can't tell you what's wrong) and at the same time have a concern for precision; who want freedom to come and go as they please, prefer to work with tangibles and to see the results of their work often, and feel the need to be of direct service to society. Values associated with self-employment as a veterinarian are discussed on pages 109-114.

For More Information, see Appendix C or write The American

Veterinary Medical Association, 600 South Michigan Avenue, Chicago, Illinois 60605.

WRITER-EDITOR

There are so many different ways of making a living as a writer or editor that covering each of them with any degree of completeness would take a book in itself. All attempted here is a brief summary, and only a suggestive one at that. The discussion is further limited to those kinds of writing-editing work which bring in a regular salary (except for a final few paragraphs on creative writers and other entrepreneurs), and by the omission of public relations and translation (foreign language worker), which are described separately elsewhere in this book. The teaching of writing and journalism is not dealt with beyond noting here that this kind of work is undertaken, in the main, full or part time, by successful writers and editors.

The Work

Editors Prepare the work of writers, and sometimes their own, for printing or to be read aloud; may give assignments to writers, evaluate and accept or reject unsolicited manuscripts, correct and amend copy, stimulate writers whose work they want and seek new writers, do make-up and write headings. They may determine editorial policy within their areas of responsibility, great or small, and if this area is a large one, the success or failure of the publication or program involved may rest on their judgment. They may be responsible for such corrolary functions as production, advertising, copyrights, art work, distribution and promotion.

Reporters and Other Staff Writers Cover news close at hand or as far away as the other side of the globe; may specialize or take what comes; may write features, editorials and other non-news pieces and rewrite the work of others; may broadcast their stories orally over radio or TV rather than writing them for publication; sometimes double as cameramen.

Technical Writers Put technical information into language which can be understood by persons unversed in the subject matter; may write manuals, publications, features, advertisements, publicity, research proposals and reports, abstracts, speeches and contracts.

Copywriters   Prepare the written material in advertisements to be printed or aired over radio or TV.

Columnists and Commentators (staff)   Comment regularly, in writing or orally, on some area of continuing public interest.

Numbers and Prospects

Editors, Reporters and Other Staff Writers and Columnists and Commentators   About 250,000 editors (some 30 per cent of them women who are concentrated in women's magazines as editors of fashion, food, society and like departments on newspapers and magazines) ; about 35,000 newspaper reporters (also about 30 per cent women) ; for the rest, no estimates are available. For those who work for newspapers and radio-TV, long-range prospects are only moderate, as newspapers tend more toward consolidation than increasing numbers due principally to production costs, and radio-TV depends increasingly on network and filmed or taped programing. To the extent that they are associated with publishing, advertising and magazines, however, prospects are good, though in regard to magazines, frequent change of employers likely (only one of 300 newly published magazines has a life expectancy of 25 years). In all cases, competition is likely to be stiff at entry and up the line, the larger the community the stiffer.

Copywriters   Estimates of numbers not available; prospects good as business expands and population grows, but continuous employment heavily dependent on the general health of the economy, consumer taste and peronal mobility and flexibility and talent.

Technical Writers   About 30,000. Prospects excellent as technology becomes more complex and, thus, the difficulty of bridging the communications gap between scientists and engineers on the one hand and the technically unlettered on the other becomes more acute.

Where Employed

Editors, Reporters and Other Staff Writers and Columnists and Commentators   By the country's 1800 daily newspapers, half a dozen wire services, 9000 weekly newspapers, 70,000 magazines and journals, 10,000 house organs, 6000 radio stations and the four national networks, 600 TV stations and the three national networks, and the movie and legitimate theatre industries; *Editors,* in addition, by all the 1500 fiction, textbook, religious, juvenile, educational, business-science-technical and scholarly book publishers, which are largely concentrated in New York, Boston, Chicago, Los Angeles, Philadelphia and Washington, D.C.

Technical Writers By business and industrial concerns, book publishers, government agencies and technical magazines.

Copywriters By all organizations in and out of business which prepare their own advertising, and by advertising agencies.

Preparation Bachelor's degree virtually essential in all areas; for work on newspapers and other periodicals, there is considerable debate on whether undergraduate specialization should be in journalism-communications or in liberal arts — the ideal combination is the latter capped by a year or two of graduate work in the former or an undergraduate curriculum which is predominantly in liberal arts but includes pre-vocational coursework. In publishing, a Bachelor's degree in liberal arts, including substantial coursework, if not concentration, in English is the best bet. Technical writers must acquire somewhere along the line knowledge of the technology of choice. High degree of on-the-job learning is a feature of all writing-editing occupations; larger publishers and periodicals look first for people who have acquired experience in smaller organizations.

Advancement Outside the book publishing field, virtually everybody starts out as a writer, be it general reporting, feature writing, technical writing or copy writing; thus editing, column writing, newscasting and radio and TV commenting usually are steps up for writers rather than entry-level occupations. Senior editorial and columnist-commentator posts are about as far as anyone can go without capital since the next and final step, publishing, normally requires acquisition of all or part of the enterprise. In book publishing, the route up is through the immediate editorial hierarchy or other editorial hierarchies (movement from firm to firm

on the way up is not an unusual pattern). Writers and editors
frequently move into public relations.

Salaries Possibly except for technical writers, somewhat below
the levels, varying with experience, seniority, responsibility
carried and field and place of employment, paid persons otherwise
employed with four-year liberal arts degrees. Senior editors, and
nationally known columnists and star correspondents can reach
upper-middle-management levels. Talent and breaks can have an
important bearing. (See Appendix A for 1967-68 benchmark
figures.)

For People Who Have at least some yen to be creative; like working under pressure occasionally or constantly, and have little concern for security — again, except for technical writing, which is
more analytical than creative and usually deliberately paced and
eminently secure. (In regard to security, writing and editing in
general are among the very few kinds of work in which frequent
moves from employer to employer and from one facet of the occupation to another are not considered to be a poor recommenda-
tion.) All other values discussed in this book can be satisfied or
may be frustrated in writing-editing, depending on the particular
kind in which one is engaged.

Entrepreneurial Writing-Editing Only a handful of creative
writers — of novels, short stories, plays, poems and the like — eat
regularly on what they sell, and only a handful of these eat well.
In general, only one out of 100 unsolicited submissions, at best, are
accepted by editors, and those accepted may never get published
because of a change of editors or plans, or may not sell well because they are ignored or adversely reviewed by critics or simply
do not attract readers. Freelance feature writers fare no better.
The stories they would like to write are usually assigned to publication staff members. Lack of private funds means in most cases that
both creative writers and freelancers must hold down regular jobs,
in or out of the writing field, to subsist.

Less hazardous, because they are undertaken only by those who
have won their spurs and reputations as writers or editors elsewhere, are such self-employments as writing syndicated columns
and offering one's services to writers or publishers as an agent,

225

consultant, editor, translator or ghost writer and rewriter (some agencies offer to write whole books for anyone).

Values associated with self-employment . . . as editor or writer are discussed on pages 109-114.

For More Information see Appendix C or write any of the following: The American Book Publisher's Council, 58 West 40th Street, New York, New York 10018; The American Newspaper Publishers Association, 750 Third Avenue, New York, New York 10017; The Society of Technical Writers and Publishers, Inc., P.O. Box 3706, Beechwold Station, Columbus, Ohio 43214; *Word Business '68,* The Yale Daily News, 241-A Yale Station, New Haven, Connecticut 06520; *The Literary Market Place,* R. R. Bowker Company, 1180 Avenue of the Americas, New York, New York 10036.

Appendix A

Salary and Earnings Benchmarks

The discussion of salaries incorporated in each of the foregoing job descriptions have been either briefly suggestive only or nonexistent. The reason is that to be fully adequate, each would have had to run to several pages to cover the important aspects of the matter, aspects which are, however, in most cases common to all. In these circumstances it obviously makes sense to confine discussion of the subject to a single section.

This section is in two parts, first some remarks on the problems faced by anyone attempting to get a firm fix on salary and earnings figures in almost any kind of work at any point in time; and second, selected— suggestive only — salary schedules and earnings data in the Federal Government, the Military Services, business and industry, public schools and colleges and universities available at the time this is written, *the spring of 1968.*

As to the problems. Let's assume, to illustrate, that you expect to get your BA or BS degree shortly and want to get into personnel work. What salary might you expect to be offered at the start and what might you be earning a decade or so hence? At this moment, the best guess would be somewhere between $5000 and $9000 to start and between $12,000 and $30,000 ten years or so from now. Not very helpful. To take starting salaries first, as of early 1968 the Federal government would pay you either $5,565 or $6,734. As an unmarried Second Lieutenant or Ensign in the Military Services, stationed in the United States, your total take would be on the order of $5,700. In both instances, these would be firm figures, applicable in whatever part of the country you were stationed and regardless of what agency or arm you worked for. But that is the end of the firm figure pattern.

In business your offers would probably be in the $6000 to $9000 range, averaging perhaps $7500. The specific offer would depend on the size and nature of the business, its location geographically, the size of the town or city in which it operated, the general affluence of the community, large or small, and your record to date. If you elected to go into education administration, the range would probably be between $5000 and $7000, specific offers being influenced by more or less the same factors which condition those made by business. The picture is closely comparable so far as state and local government and non-profit organizations are concerned. Finally, if you decided to set up in business for yourself, operating a placement agency, for instance, you would probably be in debt for a while.

Turning to eventual earnings, the future picture is even cloudier. As with initial salaries, your field of work and your employer within it and the nature and location of the community in which you worked have a bearing. But other factors also come into play. Among them are the amount of formal postgraduate training you have undertaken, your performance of the job, what your responsibilities are, especially in the general management area, the demand-supply situation so far as your skills are concerned, your seniority within the organization, the prevailing inflation and luck. You could double your starting salary over ten years or you could, in the most favorable set of circumstances, quadruple it.

The matter of advanced degrees was noted above. While they have less bearing in personnel work than in many other kinds, their impact can be pointed up by noting that, as of today, if you entered personnel work after earning a two-year Master's degree in Business Administration, the Federal Government might offer you as much as $9700 to start and a business organization, $11,000 or more. If there were a Ph.D. available in personnel work, you could add from $2000 to $4000 to these figures.

And again in the matter of the impact of degrees. Let us suppose that your undergraduate work was in accounting, the physical sciences or engineering, and that you wanted to check out what you might earn if you pursued these disciplines instead of personnel work. If you did this, business would pay you on the average about $8000 as an accountant, about $8600 as a physical scientist and over $9000 as an engineer, as against the average of $7500 they would offer you as a personnel worker. The comparable figures in Federal service (as against $5565-$6734 for personnel work) would be $6700-$7600 for accountants and $6700-$8000 for scientists and engineers. On the other hand, teaching in general puts no premium on any of the disciplines. You would be paid as much to teach history, for instance, as accounting, engineering or physics.

In what has gone before we have not touched on such traditional professions as law and medicine. Very generally, if you went to work for others, you would be paid what they pay physical science and engineering Ph.D.'s. New doctors, for instance, are currently being offered about $12,000 by the Federal government and new lawyers somewhat less because there is no shortage. However, large New York law firms are presently offering $15,000 to start. If, on the other hand, you went into private practice, you would be likely to be on a hand-to-mouth basis for a substantial number of years and, while you might eventually achieve earnings higher than are possible on any salaried job, simply a comfortable living would be the more probable prediction.

Finally, and to further confuse the issue, you must keep in mind that none of the figures cited above is accurate as of the time you read this section. They were as accurate as could be ascertained at the time they were set down in the spring of 1968, though in some cases changes were expected in the immediate future. Since that time inflation and a continued seller's market for able collegians has probably raised many of the figures, at the rate of perhaps 3 to 8 percent per year, but this is by no means a certainty and some if not many may have remained static or even gone down since then.

So much for the problems involved in trying to pin down salaries and earnings in various kinds of work. The impossibility of exactness, however, does not eliminate interest in this key aspect of any job. In these circumstances, the best that can be done here is to set down some salary figures which are available or guessable as this is written. These follow. Keep in mind as you read them that they are not only out of date, but also that they are averages, or applicable to a specific situation, and are suggestive only and thus do not cover every set of circumstances. Extrapolation may be able to fill in the picture in some instances, but don't come to immutable conclusions about any matter in which salaries and earnings are an issue without finding out what the current situation is. In this regard, you will have no great problems in getting hold of governmental, public school, college and university and Military Service schedules. As to business, your best source of timely information is your own institution's placement office.

A final note. When the words "middle management" are used in the individual job descriptions, they mean jobs which command salaries from two to four times as great as those offered new employees for that kind of work in most organizations. "Top management" means jobs at the vice presidential or equivalent level (and the presidency or top job itself) in an organization.

CHART A-1

FEDERAL GOVERNMENT SALARIES

NEW EMPLOYEES WITH COLLEGE
OR UNIVERSITY DEGREES

(Salaries as of Spring 1968. Increases ranging from 3 per cent in the lower grades to 9 per cent in the upper are in immediate prospect and further increases a strong possibility in July, 1969)

Most Positions		Accountants, Auditors	Engineers, Some Scientists and Professionals
GS- 5	$ 5,565	6,681	6,681
GS- 7	6,734	7,634	8,084
GS- 9	8,054	8,592	9,399
GS-11	9,657	9,657	10,945
GS-12	11,461	11,461	11,843

All Disciplines — Largely by Promotion

GS-13	$13,507
GS-14	15,841
GS-15	18,404
GS-16	20,982
GS-17	23,788
GS-18	27,055

Degree levels and salaries:

BA or BS . . . . GS-5 or GS-7:
depends on academic standing.
MA or MS (one year) . . . . GS-7 or GS-9:
depends on academic standing and/or experience.
MA or MS (two year) . . . . GS-9 or GS-11:
depends on academic standing and/or experience.
Ph.D. or equivalent professional level . . . . GS-11 or GS-12:
depends on discipline and/or experience.

CHART A-2
THE MILITARY SERVICES

(As of April 1968. Changes Expected Shortly)

Army Rank	Base Pay Range — Increases with Length of Service
Second Lieutenant	$ 3,852 — $ 5,328
First Lieutenant	$ 4,488 — $ 6,744
Captain	$ 5,592 — $ 9,084
Major	$ 6,024 — $10,512
Lieutenant Colonel	$ 7,128 — $12,576
Colonel	$ 8,916 — $15,420
Brigadier General	$12,036 — $17,544
Major General	$14,484 — $20,184
Lieutenant General	$15,996 — $22,380
General	$25,368
Chairman, Joint Chiefs, and Services Heads	$27,984

Allowances

Quarters: $1,010 - $2,000 per year, depending on rank and dependents.

Subsistence: $576 per year.

Flight, submarine, diving, hostile fire: $780 - $4,200 per year.

Incentive pay for hazardous duty (parachute jumping, demolition work, etc.): $1,320 per year.

Also allowances for uniform, cost of living and housing (overseas), special basic subsistence and travel and transportation, and payments for accrued leave.

CHART A-3

COLLEGE AND UNIVERSITY TEACHING
COMPENSATION* — AVERAGES 1966-67
(From the June 1967 Bulletin of the American
Association of University Professors)

	Public	Private Independent	Church
Universities			
Professor	$16,155	$19,825	$15,292
Associate Professor	12,122	13,460	12,084
Assistant Professor	10,035	10,696	9,727
Instructor	7,685	8,327	7,659
Liberal Arts Colleges			
Professor	14,398	15,086	13,019
Associate Professor	11,505	11,594	10,530
Assistant Professor	9,599	9,547	8,880
Instructor	7,661	7,738	7,366
Teachers Colleges			
Professor	12,859	14,092	
Associate Professor	10,506	11,281	
Assistant Professor	8,965	9,547	
Instructor	7,491	7,464	
Junior Colleges			
Professor	13,273	11,173	9,858
Associate Professor	11,475	10,024	8,656
Assistant Professor	9,516	9,081	7,451
Instructor	7,838	7,709	6,842
Technical Colleges			
Professor	14,367	16,927	
Associate Professor	11,406	12,411	
Assistant Professor	9,649	10,199	
Instructor	7,498	7,567	

* "Compensation" includes both salary and fringe benefits which average 7-8% of salary. Most faculty members have two to three months off each summer to do as they see fit and, on the average, get a year off in every seven with pay.

CHART A-4
PUBLIC PRIMARY AND SECONDARY SCHOOL SALARIES IN A
HIGH-QUALITY, COLLEGE-PREPARATORY ORIENTED SYSTEM

(As of Winter 1968. 4 per cent increase in prospect)

Teachers: Degree Level

Years of Teaching	AB	MA	MA plus 32 credit hours	Ph.D.
0	$ 6,300	$ 6,800	$ 7,300	$ 7,900
1	6,600	7,100	7,600	8,200
2	6,900	7,400	7,900	8,500
3	7,200	7,700	8,200	8,800
4	7,500	8,000	8,500	9,100
5	7,800	8,300	8,800	9,400
6	8,100	8,600	9,100	9,700
7	8,400	8,900	9,500	10,100
8	8,700	9,200	9,900	10,500
9	9,000	9,600	10,400	11,000
10	9,300	10,000	10,900	11,500
11	9,700	10,500	11,400	12,000
12	10,100	11,000	11,900	12,500
13	10,500	11,500	12,400	13,000

Administrators:

Salaries roughly the same for comparable degrees and time on the job. However, for most administrative jobs in most systems, one must have first become fully qualified as a teacher under state registration rules and have taught for a number of years.

CHART A-5
AVERAGE BUSINESS AND INDUSTRY
STARTING OFFERS — JUNE 1968*

	Curriculum	Amount (Approx.)
Bachelor's Degree:	Accounting	$ 8,300
	General Business	7,800
	Engineering	9,200
	Liberal Arts	7,500
	Marketing and Distribution	7,500
	Physics, Chemistry and Mathematics	8,700
Master's Degree:	Business School and Related:	
	Non-technical Bachelor's degree	10,500
	Technical Bachelor's degree	11,300
	Engineering	10,900
	Physics, Chemistry and Mathematics	10,500
Doctor's Degree:	Engineering	14,400 — 15,800 depending on branch
	Physics, Chemistry and Mathematics	14,700

*Derived from data provided in its annual *Salary Survey* of 1968 by the College Placement Council, Inc., the copyright holder.

Appendix B

First Job: The Water's Always Chilly

The estimates run between one-third and one-half as to the number of collegians who change jobs within two years after they go to work. In many cases there are good reasons for making an early change or two. Among them are not, however, failure to have done the homework ahead of time which might have demonstrated that the job probably wouldn't fit, and — the subject of this brief essay — attributing to the particular job certain disagreeable and frustrating facets which, in fact, are common to almost all first jobs.

Your first job — in business or industry, government, education, the Military Services, a private non-profit organization or even self-employment — is likely to be vastly different in many respects from what you have become used to in four or more years at college. And unless you can live without working there's nothing to do about it but accept it — and try to distinguish between what is attributable to *the* job and to *a* job. In regard to the latter, moving won't help. Some of the differences you may find galling as between full-time earning and full-time learning are noted below.

1. On campus you are to a degree the master of your own time. You can cut classes or get there late or take long weekends, within reason. When you study is your own business. Required exercises seldom consume a full day. And you have a number of vacations during the school year and two months or so off in the summer. On the job you must be at a given place consistently on time and must work all day every weekday. Over the year you'll get a handful of holidays and usually no more than two weeks off in the summer at the start.

2. At college you are judged on the results you achieve academically. How you dress and cut your hair, how often you bathe, whether or not you antagonize your classmates, how hard you appear to be working, whether or not you are given to meditation, whether you appear to put your studies first, even the extent to, and manner in which you disagree with your professors and other authority figures, are of little or no concern to the faculty if your work is good. Good work, is of course, vital to holding down a job and progressing, but it is not enough. Unless you are a genius, your dress and comportment, your ability to get along with your peers, how busy you look, the degree to which your interests in matters unrelated to your job intrude on your work and, most particularly, the extent to which you disagree with the boss and how tactful you are in expressing disagreement, all can have great influence on your job security and your immediate future.

3. At college the focus of attention, particularly your own, is on you as an individual student, your growth and accomplishments. Your first responsibility is to yourself. While your improving practical competence is obviously important to your employer on a job, he is paying you, first of all, to serve his organization and help it grow and is likely to take a dim view of anyone who appears to be principally concerned with his own development.

4. Marks and promotion from class to class give you fairly regular and frequent measures of your progress and accomplishments at college. On the job promotion and pay increases may come at pre-set intervals for the first few years. But for the most part indications of how you are doing are irregular and infrequent.

5. On campus, you choose your roommates and can change them each year if you wish. The same is true, to a substantial degree, of your courses and professors. On the job you have no choice of your immediate colleagues nor any early opportunity to change them. And the same is true of your boss and, usually, what you do, in the early years.

6. At college, the premium is on thinking globally, arguing cogently and inquiring uninhibitedly. Frequently there are no plainly right and wrong answers and even if you are wrong, you may get some credit if you were thoughtful. On the job, your first

work is to master limited subject matter of increasing complexity, sometimes by repetition. Whether you are right or wrong in your decisions will be soon apparent from results, if not immediately manifest. And you get no credit for being wrong nor can you be so often without adverse consequences.

Some or much of the above may seem to you too obvious to warrant exposition, but no harm can result from knowing in some detail the nature of a problem you may have ahead, so that you won't quit that first job for the wrong reasons.

Appendix C

Recommended Sources of Additional Information

(Many of the publications cited below may be available at your Placement or Counseling Office. Those followed by an asterisk are available, if at all, only in one or the other of these offices.)

KINDS AND FIELDS OF WORK

Occupational Outlook Handbook, 1968-69 Edition; U. S. Government Printing office, Washington, D.C. $5.00 856 pp.

The Encyclopedia of Careers and Vocational Guidance, 1967; Doubleday & Company, Garden City, N. Y. $30.00 two volumes 1500 pp.

Federal Career Directory, 1966; U. S. Government Printing Office, Washington, D.C. $.55 88 pp.

Job Horizons for College Women, 1967; U. S. Government Printing Office, Washington D.C. $.35 83 pp.

Business Careers After College, 1968; The Daily Princetonian Publishing Company, Inc., Princeton, N. J. Free 72 pp.*

College Courses and Beginning Jobs — Prospective Occupations for Liberal Arts and Science Majors, 1967; U. S. Government Printing Office, Washington, D.C. $.15 23 pp.

THE MECHANICS OF JOB HUNTING, JOB EVALUATION, ETC.

Planning Your Career, 1963; Robert Calvert, Jr., & John E. Steele; McGraw-Hill Book Company, Inc., New York. $1.95. 152 pp.

How To Go About Getting a Job With a Future, 1967; J. I. Biegeleisen; Grosset and Dunlap; $1.95. 100 pp.

Making The Most of Your Job Interview; The New York Life Insurance Company, New York, N. Y. Free. Pamphlet. 14 pp.

BUSINESS AND GOVERNMENT ORGANIZATIONS INTERESTED IN COLLEGIANS

College Placement Annual, 1969; The College Placement Council, Inc., 35 East Elizabeth Avenue, Bethlehem, Pa. Free 688 pp.*

STARTING A BUSINESS OF YOUR OWN

Starting and Managing a Small Business of Your Own, 1962; U. S. Government Printing Office, Washington, D.C. $.25 49 pp.

PRIVATE COUNSELING AGENCIES

1967-68 Directory of Approved Counseling Agencies; American Personnel and Guidance Association, 1605 New Hampshire Avenue, N. W., Washington, D.C. $2.00 192 pp.*

TERM — TIME EMPLOYMENT

How to Succeed in Business Before Graduating; Peter M. Sandman and Daniel R. Goldenson. The Macmillan Company, New York, N. Y. 1968 $1.95 278 pp.

How to Earn (a lot of) Money in College; Harvard Student Agencies, Inc., Cambridge, Mass. 1968. $1.95 238 pp.

GRADUATE EDUCATION

Guide to American Graduate Schools, 1967; Henry B. Livesey & Gene A. Robbins; The Viking Press, New York. $3.95 355 pp.

Peterson's Guides to Graduate Study, 1967-68 Edition; Peterson's Guides, Inc., P. O. Box 123, 20 Nassau Street, Princeton, New Jersey. Free. Series of looseleaf notebooks.*

FELLOWSHIPS, SCHOLARSHIPS, ETC.

Fellowships in the Arts and Sciences, 1967-68; The American Council on Education, 1785 Massachusetts Avenue, Washington, D.C. $2.25 93 pp.

Scholarships, Fellowships, Loans, Vol. III (1955) and Vol. IV (1962); S. Norman Feingold; Bellman Publishing Company, Cambridge, Mass. Vol. III 471 pp., Vol. IV 368 pp. $10.00 each.

Current Financial Aids for Graduate Students — 1966-67; Bernard C. Maxwell, Ed.; College Opportunities Unlimited, Inc., 824 North Cooper Street, Peoria, Ill. $7.50 268 pp.

OVERSEAS EDUCATION

Study Abroad XVI, 1966-68; United Nations Educational, Scientific and Cultural Organization, the United Nations, New York. $4.00 589 pp.

Appendix D

The Résumé

Your résumé is a brief written summary of your background for use as a point of departure for discussion when you are being interviewed, as a record kept for future reference by a company possibly interested in employing you, and as part of your presentation when you are soliciting work by mail. Use your résumé prodigally. In case of doubt, leave one when you make a call and enclose one when you write. A sample is given on pages 243-244.

A résumé should contain all the information about you which may be relevant to your qualifications for the particular employment you seek. The following points will help to make your presentation effective.

1. Brevity: Try to stay within a single page.
2. Neatness: A résumé should be typed and, if to be used in quantity, duplicated tidily by some means other than carbon copies. A potential employer who gets a carbon copy may assume that you consider him second best.
3. Organization: That used in the sample is a reliable guide but not inviolable. When listing work experience, start with the most recent job and continue in reverse chronological order. Avoid gimmicky formats.
4. White space: Leave substantial margins and breaks between sections, whatever the temptation to cram in more information.
5. Emphasis: Stress relevant experience of the recent past. College accomplishments recede in importance as subsequent work history accumulates. Accentuate your strong points.

6. References: Optional. Be sure the people whose names you give have agreed to respond if queried. Sophisticated employers will insist on contacting your recent superiors before hiring you, however, regardless of whom you cite as references. Do not list relatives.

7. Job objectives: It is often difficult for a collegian to leave open all the doors he would like to without appearing to lack direction. Also, the objective may vary depending on the employer applied to. Consider holding your "objective" for oral presentation, or inclusion in your covering letter when you are applying by mail.

8. Salary desired: Best ommitted unless you will not accept any job for less than the figure you have in mind. Most employers have decided in advance what they will pay to someone like you, regardless of your desires.

9. Salaries earned: Usually ommitted in résumés for general use, although they are sometimes noted in connection with summer jobs to indicate the degree of responsibility held. Company application blanks, however, often call for this information.

10. Reasons for leaving jobs: Usually omitted on résumés for general use unless they will explain away changes which might otherwise raise a question in the reader's mind. Company application blanks, however, often call for this information.

11. Currentness: When any relevant change takes place in your circumstances and history, it is better to make up a new résumé than to make corrections on the current one.

RÉSUMÉ

William A. Doe
14 Balfour Hall
State University
Middletown, Ohio
Phone: (707) LIberty 8-8330

Home Address:
1415 High Street
Albany, N.Y.
Phone: (202) REgent 4-4556

PERSONAL DATA:
Age: 21
Marital Status: Single
Height: 6'1"
Weight: 180 pounds

U.S. Citizen
Health: Excellent
Draft Status: 2-S

JOB OBJECTIVE:
To begin work in sales and marketing with the aim of moving eventually into general management. No product or geographic preferences.

EDUCATION:
State University (BA degree expected in June, 1969)
Major: Political Science
Major Subjects: Political Science, Economics, European
    History, Psychology
Minor Subjects: Mathematics, History of Art, French
Grades: Fair to excellent. Steady improvement in past two
    years. Now "B+" in Major.
Language: Read, write and speak French fairly well

EXTRA-CURRICULAR ACTIVITIES:
President of the Debating Club
Secretary of Campus Fund Drive
Intramural sports
Member of Glee Club
Pay half my colleges expenses selling grinders to students door-
    to-door in the evenings
Active in Scouting (Eagle Scout) at home

243

WORK EXPERIENCE (all in Summer):
1968 — Sales Internship with Everyman's Housewares, Inc., Philadelphia, Pa.
1966-67 — Laborer on highway construction crew. Promoted to Section Boss.
1965 — Counselor and waterfront director, Camp Winged Foot, Laconia, N.H.
1964 — Worked as waiter in France.

REFERENCES: (Furnished on request) or:

Mr. John Q. Jones, Sales Manager
Everyman's Housewares, Inc.
40 Front Street
Philadelphia, Pa.

Professor James J. Smith
Department of Politics
State University
Middletown, Ohio

Mr. Warren T. Johnson
Director, Camp Winged Foot
Home: 89 Broad Street
Cambridge, Mass.

Appendix E

Job Interviewing

Extensive brochures have been written on taking job interviews. One in wide use (see Appendix C) lists 87 "do's" and "don'ts" and 94 questions an interviewer might ask you. Such detailed discussions — your Placement Office probably maintains a selection — are worth reading to be sure you haven't overlooked any of the fine points. But it is my view that such a review is not vital if you keep two things in mind — that you want to gain as much relevant information as you can within the brief time you will have, and that you want to put your best foot forward. (Taking interviews "for practice" is a bad idea, for several reasons. The ease at dissimulation you may acquire — and that is about all you can acquire — may be detected to your cost when later your interest is sincere; you are unlikely to get helpful comments on your performance; and you waste the interviewer's time.)

In regard to gaining information, it is not necessary that your interest be confined to the organization represented by the interviewer, though you should be well acquainted with it. You can expect a courteous reception, for instance, if your principal concern is learning more about business in general — or education or government — as possible fields of work. At a time when the demand for able collegians far exceeds the supply, most interviewers welcome the opportunity to try to stir up interest in even the most undirected.

However general or specific your quest, the interview, like a college class, will be more productive if you've prepared for it. Preliminary study of available literature and discussion with knowledgeable individuals will always give you some of the answers you seek, leaving more time during the interview to acquire information not readily to be had elsewhere.

And a final word. Whatever else you ask the interviewer, you should quiz him about what kind of people thrive in the organization for which he is recruiting and what kind don't, to attempt to get some insights into the personal values the work is likely to satisfy or frustrate. An accurate understanding of this aspect of the jobs and fields you are considering is important to you and, short of first-hand experience, can be best acquired from conversations with people who, like the interviewer, have intimate knowledge of them.

You are more likely to get the information you want from the interviewer if you put your best foot forward, of course. The brochures will remind you to tie the laces. I should like to stress the word "your." (Some advisers on interviewing urge, rather, conformity to a single, presumptively most effective, pattern of comportment.) Obviously, if you intentionally purport to be something you are not in any substantial factual way and this is discovered during the interview or after you go to work, you will be summarily written off and will add an item to your record which can come back to haunt you. More subtle, but equally important, is the impression you make of the kind of person you are. If this is seriously at variance with the truth, you may be hired for a job that turns out not to fit, or fail to be hired for one that would.

Whatever may be the shape of your foot, it can be presented agreeably if you follow a simple rule. Treat the interviewer like any other human being you would like to impress. Good impressions are left by those whose appearance and manner are not offensive, who are informed, attentive, responsive and courteous, and who appear, on their side, to be impressed.